PENTAGON III

U.S.S.R.

N. KOREA
WONSAN

JAPAN

ON

KOREA

YOKOSUKA

30°

SASEBO

CHI CHI JIMA

20°

NAHA
OKINAWA
BUCKNER BAY

AN
SIUNG
NG HARBOR

GUAM

10°

PPINES

PORO PT.

150°

140°

0°

EQUATOR

30°

# MOBILITY, SUPPORT, ENDURANCE

## A Story of Naval Operational Logistics in the Vietnam War 1965–1968

by

VICE ADMIRAL EDWIN BICKFORD HOOPER, USN (Retired)

NAVAL HISTORY DIVISION

DEPARTMENT OF THE NAVY

WASHINGTON, D.C., 1972

137108

H 784

UNITED STATES
GOVERNMENT PRINTING OFFICE
WASHINGTON: 1972

For sale by the Superintendent of Documents, U.S. Government Printing Office
Washington, D.C. 20402—Price $4.25
Stock Number 0846–0057

# Dedication

Dedicated to the logisticians of all Services and in all wars, and in particular, to the dedicated, and often heroic, officers and men of the Service Force, U.S. Pacific Fleet.

NH–74351

*The globe as viewed from over the intersection of the Date Line and Equator.*

# Foreword

In narrating the naval history of a war, one approach open to a historian is to record the general story of naval operations, then complement the main history with works dealing with specialized fields. The Naval History Division plans to follow this approach in the case of the Vietnam War, focusing the Division's efforts primarily on an account of naval operations but accompanying the major history with publications in limited fields deserving of treatment beyond that to be given in the main work.

This was the practice, as it finally evolved, in World War II. One of the volumes that complemented Samuel Eliot Morison's magnificent multi–volume *History of United States Naval Operations in World War II* was *Beans, Bullets, and Black Oil.* Valuable insights on the logistic aspects of the war at sea were provided by the author, Rear Admiral W. R. Carter. Not only had he served as Commander Naval Bases, South Pacific, during critical phases of the Solomons campaign of 1942 and 1943, but also later when the United States naval offensive across the Pacific was in full swing, he had organized and commanded Service Squadron Ten, the mobile base organization so essential to sustaining the massive operations of the Third and Fifth Fleets in the violent final phase of the war. Widely used as a reference work, *Beans, Bullets, and Black Oil* did much to impart an understanding and appreciation of mobile logistic support throughout the Navy, and to keep the basic concepts alive in the post–war years. To Admiral Carter goes a considerable amount of the credit for the continuing emphasis which the Navy placed on the maintenance of its capabilities for mobile logistic support in the active and inactive fleets, on the continuance of a reasonable state of readiness in this important area, and on the refining of some of the techniques involved.

Although somewhat broader in scope, *Mobility, Support, Endurance* is a similar volume intended to complement the planned primary history of United States naval operations in the Vietnam War.

# Preface

*"The only good histories are those that have been written by the persons who commanded in the affairs whereof they write."*

MICHEL DE MONTAIGNE (1533–1592)

Over the years a number of general officers and a few flag officers in positions of responsibility have written their own accounts of what went on during a major war. Quite understandably these have tended to focus mainly on the purely combat features of the war and on overall strategy. The result has often been an unbalanced picture of the total military effort.

To complete the picture, it is necessary to place in proper perspective the logistic support actions upon which the combatant forces and the effectiveness of these forces were totally dependent. It is the coupling of combat strength and logistic support that makes victory possible, whether it be action by a small unit, a major battle, a campaign, a war, or the wide variety of peacetime operations to support the national interest. Thus, along with knowledge of combat activities, one must gain an appreciation of logistics, of its relationship to operations, and the nature of operational logistic actions for a full understanding of a war. Hopefully, this recording of the activities of the Service Force, U.S. Pacific Fleet, will advance that appreciation, and contribute to a more complete picture of the Vietnam Conflict.

Within the military itself, many logisticians in the past have complained of ignorance of others as to the importance of logistics and the nature of logistic activities. I have never endorsed the more extreme complaints, but there are measures of truth in them. In their totality, logistics and related services in a major war are so varied, complex, and extensive that they are not always easy to comprehend. Those receiving the support normally only see the immediate interface with that support. When the support is good, it is natural to take that support for granted—with little concern over why it was good and little thought to do with the portion of the total effort involved other than at the interface with the operating forces. I have too often found even logisticians who, while experts in their own specialities or their own locality, were deficient in their knowledge of the scope of the total logistic effort, of the inter–relationships of its parts, of the extent to which systems must be tailored to the nature of the operations and special environments of the various types of combat forces, and of Service and unified command responsibilities to do with logistics. This book will not attempt to fill in all the gaps, but hopefully it may shed a bit more light on some of these matters.

It is with such goals in mind that I have set forth a recording of events and of views and experiences gained in thirty–one months as commander of the Navy's foremost operational logistic command.

Although concentrating on the period from 20 July 1965 to 17 February 1968, when I commanded the Service Force, U.S. Pacific Fleet, the stage will be set by a limited discussion of earlier events, and for completeness, some subsequent developments also will be mentioned. While the bulk of the treatment has to do with operational logistics I have not been able to avoid completely the temptation to make a few observations on broader matters.

The initial urge to write this book came from the difficulties encountered when, in the summer of 1965, I sought guidance from history as to the solution of the growing problem then being faced. Some useful information was obtained from Rear Admiral Carter's *Beans, Bullets and Black Oil.* However, that informative book concentrated almost exclusively on the mobile support forces in the Pacific in World War II. It did not extend to meaningful treatment of many other aspects of naval logistics in the Pacific, such as planning, organizing, preparing, establishing, and operating advanced bases. For the latter it was necessary to draw on the files of Rear Admiral Eccles, USN (Retired), who had been in charge of the Advanced Base Section of the Service Force during the final stages of World War II. In the hope that more complete information would aid those faced with the problems of the future, it seemed desirable to provide a more comprehensive record of operational logistics in the case of the Vietnam Conflict. For the naval officer who would go deeper there are in the classified files not only the annual Command Histories, but also a weekly history started soon after I arrived and "Operations of the Service Force" for Fiscal Year 1966 and subsequent years.

The preparation of this book was very nearly completed during evenings and weekends in 1968 while I served as Assistant Deputy Chief of Naval Operations (Logistics). At the time of setting down on paper the vast majority of what follows, there was no hint of the fact that a Joint Logistics Review Board would be convened to study logistic support in Vietnam, or that I would be a member of that board. Nor did I have the slightest suspicion that I would later become Director of Naval History. I set aside further work on this book until the Joint Logistics Review Board's efforts had been completed.

Special attention has been given to those operations of the Service Force which differed most from those of more normal periods. Particular emphasis is placed on the extensive Navy logistic operations in the Republic of Vietnam. Support of the Fleet itself, which is the primary role of the Service Force, is given less detailed treatment. Since it is the practice of the United States Navy to operate in peace on the same basis as in war, to the extent this is reasonable and practicable, the changes required to meet the needs of the Fleet in the Vietnam Conflict were relatively straightforward.

One other purpose to which I hope this book contributes is imparting some feeling of the fact that operational logistics is far from being as dull as many assume it to be. During the period of this conflict, I found command of the Service Force to be extraordinarily challenging and exciting. Not only was the command a vast and diversified one but the responsibilities were heavy. There was never a letup from the seemingly unsolvable problems that had to be solved in timely fashion in the face of the forbiddingly long lead times that are inherent in so much of logistics. The challenges and excitement of logistics in time of war are not confined to the commander. This is particularly true in the combat theater. It is true elsewhere as well. For, the effectiveness and responsiveness of the combat forces are strongly dependent on many decisions in the logistic chain of command and on the day–by–day staff actions to provide for the changing needs of support of dynamic warfare, actions which must in many cases anticipate needs well before they are even recognized in the field. I was supported by two able Chiefs of Staff, Captains Francis C. Rydeen and Dan T. Drain, and many other outstanding officers throughout the staff.

Finally, I wish to give some recognition to the imaginative, hard working and, at times, heroic efforts of those under my command. I deeply regret that space permits not much more than a sampling of these efforts of superlative performance of the many individuals involved.

One of the sources of satisfaction was the extent to which this performance was recognized by others. Typical of the reactions of those in the Fleet were the statements by one destroyer commander that

> logistic readiness support rendered by the Pacific Navy was nothing short of magnificent. If you needed it, you got it with speed and a minimum of on board supply effort. . . .

\*     \*     \*

Repairs provided ashore at Subic and Yokosuka . . . were superb. The word 'no' simply does not exist in their vocabulary. . . .

\*　　\*　　\*

Mail delivery during WESTPAC deployment was the black oil that kept our morale going. In light of the tremendous distances involved, great bulk, sheer number of ships, and ever-changing schedules, SERVPAC mail officers work miracles.[1]

In the words of General Lewis K. Walt, USMC, after his return from duty as Commanding General, III Marine Amphibious Force and Senior Advisor to I Corps:

There is a tendency to think of Vietnam as a land and air war. All too often, the tremendous contribution which our Navy is making is overshadowed by the more dramatic ground clashes or bomb damage reports. We are prone to forget that without the support our Navy gives, those reports might not be so favorable. . . .

We Marines are particularly aware of the Navy's outstanding job. We've watched the Seabees, for example, transform sand and swamp into modern, well-developed bases at Chu Lai, Danang East, Phu Bai, Quang Tri, and Dong Ha. We've seen them work around the clock building hospitals, airfields, barracks, roads, and fuel storage farms. They've built Special Forces Camps and fortified combat outposts like Khe Sanh and Con Thien—and much of this work was done under enemy fire. In fact, as in past wars, they have fought shoulder to shoulder with Marines, and our long–standing respect for Seabees as builders and fighters has increased daily in Vietnam.

\*　　\*　　\*

They've also distinguished themselves in combat. One of them won the Medal of Honor, and their other decorations include a Distinguished Service Medal, seven Silver Star Medals, 25 awards of the Legion of Merit, 59 Bronze Star Medals, and 231 Navy Commendation Medals.

The U.S. Naval Support Activity at Danang has done a truly remarkable job in providing extensive logistics to Free World Forces in I CTZ. . . . Through the port city of Danang, over four million tons of supplies a year are moved in order to provide I Corps Marines with logistical support. Ammunition, soap, rations and fuel are only a small portion of the 11,000 supply items helping to keep the fighting Marine equipped with the tools of his trade. In addition, NSA Danang operations have included extensive logistic common item support to tens of thousands of other Free World Fighting Forces in the five Northern Provinces.

NSA Danang has also functioned in a most effective manner in ensuring the flow of supplies through enemy exposed forward areas, such as the Cua Viet River just below the DMZ. The NSA motto, 'They shall not want,' best describes its mission—keep the troops supplied.

---

[1] Commander W. P. St. Lawrence, Jr., USN, "Mobile Logistic Support," *Combat Readiness* (Jul.–Sep. 1968), pp. 14–15.

To the Marine infantryman, though, undoubtedly the greatest guy going is the Navy corpsman attached to his platoon. He's the man on the spot ready to apply a band–aid to a blister or a tourniquet to a severed artery; and he's there no matter how grim or dangerous the situation gets. He's backed up by some of the finest doctors in the world and by a medical system which evacuates a wounded Marine from the battlefield within minutes after he's been hit and has him aboard the hospital ship *Repose* or *Sanctuary* or at one of our fine hospitals ashore for expert medical attention shortly thereafter. Thanks to this system, we have lost only 1.6 percent of those Marines who have been wounded. Of the remaining 98 percent plus, a majority have returned to duty in Vietnam.

*    *    *

The simple fact is that we couldn't be in Vietnam today in the strength we are if it weren't for our Navy and its undisputed use of the seas. In addition to the 68 ships and more than 82,000 Navy men in Vietnam or in the waters offshore, roughly 98% of all materials and supplies used in Southeast Asia come to us by sea transport. This amounts to 800,000 measurement tons per month.

It's true that most of the public attention and much of the credit for success goes to the man in the foxhole or in the cockpit, but one thing is certain—he is there only because he's backed up 100% by the mightiest Navy the world has ever known.[2]

The title of this book, *Mobility, Support, Endurance*, is taken from the names given the three prongs of Neptune's Trident on the seal of the Service Force, U.S. Pacific Fleet.

I would like to express appreciation to several members of the Naval History Division staff for their assistance in the final stages of the manuscript. Mrs. Sandra Doyle undertook a number of editorial tasks associated with the final preparation of the manuscript and its publication. DM2 Dennis A. Hodgin, USN, prepared the excellent charts that appear in the volume. Mrs. Agnes Hoover assisted in the selection of the book's photographs.

The views and assertions expressed herein are the private ones of the author and are not to be construed as official or reflecting the views of the Navy Department or the Naval Service at large.

EDWIN B. HOOPER<br>Vice Admiral, U.S. Navy (Retired)

Chevy Chase, Md.

---

[2] Lewis Walt, "Fire One," *Leatherneck*, LI (Oct. 1968), pp 20–21.

# Contents

| Chapter | Title | Page |
|---|---|---|
| | FOREWORD | v |
| | PREFACE | vii |
| I | THE VIETNAM CONFLICT | 1 |
| | A "Logistic War" | 4 |
| II | THE EARLIER STAGES OF THE CONFLICT | 8 |
| | Early Role of U.S. Navy | 10 |
| | Republic of Vietnam | 12 |
| | Navy Logistic Involvement | 14 |
| III | LOGISTICS AND COMMAND RELATIONSHIPS | 16 |
| IV | THE SERVICE FORCE | 21 |
| | Forces Afloat | 24 |
| | Shore Activities | 25 |
| | Tasking | 29 |
| | Principal Logistic Agent | 31 |
| | Flexibility and Economy of Resources | 32 |
| V | THE CRITICAL SITUATION IN 1965 | 34 |
| VI | THE SEVENTH FLEET IN ACTION | 40 |
| | Sustaining Operations | 45 |
| | Underway Replenishment | 47 |
| | Fuel | 48 |
| | Ammunition | 53 |
| | Provisions | 54 |
| | New Types | 54 |
| | Mobility, Support, Endurance | 57 |
| | Hard, Unglamorous Work | 57 |
| VII | COUNTRY-WIDE SUPPORT | 59 |

| Chapter | Title | Page |
|---|---|---|
| VIII | I CORPS TACTICAL ZONE | 67 |
| | Amphibious Landing | 68 |
| | Naval Support Activity, Danang | 73 |
| | Medical | 75 |
| | Establishment of the Naval Support Activity | 78 |
| | Port and Terminal Operations | 81 |
| | Port Development | 86 |
| | Harbor Defense | 90 |
| | Civil Disturbances | 91 |
| | Small Craft Repair | 94 |
| | Supplies | 94 |
| | Fuel | 95 |
| | Provisions | 95 |
| | Real Estate | 96 |
| | Public Works | 97 |
| | New Responsibilities | 97 |
| | Security | 98 |
| | Civic Action | 101 |
| | Award | 102 |
| IX | SOUTHERN I CORPS | 103 |
| | Chu Lai | 103 |
| | Starlight | 105 |
| | Base Development | 106 |
| | Duc Pho | 109 |
| X | THE CRUCIAL FIGHT FOR THE NORTHERN PROVINCES | 110 |
| | Hue, Tan My and Phu Bai | 112 |
| | Tet | 117 |
| | Cua Viet and Dong Ha | 119 |
| | Enemy Action | 122 |
| | Weather | 124 |
| | Khe Sanh | 126 |
| | Major Military Feat | 127 |
| XI | INSHORE AND INLAND WATERWAYS | 128 |
| | Market Time | 129 |
| | Game Warden | 133 |
| | Naval Support Activity, Saigon | 136 |
| | Supply | 141 |
| | Maintenance | 142 |
| | New Tasks | 143 |
| | Public Works | 144 |
| | Resupply by Water and Air | 144 |

| Chapter | Title | Page |
|---|---|---|
| | Mobile Riverine Force | 147 |
| | Personal Response Project | 151 |
| XII | BASES FOR THE SUPPORT OF NAVAL CRAFT IN VIETNAM | 153 |
| | I Corps | 153 |
| | Qui Nhon | 155 |
| | Cam Ranh Bay | 157 |
| | Vung Tau | 159 |
| | Cat Lo | 162 |
| | An Thoi | 163 |
| | Long Tau River | 164 |
| | Nha Be | 165 |
| | Bases in the Delta | 169 |
| | My Tho | 170 |
| | Dong Tam | 172 |
| | Vinh Long | 174 |
| | Sa Dec | 175 |
| | YRBM–16 | 175 |
| | Long Xuyen | 177 |
| | Binh Thuy | 177 |
| | Support Effectiveness | 179 |
| XIII | CONSTRUCTION | 180 |
| | Defense Construction Agent | 180 |
| | Build-up of Contractual Effort | 184 |
| | Controls | 185 |
| | Seabees | 186 |
| | Seabee Teams | 192 |
| XIV | SALVAGE | 194 |
| | *Frank Knox* | 197 |
| | Combat Salvage | 201 |
| | Rescue Tows | 202 |
| | The Threat of Blocked Channels | 202 |
| | Harbor Clearance Unit One | 203 |
| | Accelerating Tempo of Salvage Operations | 206 |
| | *Excellency* | 207 |
| | River Clearance | 207 |
| | *Prairie Grove* | 210 |
| | *Mahnomen County* | 211 |
| | *Jamaica Bay* | 211 |
| | Diversified Operations | 213 |
| | *Minot Victory* | 214 |

| Chapter | Title | Page |
|---|---|---|
| | *Stoner* | 215 |
| | *Guardfish* | 217 |
| XV | SURVEILLANCE AND SPECIAL OPERATIONS | 219 |
| | *Banner* | 220 |
| | *Pueblo* | 221 |
| | "Blocking Ships" | 225 |
| | Survey Operations | 227 |
| | Mobile Communications Support | 229 |
| | Other Operations | 229 |
| | Postal Services | 230 |
| XVI | WESTERN PACIFIC BASES | 231 |
| | Repair | 233 |
| | Supply | 237 |
| | Other Activities | 239 |
| XVII | AMMUNITION | 240 |
| | Responsibilities | 244 |
| | Forecasting | 245 |
| | Management | 246 |
| | Shortages | 249 |
| | Subic | 251 |
| | Mines | 253 |
| | Northeast Asia | 253 |
| XVIII | THE LIFELINE BY SEA | 254 |
| | Military Sea Transportation Service | 255 |
| XIX | EPILOGUE | 259 |
| Appendix I | TYPES OF SHIPS AND CRAFT IN THE SERVICE FORCE, U.S. PACIFIC FLEET | 263 |
| | INDEX | 267 |

# Illustrations

(All illustrations are from the historical collection in the U.S. Naval Photographic Center, Washington, D.C., except one illustration identified by a number preceded by 80–G which is in the official U.S. Naval photo collection in the National Archives.)

| | Page |
|---|---|
| Western Pacific (chart) | end paper |
| Service Force seal | title page |
| Global view of the Pacific (chart) | iv |
| Southeast Asia (chart) | 3 |
| Tonkin, Annam, Cochin China (chart) | 9 |
| *Bayfield* off–loading refugees | 12 |
| Admiral Sharp, Rear Admiral Veth, and Captain Wells | 19 |
| Admiral Johnson, Rear Admiral Ward, and Commodore Chon | 20 |
| Service Force organization (chart) | 27 |
| Bridges severed at Haiphong | 41 |
| Recommissioned battleship *New Jersey* | 43 |
| Replenishment cycles, 1965 and early 1966 (chart) | 49 |
| Replenishment cycles after June 1967 (chart) | 50 |
| Oiler *Hassayampa* refueling carrier *Ranger* | 51 |
| Eight-inch powder casings highlined from *Pyro* | 52 |
| Aircraft fuel tanks delivered by vertical replenishment | 55 |
| Combat stores ship *Mars* | 56 |
| Entrance to Headquarters Support Activity, Saigon | 62 |
| I Corps Tactical Zone (chart) | 66 |
| Only Danang pier prior to port development | 69 |
| Small oiler *Genesee* | 72 |
| The White Elephant | 74 |
| Naval Base Hospital, Danang | 76 |
| Change of command of NAVSUPPACT Danang, February 1966 | 80 |
| Tien Sha ramp | 82 |
| Site of the Bridge Cargo Complex | 87 |
| Bridge Cargo Complex | 87 |
| Observation Point, 1965 | 89 |
| Observation Point after construction of piers | 90 |
| Tourane River Bridge | 92 |
| Danang area (chart) | 99 |
| Rosemary Point, January 1966 | 105 |
| Rosemary Point, September 1967 | 108 |

Hospital ship *Repose* ........................................................................... 112

Hue ramp ........................................................................................... 116

Cua Viet River mouth before dredging ............................................. 120

New cargo lift craft ........................................................................... 121

Saigon and the Delta areas (chart) ................................................. 135

The author and Captain Herbert King ............................................. 138

AKL *Mark* ......................................................................................... 145

*Benewah* acting as tender ................................................................ 150

Mobile Support Base ......................................................................... 154

Future site of Naval Support Detachment, Cam Ranh Bay ............. 157

Repair ship *Tutuila* .......................................................................... 160

Naval Support Detachment, Cat Lo ................................................. 163

Barracks craft and *Krishna* at An Thoi ........................................... 164

Nha Be, 1965 ..................................................................................... 165

Nha Be, 1968 ..................................................................................... 168

Base under construction at My Tho ................................................. 171

YRBM–16 after mining ..................................................................... 176

New base at Binh Thuy ..................................................................... 178

Liberty Bridge under construction ................................................... 188

Salvage ship *Deliver* ........................................................................ 195

Refloating destroyer *Frank Knox* .................................................... 199

Light lift craft ................................................................................... 204

Heavy lift craft ................................................................................. 205

Salvage of *Paul Bert* ......................................................................... 208

Lieutenant DeLanoy receiving the Bronze Star ............................... 209

Refloating *Jamaica Bay* .................................................................... 212

SS *R.C. Stoner* ................................................................................. 216

*Banner*, first of the "environmental research ships" ...................... 220

Fleet ocean tug ................................................................................. 226

*Annapolis*, first of the communications relay ships ........................ 230

Ship Repair Facility, Subic Bay ........................................................ 236

Carrier catapult of A–7 Corsair ....................................................... 242

Pier at Naval Magazine, Subic Bay ................................................. 252

USNS *Core* delivering aircraft ......................................................... 257

CHAPTER I

# The Vietnam Conflict

United States participation in the conflict in Vietnam was one of gradual involvement, starting with a small advisory group and expanding into the employment of combat and support forces in a major war of long duration. The war differed in many respects from any previous one in our history and presented unique problems, both of a combat and a logistic nature.

The uniqueness stemmed in part from the fact that the localized combat actions were but one segment of a struggle of world–wide proportions. It stemmed in part from the strategy which evolved and from the self–imposed restraints. It stemmed also from the guerrilla nature of the actions and from the environment in which the war was fought.

The world–wide struggle was between the Communists and the "Free World." The start of the U.S. military assistance and advisory program in 1950 had been preceded by the establishment of Communist control over several nations formerly independent, and by "Cold War" confrontations at scattered locations throughout the globe—including Poland, Iran, Turkey, Yugoslavia, Greece, Trieste, Bulgaria, Hungary, Czechoslovakia, North Korea, Rumania, East Germany, and China. As a natural outgrowth of the need to block Communist efforts toward their avowed goal of world domination, the involvement in Southeast Asia was in many respects an extension of the United States policy of containment.

The world–wide nature of the struggle was to have many direct and subtle effects on the use of military forces and on the way in which the localized war was fought. It strongly influenced strategic decisions. Fighting the war in Southeast Asia was but one of the military tasks in the global struggle. Many other requirements were placed on the Navy and other services, and new trouble–spots were forever erupting. It was necessary to maintain continuous deterrence against nuclear attack. It was necessary to establish control of the sea wherever and whenever the situation demanded and to counter threats to that control, such as those posed by submarines. "Keeping the peace" functions were required in widely scattered areas. Thus, the Fleet was committed to many operations in addition to those off

1

Vietnam, and had to be instantly ready for redeployments in response to new challenges. The result was the placing of extensive demands on naval logistics, including demands well beyond those of a localized nature.

From their early beginnings, the Indochinese Communists considered their efforts a part of the world–wide "struggle between two social systems." Gaining control over the nationalist movement was but a step along the way. Thus, as the other side saw it, the "victory" over the French in 1954 was considered to be "one of the great historic events in the period of transition from capitalism to socialism," and it was declared that Vietnam "has now become one of the outposts of the socialist world." The goal clearly set forth was "to win complete victory for socialism and communism in our country as well as in the world." [1]

In the continuation of their struggle against the Republic of Vietnam after Ngo Dinh Diem had taken over from the French, the Communist offensive included "armed propaganda," a combination of "political activities," "propaganda," and "military activities." The strategy closely followed the previous concepts of General Vo Nguyen Giap whereby initial priority was placed on the "political struggle," with the "armed struggle" in the form of guerrilla warfare growing in intensity. After gaining a co–equal status with the political struggle, the armed struggle was to become the key role in the form of "mobile war." The deployment of North Vietnamese combat forces south in 1964 and 1965 indicated a Communist decision to enter that stage in which the armed part of the conflict would include "regular warfare" actions in addition to guerrilla activities.

It was under these circumstances that United States assistance to the Republic was expanded to include the deployment of organized military forces as an aid to safeguarding the freedom of the people of the Republic and to ensuring the containment of Communist expansion.

From the start ours was a limited, a tightly controlled, and a restrained effort. The deliberate strategy of the war on our part was closely aligned with the "measured response" concept which had grown so popular in the writings of some political scientists since the Korean War, a concept stemming at least in part from concerns over the dangers of a nuclear exchange and "general war."

The fact that a strategy of "graduated military actions" required implementation of many individual decisions from time to time as the assessment

---

[1] Vo Nguyen Giap, *People's War, People's Army* (New York: Frederick A. Prager, 1962), p. 37.

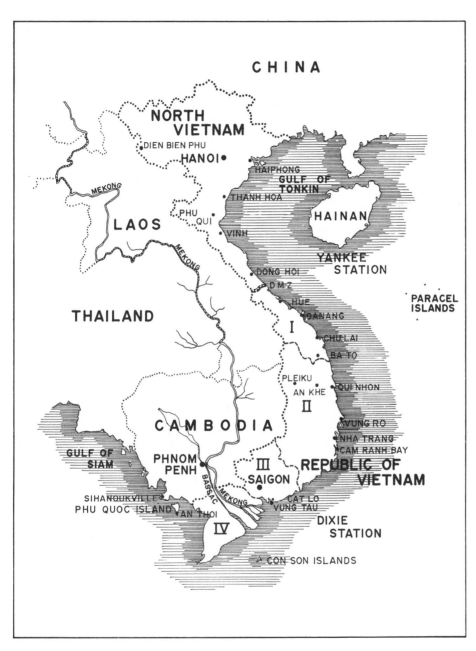

*Southeast Asia.*

NH–74354

of the future changed inevitably complicated the problems of providing timely and adequate logistic support. The support of the war and the way it was fought was influenced as well by the fact that there was no national mobilization or call-up of Reserves, until the *Pueblo* crisis. Annual budgeting tended to be done on an optimistic basis including, for a time, the budgetary assumption that the war would cease at the end of the fiscal year. All these factors greatly complicated the problems of providing timely and adequate logistic support.

In contrast with the United States, the strategy of the North Vietnamese and Viet Cong remained almost purely offensive, except in North Vietnam itself—a strategy combining politics, propaganda, invasion, guerrilla action and subversion, all with a political objective. The enemy military effort was clearly so shaped as to produce political and psychological effects, and propaganda was consistently and persistently aimed at influencing those in Vietnam and those in the non–Communist world, including those susceptible in the United States itself.

All this was reminiscent of the war against the French during 1946–1954. In the Viet Minh War many claimed the overthrow of the French control stemmed more from the defeatist attitude in Paris than from the military actions in Southeast Asia.[2]

Extensive assistance was provided to the North Vietnamese by other Communist nations. Weapons, aircraft, munitions, equipment, and supplies were provided by the Soviet Union, its satellites, and Red China. Russian technicians trained and aided the missile force, the air force, and its ground control in North Vietnam. China provided logistic and construction help near their common border. North Korea provided aviators.


## A "LOGISTIC WAR"

Early in 1966 Lieutenant General Victor H. ("Brute") Krulak, Commanding General, Fleet Marine Force, U.S. Pacific Fleet, expressed to me the view that this was a "logistic war." He said this in such a fashion as not to downgrade the forces in contact with the enemy on the ground, in the air, and on the water. Rather, his statement revealed a keen awareness of the

---

[2] General Vo Nguyen Giap stated that the "victory" in that war "cannot be isolated from the sympathy and support of progressive peoples throughout the world, among whom are the French people under the leadership of the Communist Party. . . ." *Ibid.*, p. 36.

importance and difficulties of the logistic problems faced by the enemy in this strange war, and those faced by ourselves.

In the case of the enemy, the Communists had their own logistic problems, as the Vietnam military effort depended heavily on the receipt of weapons, vehicles, and other equipment and materials from abroad. Some came from China by rail lines to Hanoi from the north and northwest. For part of the Vietnam Conflict, this flow was subject to interdiction by American air strikes—although within controlled limitations.

The great bulk of weapons, and military supplies necessary to sustain the North Vietnamese efforts came by sea in ships which delivered their cargoes mainly through the river port of Haiphong. One measure of the build–up of cargo shipments was that 47 Soviet ships delivered war material to North Vietnam in 1964, 76 in 1965, 122 in 1966, and 433 in 1967. Some came in Soviet bottoms, some in ships of the satellite nations of Eastern Europe, some in ships of Red China, some in ships of the Free World, and some in vessels of Hong Kong registry.

It was within the capability of the United States Navy to shut off this flow by sea but, after weighing all considerations, blockading and mining of the approaches to Haiphong were never authorized by U.S. officials during the period covered by this book. Such actions would undoubtedly have had a major impact on the war, conceivably even decisive, had it ever have been deemed wise to make this additional use of our sea power. Lacking such a decision, emphasis was required on the more costly and less effective efforts to impede, to the extent controls permitted, the movement of military cargoes south through North Vietnam and Laos and to seal the coast of the Republic of Vietnam.

The enemy's problems of inland supply down through the jungle of the "Ho Chi Minh Trail" through Laos, were formidable. Water routes were by far the preferable means when the forces were near the coast. It was never clearly established how much enemy cargo got into the Republic of Vietnam by the sea route, but there was early evidence of steel trawlers being used for this purpose. Further evidence was provided by the existence of well–stocked VC supply areas at several points along the 1,100–mile coast. As of April 1965, some 50,000 junks were licensed by the South Vietnamese Government. The myriad of sampans one would see off the coast during good weather made it seem certain that there was much undetected lateral movement from point–to–point as well. My personal opinion was that far more came in this way than was ever officially verified.

In addition to Communist deliveries along the Vietnamese coast, there was also evidence of cargoes being brought into Cambodia through the port of Sihanoukville—with or without the consent of Prince Sihanouk. It was suspected also that some cargoes destined for the Communists were included in ships which were permitted passage up the Mekong River. A Mekong convoy system, initiated in November 1966 by the Vietnamese, at least inhibited direct resupply en route.

Despite the fact that Sihanouk announced on one occasion that the National Liberation Front was the sole representative of South Vietnam unless they were unified, and took actions which seemed invariably weighed against the United States, Cambodia was cautiously treated as a neutral. There had been historical precedent for countering the flow of war materials through neutral nations. The British had, in World War I, declared cargoes going to neutral European countries as contraband on the assumption that they were destined eventually for Germany. No similar decision was reached in the Vietnam War. As it was, the full extent of the flow of supplies to the North Vietnamese in Cambodia by sea and through the port of Sihanoukville was not officially acknowledged until Prince Sihanouk was overthrown and this source finally cut off.

On our side, many factors were to complicate the problems of providing logistic support in the expanding Southeast Asian conflict. In the first place, the theater of operations was a vast distance away, on the other side of the globe across the broad span of the mammoth Pacific Ocean. The quantities of supplies, material, equipment, and munitions far exceeded those required by comparable forces in earlier wars.

At the start of the war there was but one major deep–draft port in the Republic of Vietnam, the port of Saigon, and that was limited in the depth of its water and in its pier space. The only other port that could accommodate ocean–going ships was Cam Ranh Bay, equipped with but one small pier. Elsewhere, initial dependence had to be placed almost entirely on logistics–over–the–shore type operations.

Further complications arose from the fact that operations had to be conducted throughout an entire country harassed by guerrillas, an undeveloped country with little logistic capability of its own, and a country with but one easily interdicted, narrow–gauged railroad and an inadequate system of roads.

Monsoonal weather was to add to the difficulties.

As has always been the case, timely and effective logistic support was a prerequisite to every action undertaken by the operating forces. In this war there were a number of conditions which added to the complications of providing such support. On the part of the United States, the war was fought without full mobilization or call-up of Reserves. Limitations of active logistic forces, particularly in the Army, resulted in the assignment of additional logistic responsibilities to the Navy within Vietnam, and influenced ways in which support was rendered. Problems of support were further compounded by the often inadequate provision for escalation, by the marginal nature of many of the assets, and extraordinarily restrictive controls. Country-wide guerrilla actions, the geography of Vietnam, and its climate added further complications. All these conditions and considerations placed severe demands on the flexibility, adaptability, and responsiveness of the logistic system of the Pacific Fleet; on anticipation of future needs in radically changing situations; on full and efficient use of all available assets; on mobile means of support; and, above all, on ingenuity.

CHAPTER II

# The Earlier Stages of the Conflict

Fighting for independence and resisting invasion from the north were not new to the Vietnamese. After being ruled for a thousand years as a Chinese colony, they had repulsed the Chinese and established an independent state in 939 A.D. Then, with the exception of nineteen years as a Chinese province in the fifteenth century, independence had been maintained until colonial conquest by the French began in the nineteenth century. Often the Vietnamese had fought to protect their independence and to repulse invasion attempts, including those by the Mongols under Kublai Khan in the thirteenth century. In the nineteenth and twentieth centuries sporadic resistance to French rule continued until the establishment of the Republic of Vietnam in 1956. Thereafter, the fighting for independence and resisting of invasion from the north was to be that of the South Vietnamese.

The efforts of the Communists to gain control of Vietnam had their start when Nghe An, alias Nguyen Ai Quoc, alias Ho Chi Minh, drew upon the Vietnamese colony in Canton to form a Revolutionary Youth Association whose members returned secretly to Vietnam to establish cells. A member of the French Communist Party early in the twenties, Ho Chi Minh had remained in China from 1925 to 1927. In 1930, as a representative of the Communist International, he unified Communist groups into the Indochinese Communist Party.

Intervention by the Japanese in World War II in 1940, their final seizure of control in March 1945, and the surrender later that year gave Ho Chi Minh the opportunity he had been looking for. The Viet Minh, which had been formed by the Indochinese Communist Party in 1941 in coalition with other nationalist groups, provided the means. In the name of the Viet Minh, Ho Chi Minh declared the independence of the Democratic Republic of Vietnam on 2 September 1945.

Further instabilities occurred as Chinese troops arrived in September to

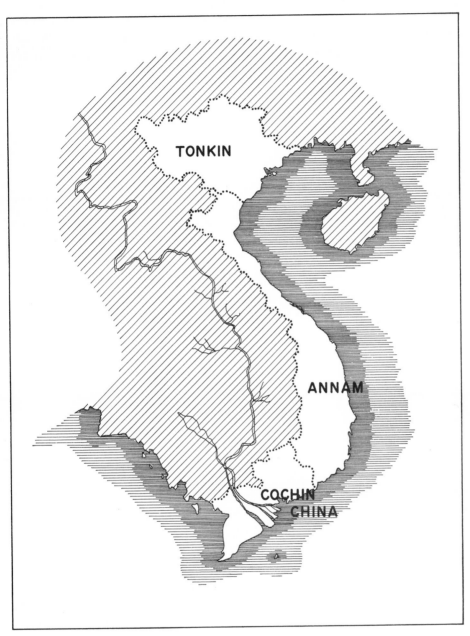

NH–74355

*Tonkin, Annam, Cochin China*

supervise the surrender of the Japanese north of the sixteenth parallel, while British forces accomplished the mission south of the parallel. The British soon made way for the French but it took several months to negotiate the departure of the Chinese. As a result of the unfolding events, France recognized the Democratic Republic of Vietnam as a "free state," part of the Indochinese Federation of the French Union.

Following the Communist script further, the Communists abandoned their pretense as a front organization, seized control, and started the Viet Minh War with an attack on the garrison in Hanoi on 19 December. In response, the French established a rival government under Bao Dai.

The guerrilla war against the French was to last seven and a half years and terminate with the Geneva Agreements on 20 July 1954, although the final declaration was not signed by the State of Vietnam or the United States. A temporary line of demarcation was drawn at the seventeenth parallel with the State of Vietnam to be in control south of that line. This was accompanied by a French pledge to withdraw its troops. Thus, the Communists now ruled what had been Tonkin and the northern part of former Annam, while a "free–world" state ruled the remainder of Annam and the Cochin China region with its Mekong Delta. Guerrilla war continued to be fought by the Communists as they attempted to extend their area of control to the South as well as the North.

## EARLY ROLE OF U.S. NAVY

The United States had extended diplomatic recognition to Vietnam, Laos, and Cambodia on 7 February 1950. This was followed on 8 May by Secretary of State Acheson's declaration that, because Soviet imperialism endangered nationalism and democracy in Indochina, the U.S. was preparing to extend economic aid and military assistance to the three emerging nations and to France. On 27 June, President Truman promised additional military assistance to France and the Associated States of Indochina.

The advisory group sent to Vietnam in the summer of 1950 included four officers and men of the U.S. Navy, the primary objective of naval assistance being to strengthen the river and coastal forces of the French and the Vietnamese. Old French craft were replaced with more modern craft, modified for the jobs to be done. A secondary objective was a build–up of the Vietnamese seagoing forces. In fulfillment of both of these objectives, the Service Force, U.S. Pacific Fleet, had an early role in helping improve ship repair facilities in Vietnam, in training personnel for repair and supply functions, in planning bases, and in providing other forms of logistic assistance.

For a time, in the final phases of the Viet Minh War, it looked as if United States sea power would come more actively to the aid of the French. As a result of the seriousness of the siege of Dien Bien Phu, the French made an appeal on 20 March 1954 for U.S. intervention, stating that only an immediate air strike against besiegers and their supply lines could prevent disaster. Portions of the Seventh Fleet steamed in readiness in the Tonkin Gulf, but no further actions were taken by that force. Dien Bien Phu fell on 7 May. Although not in itself militarily decisive, the psychological impact of the fall of the garrison provided the crowning blow in Paris.

Despite the fact that the Fleet never went into action, its display of strength appears to have influenced the subsequent course of events. It has been stated that fear of American intervention influenced Ho Chi Minh to accept the split of Vietnam rather than go for higher stakes.[1]

The U.S. Navy played yet another peacetime role as 860,000 Vietnamese, including the hard–core opponents of Communism, fled to the south. Over a period of nine months, one hundred ships of the Fleet and ships under the Navy's Military Sea Transportation Service carried 310,000 Vietnamese, 69,000 tons of supplies, and 8,135 vehicles from North to South Vietnam in Operation "Passage to Freedom."

On 8 September 1954, the United States, Britain, France, Australia, New Zealand, Philippines, Pakistan, and Thailand signed a collective defense pact, thus forming the Southeast Asia Treaty Organization (SEATO). The treaty provided for "effective self–help and mutual aid" to "maintain and develop their individual and collective capacity to resist armed attack and to prevent and counter subversive activities directed from without against their territorial integrity and political stability." Each party recognized that "aggression by means of armed attack in the treaty area against any of the Parties or against any State or territory which the Parties by unanimous agreement may hereafter designate, would endanger its own peace and safety," and agreed that "it will in that event act to meet the common danger in accordance with its constitutional processes." The United States made clear its understanding that its agreement to the latter provision applied "only to communist aggression."

---

[1] Ellen Hammer, *Vietnam, Yesterday and Today* (New York: Holt, Rinehart and Winston, 1966), p. 142.

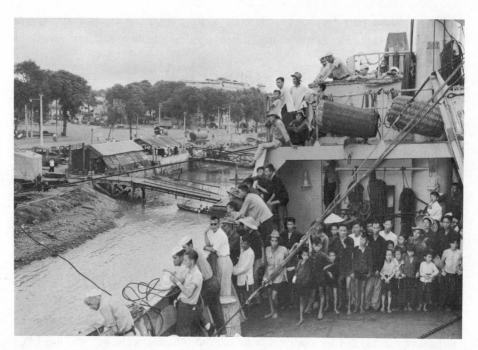

80–G–646775

*Bayfield (APA–33) docked at Saigon to off–load refugees from North Vietnam in Operation "Passage to Freedom."*

## REPUBLIC OF VIETNAM

During the period from the end of World War II until the Geneva Convention, Ho Chi Minh had covered the country with an intricate network of subversive agents. Control was exercised through a pyramid of Administrative Committees with villages at the base, and over which were superimposed intervillages, districts, provinces, zones, and interzones. This organization, which went underground in 1954, was to provide a strong infrastructure for the efforts of the Communists to gain control of South Vietnam.

In 1954, a patriot who preferred to gain independence through peaceful means, Ngo Dinh Diem, became Prime Minister of South Vietnam under Bao Dai. The latter remained in France.

In February 1955, the U.S. agreed to train the South Vietnamese armed forces. On 23 October 1955, a South Vietnamese national referendum deposed Bao Dai and created a Republic with Diem as its first president. Then, in early 1956, the French, at Diem's request, withdrew their troops.

Enemy activities intensified with North Vietnam's announcement of formulation of the National Front for the Liberation of South Vietnam, the political arm of the Viet Cong. North Vietnam infiltrated many Communists who had been trained in the North and who joined and helped organize the Viet Cong guerrilla forces. With North Vietnam remotely directing and supplying the guerrillas, campaigns of terrorism were waged to destroy local leadership and gain control of villages and hamlets in the south.

On 5 May 1961, President Kennedy announced that considerations were being given to the use of U.S. forces, if necessary, to help South Vietnam to resist Communist pressure. U.S. Naval forces became actively involved when, on 22 December 1961, U.S. minesweepers joined Vietnamese PCs in a patrol extending eight to thirty miles to sea just south of the Demilitarized Zone. This was augmented in February 1962 by air patrols of the Seventh Fleet extending in random fashion to the Paracel Islands. U.S. destroyer escorts and Vietnamese units started patrols from Phu Quoc Island to the mainland in the Gulf of Siam.

The Indian and Canadian members of the International Commission, established under the Geneva Accords to supervise and control provisions of the agreement, concluded in 1962 "that armed and unarmed personnel, arms, munitions, and other supplies have been sent from the zone in the North to the zone in the South with the objective of supporting, organizing, and carrying on hostile activities, including armed attacks, directed against the Armed Forces and administration of the zone and the South." The representative from Communist Poland dissented and made accusations against the United States.

As Commander Amphibious Group One, I served in the Far East from January to July 1962. Weighing daily intelligence and operational briefings, I was then convinced that under Diem steady progress was being made at controlling the Viet Cong and that the Republic was finally evolving into a coherent nationalist regime. There were, however, many expressions of dissatisfaction with Diem by U.S. officials and news media.

The assassination of Diem and the overthrow of his government on 1 November 1963 is a matter of history. The immediate result was instability, with something like nine governments in two years and the major gains in the relative power of the Viet Cong in many parts of the Republic.

## NAVY LOGISTIC INVOLVEMENT

As "Administrative Agent" in the Pacific area, the Navy was responsible for providing logistic services to the Military Assistance and Advisory Group. Following the establishment of the U.S. Military Assistance Command, Vietnam, on 8 February 1962 under General Paul D. Harkins, and substantial growth in the number of advisors, the Secretary of the Navy activated the Headquarters Support Activity, Saigon, on 1 July 1962. Its mission was to provide "administrative and logistic support to the Headquarters U.S. Military Advisory Group, Vietnam, and other activities and units designated by the Chief of Naval Operations." On 1 January 1965, HEDSUPPACT Saigon, was placed under the command of Commander Service Force, U.S. Pacific Fleet, as will be discussed in more detail later in this history.

Other early contributions by the Service Force were by Seabee Technical Assistance Teams (STATS). Of the ten authorized on 19 February 1962, two teams (one officer and twelve enlisted men in each) were deployed to Vietnam in July 1962 to serve with U.S. Army Special Forces. Organized primarily for working with and training natives, these "well digging" teams also had military construction capabilities. They built camps, bridges, roads, and water supplies. In November 1963, two more were deployed, one to Hue and one to Quang Tri—at both ends of the famed "Street without Joy" of the Viet Minh War.

Later organized into Seabee "construction detachments," Seabee "well digging" teams were the subject of an agreement between the Department of Defense and the Agency for International Development. The agreement, which became effective in 1963, provided for teams to be deployed to the Republic of Vietnam under joint sponsorship of DOD and AID. Enthusiastically received by local officials, the original two teams were to grow to fifteen by 1968.

Another step taken by the U.S. Navy in 1962 was the establishment of Seal teams with a primary mission of conducting unconventional warfare at sea, in restricted waters, rivers, and maritime areas. These would later see extensive combat in Vietnam. An additional Navy task arose in 1963 when the Bureau of Yards and Docks was made responsible for contractor construction and design in the case of all Department of Defense projects, and others as designated, in Southeast Asia.

On 19 May 1964, reconnaissance flights were started against the "Ho Chi Minh Trail" in Laos by carriers of the Seventh Fleet.

On 2 August 1964, North Vietnamese torpedo boats attacked destroyer *Maddox* in the Gulf of Tonkin. One boat was sunk and the other driven off by gunfire and *Ticonderoga* aircraft. Two days later *Maddox* and *Turner Joy* fired at attacking craft. Carrying out President Johnson's orders, retaliatory strikes against patrol boat bases and oil depots were conducted by aircraft from *Constellation* and *Ticonderoga.* Again in September, fast closing radar contacts were detected by *Morton* and *Edwards*, but the evidence at this time was inconclusive.

Late in 1964, evidence began to mount of the southward movement of North Vietnamese troops in organized combat units of regimental size and larger. This and a deteriorating situation in the Republic resulted in an expansion of the involvement of United States military forces. In addition to the continuing role as "military advisors," we were soon to commit our own units to combat action in support of the forces of the Republic of Vietnam.

On 7 February 1965, forty–nine planes from *Coral Sea, Hancock*, and *Ranger* of Task Force 77 bombed North Vietnamese barracks and staging areas near Dong Hoi in retaliation for a mortar attack against Pleiku Air Base. On 11 February more than one hundred planes from *Ranger, Coral Sea*, and *Hancock* struck similar areas at Thanh Hoa in retaliation for a bomb exploded in U.S. enlisted barracks at Qui Nhon.

This was followed by the Seventh Fleet's landing of Marines at Danang on 8 March, after evidence had been gained of North Vietnamese regular forces in the area.

Before resuming the story of the Vietnam conflict and its logistic support an attempt will be made to place what will follow in proper perspective by a review of logistics and command relationships in the Pacific, and of the Service Force, U. S. Pacific Fleet, as it had evolved since the start of World War II.

# CHAPTER III

# Logistics and Command Relationships

Logistics is not an activity that can be treated as an end in itself. It furnishes a majority of the essential ingredients by which the readiness of operational forces is achieved. It and its responsiveness are as essential to operational effectiveness as are training and tactics. While support is provided at times by other Services and common support agencies, combat effectiveness can only be ensured by each Service exercising the ultimate responsibility for all the ingredients of readiness for its forces, including logistics for which basic requirements are often unique to the Service concerned. This had been recognized by making Secretaries of the Military Departments responsible for such matters as logistical support and maintenance of their forces a matter of law.[1]

The deployment of these forces and their operational control could be and was changed to meet the world–wide situation at the time without major disruptions in the Service responsibilities of readiness and command. This was recognized in pertinent directives; e.g., "The chain of command for purposes other than the operational direction of unified and specified commands runs from the President to the Secretary of Defense to the Secretaries of the military departments."[2]

Whether by design or by accident, the basic overall setup was, in many respects, an extension of concepts developed over the years by the United States Navy. In the dynamic and complex environment of the second half of the twentieth century, these same concepts have become increasingly well adapted to optimizing the readiness, flexibility of response, and economy of force of our total military effort.

The basic ingredient of these concepts was a command structure which balanced continuity of command responsibility with flexibility in the combining of military forces and in the operational control of such forces.

---

[1] *United States Code*, Title 10, Articles 3012, 8012.

[2] DOD Directive 5100.1, "Functions of DOD and Its Major Components," 31 Dec. 1958.

Naval operations in World War II saw major advances in the art of attaining such a balance. Numbered fleets had been established, along with a decimal system of task force, task group, task unit, and task element designators. Ships and other forces were shifted from one operational command to another, and regrouped as the occasion demanded. This was a frequent occurrence in the Pacific where shifts not only were made from task group to task group and task force to task force, but even between the Third, Fifth, and Seventh Fleets as the situation changed and as new campaigns were launched. Yet, in all this shifting, continuity of command, other than operational control, was maintained as a result of the "type command" structure. If it had not been for this operational flexibility many more forces would have been required and the conflict would have been longer and far more costly. If it had not been for the continuity of other command functions, the result would have been chaotic.

In the Vietnam War a similar balance between flexible operational control and continuity of command existed not only within the Navy but in the relationships of naval forces with the unified combatant commander and subordinate combatant commander as well.

Internal to the administration of the Department of the Navy, the Chief of Naval Operations was charged with command of the Operating Forces of the Navy, the Bureaus of Naval Personnel and Medicine and Surgery, and assigned shore activities.[3] Much of the unparalleled success of the Navy's logistic efforts in this conflict stemmed from these command responsibilities.

Thus it was that personal responsibility was exercised up the Navy chain of command through the type commanders and fleet commanders to the Chief of Naval Operations—responsibility for training, readiness, performance, and support. Thus it was that initiative was exercised up this same chain of command, with resources applied at all levels to get the job done as effectively and efficiently as possible. Rather than conflicting with operational control, it complemented and assisted it.

Such was the case within the Marines as well, through the Commanding General of the Fleet Marine Force, who had responsibilities as a "Type Commander" to the Commander in Chief, U.S. Pacific Fleet, as well as command responsibilities under the Commandant of the Marine Corps. The self–sufficiency of the Marines was intentionally limited. A part of the Department of the Navy, many Navy commands, bureaus and offices had

---

[3] General Order No. 5, "Assignment and Distribution of Authority and Responsibility for the Administration of the Department of the Navy," 29 April 1966.

roles to play in logistic support of the Marines as well as Navy forces. This was the case in the Pacific as well as in the continental United States. Under the Commander in Chief, U.S. Pacific Fleet, the Commanding General, Fleet Marine Force, was responsible for "Marine Corps peculiar" logistic support. Commander Naval Air Forces supported Marine, as well as Navy, aviation. The remaining responsibility for logistic support was assigned to Commander Service Force.

The day–by–day operations of the Pacific Fleet were such that a powerful operational logistic system was in being and functioning effectively in supporting Fleet forces and in carrying out the other logistic responsibilities of CINCPACFLT. The flexible application of the system was the key to carrying out the Navy's logistic responsibilities in Southeast Asia, both with regard to the Seventh Fleet and the forces in Vietnam.

To understand how this logistic support functioned it is necessary to have an appreciation of the responsibilities of the Services and unified commands and their relationships. These had changed significantly since World War II as a result of the National Defense Act of 1947, and the amendments to that Act. Through the latter, the Secretary of Defense had obtained direct and extensive authority, under the President, over the combatant forces.

The amendments to the Act provided for the establishment of "unified combatant and specified combatant commands . . . to perform military missions" and—quite properly—it had been made clear that "a force so assigned is under the full operational control of the commander of the command to which it is assigned."

Within the Pacific, the commander of the "unified combatant command" was Commander Pacific (CINCPAC), Admiral U. S. G. Sharp who had relieved Admiral Harry D. Felt on 30 June 1964. Under CINCPAC were the three component commanders, the Commanders in Chief, U.S. Army Pacific, U.S. Pacific Fleet and U.S. Air Forces Pacific. Operational control of forces in Vietnam was through Commander U.S. Military Assistance Command, Vietnam, a subordinate unified commander. The latter was delegated extensive authority over operations in Vietnam, but this did not extend to operations outside the Republic. Thus CINCPAC exercised his operational command of the Seventh Fleet through CINCPACFLT, Admiral Roy L. Johnson.[4]

---

[4] Admiral Johnson was relieved by Admiral John J. Hyland on 30 November 1967. Vice Admiral Bernard A. Clarey was Deputy CINCPACFLT, followed by Vice Admirals Lawson P. Ramage and Walter H. Baumberger on 4 August 1966 and 16 March 1967, respectively.

NH–74283

*The Commander in Chief, Pacific, Admiral U. S. G. Sharp (center) on board Benewah. To the right Rear Admiral Kenneth L. Veth, Commander U.S. Naval Forces, Vietnam. To the left Captain Wade C. Wells, Commander Mobile Riverine Force. November 1967.*

Through this arrangement many resources under the operational control of CINCPAC could be and were brought to bear on the Vietnam Conflict and its support. However, important as the Vietnam War was, CINCPAC had to concern himself with other areas throughout the vast Pacific as well. The forces under his command could not be committed irrevocably to Vietnam. Rather it was his responsibility to direct operations throughout the Pacific in the nation's interest, maintaining readiness for limited combat actions as necessary and even for general war. There were a number of situations in critical and volatile Western Pacific areas which required redeployment of forces, including the *Pueblo* incident of the winter of 1968.

The combat and support forces which provided the military strength of this command were those of the Military Services stationed in the Pacific. Thus there were two complementary chains of command; that of the unified command structure through which operational control was exercised and Service efforts coordinated, and that of the Military Services which trained, prepared, and supported the forces and were responsible for their readiness

NH–74282

*Admiral Roy L. Johnson, Commander Pacific Fleet; Commodore Tran Van Chon, Vietnamese Chief of Naval Operations; and Rear Admiral Norvell G. Ward, Commander Naval Forces, Vietnam (left to right). April 1967.*

and performance. This division of responsibilities was crucial to success. The build–up of U.S. forces in Southeast Asia and the increased tempo of combat operations was made possible only by the fact that each Service provided or arranged for its own logistic support. Such support was crucial in the early months of deployments and redeployments. Common support and common services were established within Vietnam, but it took time to develop the capabilities to take care of deployments in force. As might be expected, a phasing over of the channels of support took time, and confidence had to be established as to the effectiveness, reliability, and responsiveness of the common support before full reliance could be placed on it.

Under CINCPAC, COMUSMACV had the authority to control and coordinate logistic elements within Vietnam itself, through the component (Service) commanders and, to the extent necessary, to provide logistic support to U.S. and Allied forces engaged in joint, coordinated or combined operations. CINCPACFLT and the other CINCPAC component commanders were charged with ensuring the responsiveness of logistic forces in Vietnam to these requirements, subject to the authority of COMUSMACV.

CHAPTER IV

# The Service Force

Over the years, the United States Navy had developed an extraordinarily effective operational logistic system in the Pacific. It was specially structured to optimize the employment of naval forces under dynamic and varying warfare conditions, and was unequaled in its mobility, its flexibility, and its versatility. The keys to this system are in the Service Force, established at the start of World War II, and in the continuing refinement of the Service Force concept.

In early years, a "train" of supply ships would at times accompany or follow a fleet in far-flung operations. The need for such support increased with the change from sail to steam and with the growing complexity of weapons, ships and their equipment. Prior to our entry into World War I, a realignment of responsibilities had been recommended whereby the Commander of a Fleet would be served by a "train" without being burdened with the details. Under the concept, extensive authority would be assigned to a commander over the "fleet's permanent train" (consisting of colliers, supply ships, ammunition ships, tank ships, repair ships, hospital ships, refrigerator ships, mine depot ships, and torpedo and submarine tenders). His authority would be supreme over his command, and upon occupying a base, he would also become base commander.[1]

Further refinement of the conceptual idea resulted in recommendations concerning an "auxiliary squadron" as evidenced by the following remarks, written in 1917:

> One principal purpose in forming an auxiliary squadron in the fleet is to relieve the commander-in-chief of the burden of logistics, so that he may devote his attention to tactics and strategy, uninterrupted by any but the large questions of administration that he can decide. The success of such an organization is proportionate to the degree with which the admiral is relieved of matters which subordinates, cognizant of his general plans, can settle quite as well for all concerned as if decided by the admiral himself.

---

[1] Commander Reginald R. Belknap, "The Naval Base at Key West in 1898," *U.S. Naval Institute Proceedings*, vol. 41 (Sept.–Oct. 1915), p. 1459.

To be effective, the auxiliary squadron should comprise all the elements and business which do not pertain directly to the military employment of the fleet, and also those necessary to sustain and prolong its military activity. By military employment and activity are meant the use of the fleet against an enemy, real or simulated, as distinguished from activities internal to the fleet, necessary to routine life and sustenance. In a word, the auxiliary squadron business has to do with supplies and facilities for maintaining the fleet's military powers.

The highest authority afloat has the gravest problems. He cannot delegate them, even if he would, for there is no other authority in a position to fulfill such a responsibility. Hence, unless the admiral be freed from distraction by minor matters, the larger ones cannot receive the continuity of concentrated thought which alone brings out true proportion. The organization should be such, therefore, that the commander-in-chief can count upon the various subordinate commands fulfilling their parts in his scheme of employment, without his paternal—one might almost say maternal—care in their preparation. He should no more have to deal with their coaling, provisioning and manning than a captain should be referred to every time an ordinary seaman needs a new white hat. At inspection and in the course of every day duty a captain notes whether his division officers have cared for their men's being properly clad. So with the fleet units. The admiral, having assured himself that the fleet's requirements have been seasonably arranged for, need not attend to their serving out.

*    *    *

Staff officers do not exercise military command and could not, therefore, relieve the admiral of certain administrative details. . . . An auxiliary squadron commander and his staff, however, could take over all the fleet maintenance duties; and for disciplinary and other administration among the auxiliaries, their squadron commander would have the same status as in other squadrons. . . .[2]

The above words deserve to be read by all in high positions of authority. There is no trend more potentially disastrous than that of high level commanders, influenced by ambitious staff members, involving themselves unnecessarily and wastefully in logistic details that should be delegated to subordinate commanders—with the result that they cannot occupy their full attention to the difficult matters of greatest basic importance.

The Base Force, Pacific Fleet, was established 17 December 1921, its general mission being to defend the bases and supply the vessels of the Pacific Fleet. Its direct successor, the Fleet Base Force, United States

---

[2] Commander Reginald R. Belknap, "The Auxiliary Squadron," *U.S. Naval Institute Proceedings*, vol. 43 (April 1917), pp. 639, 640, 641.

Fleet, was established on 8 December 1922. Then, on 1 April 1924, this force was augmented by gaining control over the Train, Scouting Fleet. It was renamed the Base Force, U.S. Fleet, on 1 April 1931. For a time, 1933 to 1937, patrol planes their tenders and Fleet Air Bases at Coco Solo and Pearl Harbor were brought under the Base Force commander.

On 1 February 1941, the Base Force, U.S. Fleet, became Base Force, U.S. Pacific Fleet. At the start of World War II, it included Train, Base Force; Utility Wing; Mobile Target Division One; various Fleet bases; Transports, Base Force; minecraft; auxiliaries of all types, motor torpedo boats; and other functions ashore. The service and logistic units would form the nucleus of the Service Force.

Recognition of the tremendous problems which would be faced by all–out naval warfare in the vast reaches of the Pacific resulted in the establishment of the Service Force, U.S. Pacific Fleet, on 17 February 1942, under the command of Vice Admiral W. L. Calhoun, USN.

This force was to earn a substantial share of the credit for success in extensive warfare in the wide expanse of the Pacific Ocean. It provided our forces with the ability to operate at such long distances from our established bases. It provided a support organization which facilitated the rapid shifting of campaigns from one objective to another and the means of sustaining the momentum. As stated by Fleet Admiral Chester W. Nimitz, "Our Navy's ability to remain at sea for long periods without resort to shore bases constituted a real secret weapon that surprised our enemy." Drawing upon the art of fueling alongside at sea, developed in World War I in primitive fashion and refined by our Navy between the wars, the underway replenishment techniques had been extended to ammunition, provisions and supplies during World War II. New concepts for the rapid establishment of advanced bases were implemented. Combat salvage capabilities were developed. Wherever ships of the Fleet might go, ships and craft of the Service Force would establish floating bases with ships, floating drydocks, barges and craft at suitable locations to provide repairs, fuel, ammunition, provisions and other supplies, and to furnish support and services of many varying kinds. When it was desirable to establish bases on distant islands for the support of the Fleet or its aircraft, it was the Service Force which organized the effort and established the necessary support capabilities, using special techniques designed to meet a wide variety of requirements in a minimum of time.

Further advances were made in underway replenishment after World

War II.  Other areas remained relatively dormant.  In some, such as establishment and operation of advanced bases, much of the know–how was forgotten.

With very few exceptions, the ships of the Service Force to be used in the Vietnam Conflict were of World War II vintage.  In ship construction, the shipbuilding program often had started with a balanced program which included both combatants and support ships. Step by step, in the annual reviews of programs and budgets, it was understandable that auxiliaries would be whittled away.  Few were able to stand the competition against the increasingly expensive ships of the line and their lesser combatant sisters.  Had this new conflict been a normal war, with full mobilization of resources, a modernized mobile support force might have been built.  But, in the environment of a peacetime economy, progress in the form of new construction of such ships was slow.

We were in debt to World War II for many of our other resources as well.  A wide variety of craft ranging in size from floating drydocks to small harbor craft were needed by the Navy in the Vietnam War.  Some were serving the Fleet at the time but many had to be activated or converted from assets wisely retained after 1945 and the Korean War.  A substantial portion of equipment and material destined for the Advanced Base Functional Components used to develop the initial Navy facilities in Vietnam was also left over from World War II.  Whether or not similar assets will be available in usable condition for another war will depend on decisions yet to be made at the time of this writing.  This indicates the importance of planning for and retaining assets for the future as soon as a war is concluded.

Despite the obsolescence and old age of the assets, the Vietnam War was to see a tremendous growth in Service Force capabilities, an unprecedented expansion of responsibilities, and a molding of the force into an integrated operational logistic support system unexcelled in flexibility and responsiveness in the support of combat forces, at sea and ashore.

## FORCES AFLOAT

Ships and other mobile units of the Service Force had been organized under two Service Groups and four Service Squadrons by my predecessor, Rear Admiral William D. Irvin.  Commander Service Group One was homeported in San Diego, where he served also as Commander Service Squadron One and acted as a Task Force Commander in the First Fleet.  Under him and homeported in San Francisco was Commander Service Squadron Seven. Commander Service Squadron Five, homeported in Pearl Harbor, reported directly to Commander Service Force. Commander Service Group Three was homeported in Sasebo, and served also as Commander Service Squadron Three and a Seventh Fleet task force commander. These officers were in command of the ships and craft of the force, and of the various other mobile units assigned to them. The Seabees were under Commander Construction Battalions, Pacific, with headquarters in Pearl Harbor.

## SHORE ACTIVITIES

A reorganization of the Navy on 1 January 1965 laid the groundwork for later advances in scope, effectiveness, responsiveness, and efficiency of operational logistic support—far greater than ever before achievable. The Naval Ship Repair Facilities, Guam, Yokosuka and Subic; the Naval Supply Depots at the same locations; the Naval Magazines, Guam and Subic; the Naval Ordnance Facilities, Yokosuka and Sasebo; the Headquarters Support Activities, Taiwan and Saigon; and the Fleet Post Office, San Francisco, were then placed under Commander Service Force. This meant that logistical support forces, ashore as well as afloat, were now under one command, the commander who had the primary responsibilities for logistic support of the Pacific Fleet. Prior to 1965 the command of shore facilities in the forward area had been fragmented among the bureaus concerned.

It took time for the new relationships to mature. Admiral Irvin took early steps to establish the basic responsibilities in a sound fashion, thus providing a solid foundation on which to build.

A few words on the rearrangement of responsibilities are in order. Through General Order Number 19 and OPNAV Instruction 5400.24, the Chief of Naval Operations chain of command of these and many other "shore (field) activities" was established to "insure effective support of the fleet." The chain of command in the cases cited above was through the Commander in Chief, U.S. Pacific Fleet, and Commander Service Force.

When I first took over, several staff members told me nothing had really changed, in that COMSERVPAC had long had the authority, as the Principal Logistic Agent of CINCPACFLT, to assign work to the activities in question. It was clear from the start that the change was more fundamental. The true significance became vividly apparent on my first trip west in

August 1965. In the middle of the first briefing by an activity commanding. officer, I suddenly realized that it was I who was personally responsible for all that activity did, for the effectiveness of the support it provided, and for its readiness for the future. This was accompanied by the realization also that I had authority to do something about it.

Many things came to light. To cite but one, I discovered that the mission of the Naval Supply Depot, Guam, did not even mention the Fleet or the operating forces. Only the support of command and activities ashore were mentioned. Steps were initiated to correct this. Then, under the guidance of the Fleet and Support Supply Officer on my staff, Rear Admiral B. H. Bieri, Jr., (SC), USN, and the help of the Bureau of Supplies and Accounts, specially tailored items of fleet supply were added, over the months, to meet the needs of the growing numbers of ships homeported there. As a result, this depot was able to make increasingly valuable contributions to the support of the Fleet.

Beneficial as the CNO–CINCPACFLT–COMSERVPAC chain of command over these shore activities was, it is important to note that success was also dependent on continuing assistance from the offices and bureaus, or systems commands, and of the Navy Department as a whole. By the assignment of "primary support" to the appropriate office, bureau, or command, and by stipulating that "primary support is intended to complement command and to relieve the commander, to the maximum extent feasible, of providing shore (field) activities with necessary guidance, assistance and direction in administrative, fiscal and technical matters," the chain of command was able to draw upon the expertise and experience of these specialized organizations.

As revealed so clearly by the Vietnam Conflict, one of the major sources of strength in Navy logistics was the assignment of responsibilities to the bureaus (later systems commands) for "technical direction" in their areas of expertise. Thus, in areas such as supply and maintenance of ships, aircraft or ordnance, the Navy throughout the world, ashore and afloat, had the same or consistent systems and procedures. A man trained to do his job one place was ready to perform a similar job elsewhere with a minimum of adjustment.

The shift of command over the shore activities was accompanied by the designation of Area Coordinators. In the Western Pacific these were, Commander Naval Forces, Marianas; Commander Naval Forces, Japan; and Commander Naval Forces, Philippines. Under the latter, Commander

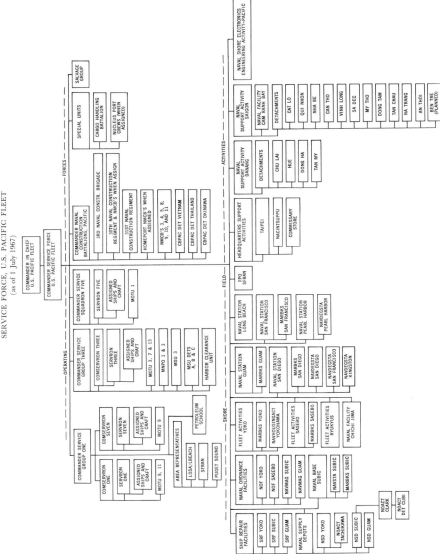

SERVICE FORCE, U.S. PACIFIC FLEET
(as of 1 July 1967)

Naval Base, Subic, served as a Local Area Coordinator. Commander Fleet Activities, Sasebo, was another Local Area Coordinator.

This part of the change was tinged with at least a hint of controversy. A number of the Area Coordinators, throughout the Navy, quite understandably would have preferred to have command rather than coordination authority. Perhaps the title "Area Commander" would have been more palatable. Be that as it may, the OPNAV Instruction gave the Area Coordinators extensive authority over area matters—to the point of consolidation of services, etc.—although direct authority over internal management of the individual activities was limited. However they may have felt, the Area Coordinators cooperated very closely with Commander Service Force. One even went so far as to say that he felt he had more authority than before the change.

Later, on 1 July 1967, funding and personnel support were shifted so as to coincide with the chain of command. At this time, care was taken by COMSERVPAC to ensure continuation of assistance by the Ships Systems Command in the case of Ship Repair Facilities, the Supply Systems Command in the case of Supply Depots, and the Ordnance Systems Command in the case of Naval Magazines and Ordnance Facilities. The teamwork could not have been better.

The accompanying change in funding responsibility had many beneficial effects. It meant a better alignment of responsibility, accountability, and authority, with controls exercised by those responsible at the various levels for the effectiveness of the operating forces. It meant better accountability for resources and improved planning up the chain of command. From our point of view, the funding channels were greatly simplified. For instance, rather than the previous three sources in Washington for operations and maintenance funds, there was but one. The variety of funding channels in the Fleet was reduced by their alignment with the well–defined chain of command.

The changes in funding responsibility were accompanied by certain command changes. Foremost among these were the placing of still more activities under Commander Service Force in the summer of 1967, namely: Fleet Activities, Yokosuka, Sasebo, and Ryukus; the Naval Base, Subic; Naval Stations, Subic, Guam, Pearl Harbor, Treasure Island, San Francisco, Terminal Island, Long Beach, and San Diego; and the Naval Facility, Chi Chi Jima. The latter was placed, at my request, under the Naval Station, Guam. Before long we were to transfer Chi Chi Jima to the Japanese, despite the fact that most of the inhabitants were descendants of American sea–faring men.

By now, COMSERVPAC commanded four of the fourteen Naval Stations in the United States, two of the eleven Naval Stations overseas, both of the Fleet Activities, all three of the Supply Depots, both of the Naval Magazines overseas, both of the Naval Ordnance Facilities, and four of the five Support Activities overseas in the entire Navy. In addition, the Public Works Centers in the Pacific and the Construction Battalion Center, Port Hueneme, California, reported to COMSERVPAC for additional duty.

I had recommended against the assignment of these additional commands, particularly in the case of those in the Eastern Pacific, fearing that attention to their problems would dilute the command attention required in the Western Pacific. However, a number of benefits were in fact realized, such as increased emphasis on fleet support and the solving of common problems through one commander rather than the six previous ones.

In November 1966 Commander Service Force was made the "agent" for the Commander in Chief, U.S. Pacific Fleet, for "resource management." This was a heavy added load, particularly since several months went by before additional officers were assigned. When the effort was sufficiently organized and functioning, the Fleet Resource Office was in October 1967 shifted to the staff of CINCPACFLT.

A number of times, I gave consideration to grouping the shore activities under subordinate commands, but never did so. One controlling reason was a belief in the importance of the direct command relationships. Another controlling reason was that no subordinate staff had the depth of expertise that existed at the Service Force headquarters, in the Fleet Maintenance Office, the Fleet and Force Supply Office, the Weapons Division, the Advanced Base and Shore Activity Division, and other staff divisions. The Activities were thus closely coupled to the sub–systems of which they were a part, and common problems received common treatment.

## TASKING

The basic responsibilities assigned Commander Service Force by the Commander in Chief, U.S. Pacific Fleet were to "provide logistic support to naval forces in the Pacific; to bases for which CINCPACFLT has command, administrative or logistic responsibilities; and to other services as directed." In addition to this basic tasking a multitude of specific and detailed responsibilities were assigned, and these continued to grow in number and scope as time went on. All were a part of the overall responsibilities.

Many of the most challenging problems of command of the Service Force rose from the fact that operational logistics is inherently a complex business. It embraces a wide variety of functions of supply, support and services. Its scope varies from command to command and from situation to situation. Whereas individual functional areas are often relatively straight–forward and easy to understand, in combination comprehension of their many facets and interrelationships is difficult. A simple diagram cannot describe the multi–dimensional and intertwining nature of the whole. Yet the degree of success in logistic support of a wide range of combat forces is dependent on how well the total capabilities are understood and controlled.

Each logistic sub–system is by itself important. Understandably, there is a strong tendency toward functional centralization, particularly wherein large groups of specialists are concerned. A reasonable degree of this is good, provided it recognizes the primary overall goals beyond those of its own area. But carried too far such centralization can have adverse effects. This is true within each Military Service. The danger of adverse effects is even greater when the detailed controls are exercised at a joint or Department of Defense level.

Closely associated with the problem of functional sub–divisions is another source of potential difficulty, the double–hatting of key individuals. In the Pacific the Fleet Supply Officer, the Fleet Maintenance Officer, and the Force Civil Engineer all had additional duties to CINCPACFLT. I am sure that there often was a temptation to take line–type actions at the Fleet level which would have tended to by–pass COMSERVPAC, but, fortunately, the individuals concerned were careful to recognize at all times the basic responsibilities of each of the commanders they served. Double–hatting should be avoided whenever possible. However, as a result of the good judgment of these officers, conflicts of interest in this case were held to an absolute minimum and the links were basically helpful.

Thus, one of the basic problems faced by the Service Force Commander was that of integrating the many and varied areas of services and support into one system while still taking full advantage of the organizations, procedures, and expertise which make up the sub–systems. For example, maximum effectiveness in maintenance could only be achieved through close relationship of actions taken in supply and maintenance. Repair of a ship or its equipment depended on the availability of materials and repair parts as well as on the repair actions themselves. The closer the supply of materials and parts were coordinated with these actions, the more effective, responsive, and timely were the repairs. The Service Force headquarters was the focal point of bringing these and other sub–systems together to achieve common objectives in the logistic support of the operating forces. I was particularly grateful for the high caliber of the specialists provided to the staff, the supply officers, the engineering duty only officers, and the civil engineering officers.

Another source of difficulty faced by an operational logistic commander was that basic decisions to do with the build–up and employment of combat forces were sometimes reached prior to providing for many of the support needs. The time for logistics to catch up was often short, yet long lead times characterize most of logistics. This emphasized the importance of concurrent logistic planning, not just at the highest command levels but at lower levels in the Service's chains of command as well. The long lead times also placed a premium on anticipation, and on making adequate provision for surges in demands and for operational contingencies. Action at the operational logistic levels can avoid many of the adverse effects of over–control farther from the scene of action. With due allowance for the time lag in response, undue excesses or deficiencies in responding to the step functions of changing requirements can be largely avoided. With regard to excesses, over–reaction to logistic deficiencies can lead to what Rear Admiral Eccles, USN (Ret.), has called the "logistic snowball." The point is that those involved in operational logistics can keep this under reasonable control if there is a true understanding of the dynamics involved. These dynamics were to occupy much of my attention in the early stages of the Vietnam build–up.

## PRINCIPAL LOGISTIC AGENT

In addition to the detailed logistic support tasking, COMSERVPAC was designated the "Principal Logistic Agent" of CINCPACFLT and, as such, was charged with responsibility for "supervision and coordination of the planning, conduct and administration of logistic services and supply of material to the Pacific Fleet, except for those logistic functions specifically assigned to other commanders."

The exceptions were almost all those of a unique or organic nature. For instance, the Commanding General, Fleet Marine Force, was responsible for

Marine peculiar items; COMNAVAIRPAC for aircraft; and COMSUBPAC for the Polaris system.

In many respects, logistics must be everyone's business. Commands at all levels must have logistic responsibilities within their cognizance. These stem from and are part of command responsibilities for the readiness of units under the commanders concerned. As a result, the type commanders (Commander Cruiser–Destroyer Force, Commander Mine Force, etc.) had responsibilities for the logistic readiness of ships and units under their command. Rarely was there any conflict with the overall responsibility of COMSERVPAC, and almost any that did arise was the result of inadvertent actions. As a result, conflicts were readily resolved. To guard against difficulties of this nature, great care was required to define what was common support and what was organic, and to clarify the interfaces when new situations were encountered. This became especially important in the establishment of new naval commands in Vietnam.

Thus, while recognition was given to the responsibilities of all the commands in the Fleet, overall responsibility and the means of providing common support were vested in Commander Service Force—subject to the policies and direction of the Commander in Chief, U.S. Pacific Fleet. This was a sound concept. It permitted the tremendous advances in the period of 1965 to 1968, and made possible the further development and maturing of an effective integrated operational logistic system.

To achieve these advances, many competing influences and forces, which uncontrolled would have diluted the responsibilities and "commensurate" authority of the Principal Logistic Agent, had to be held in balance. There was the ever–present tendency on the part of some staff members in higher level commands and offices to initiate actions or seek information outside proper channels. Although seldom, if ever, intentional, the results invariably did more harm than good. Corrective action in these cases was difficult and time consuming, taking much more effort than would be required to do the job through proper channels in the first place. But month by month matters improved as the system became better understood, and there was always the fullest support up the line.


## FLEXIBILITY AND ECONOMY OF RESOURCES

In summary, the Service Force, U.S. Pacific Fleet, and its operational logistic system were well designed to meet the extraordinary naval support responsibilities in the Vietnam Conflict, responsibilities which in many cases involved new and different tasks from those of past experience. The secret of success lay in the assignment of overall naval logistic responsibilities to one commander under the Fleet Commander in Chief and accompanying the command authority with the means of providing the necessary support, afloat and ashore. The coupling of control over resources and authority with responsibility meant a maximum of responsiveness and flexibility. It meant that support could be furnished a wide variety of forces by a minimum of total resources, regardless of shifts in operating areas and operational control.

# CHAPTER V

# The Critical Situation in 1965

The summer of 1965 was an exciting time to take over command of the Service Force, U.S. Pacific Fleet.  The transition had been made from a "cold" to a "hot" war insofar as United States forces were concerned.  Combat actions by the Navy had started on a continuous basis in February and had been growing in scope and intensity.  Logistics was faced with the challenge of sustaining these operations in such a fashion as to optimize the effectiveness of the operating forces.  The support of forces within Vietnam were presenting naval logistical forces with extraordinary problems, many of which differed from any encountered since World War II.

I must admit that I viewed my shift from duties as Deputy Chief of Naval Operations (Development) to COMSERVPAC with mixed emotions.  I was happy to be joining the Fleet, particularly in view of the fact that we were now engaged in active warfare, but, as is the case with the vast majority of unrestricted line officers,[1] my strong preference was for combatant assignments.  Little did I expect the true depth of the challenges of the next thirty–one months, the excitement to be involved in meeting these challenges on a daily basis, and the degree of satisfaction to be realized from seeing the combat effectiveness of varied forces being maximized by the superior achievements of those under my command.

I thought I had an appreciation of the importance of the Service Force and the complexity of its tasks, but was soon to learn that there was far more to the assignment than I had realized.  As I relieved Rear Admiral William D. Irvin on 20 July 1965, I was amazed at the scope of his responsibilities and the number of important problems he was facing.  Some were problems such as I expected.  Others were new and different.  I was fortunate in having as my predecessor an officer with the competence and imagination of Admiral Irvin.  By his many sound actions, he had laid a solid foundation upon which to meet the needs of an expanding war.

While none of the many problems could be neglected, five stood out in particular as requiring immediate and special attention.

---

[1] Officers eligible for command at sea.

One set of urgent problems had to do with providing logistic support and services to the Seventh Fleet, whose tempo of operations off Southeast Asia was rapidly increasing. Although all the implications were not yet apparent, the unique nature of many of the problems of supporting that Fleet were becoming clear. Never before had carriers and other ships been engaged in such sustained combat operations day–in and day–out. The operating areas were 700 to 1,500 miles from the nearest fleet base at Subic Bay, Philippines, and extended from the Tonkin Gulf some 1,100 miles to the Gulf of Siam. Demands on the underway replenishment forces, gradually increasing since April 1965, had taken a substantial jump in July. The underway replenishment ships were too few and almost all were twenty years or more of age. We needed more ships, and the highest readiness and efficiency we could achieve with those already in the force.

The center of gravity of fleet operations was now in Southeast Asia. This placed a tremendous load on Subic Bay. Although a magnificent harbor, far better for a naval base than the vast and shallow expanse of Manila Bay, most of the facilities there were of a temporary type, Quonset huts and the like. Their capabilities and capacities had not been developed for full support of a large fleet. Personnel manning had also been geared to lesser operations. All in all, the imbalance between demands and capabilities were so great that, on my August visit, I was concerned that a total breakdown might occur. There was much to be done in the shortest possible time frame. As will be related later, the facilities themselves, the SERVPAC staff, the Office of the Chief of Naval Operations, and the Bureaus of the Navy Department combined in many actions to improve the situation. The low point in the Naval Ship Repair Facility was reached in September, that in the Naval Supply Depot in December. Thereafter, the upswing was continuous.

The seriousness of the situation at the Naval Magazine became apparent about the first of August, when I learned that a ship loaded with ammunition had been in port in Subic since late June. Subic had become the main ammunition transshipment and stowage point not only for the increasing demands of the Fleet and of the Marine Air Wing, but in those early days, it often handled ammunition destined for the Air Force as well. Emergency steps were taken in collaboration with Commander Naval Base, Rear Admiral Donald G. Baer, to increase throughput. These included improvement of off–loading facilities, buoys, barges, handling equipment, and increases in cargo handling gangs provided under Supply Depot contract.

As a result throughput capabilities were doubled within a month. Thereafter, by hard work and good planning, backlogs were kept down.

The stowage capacity of NAVMAG Subic was totally inadequate. Every conceivable means was taken to increase explosive stowage, by the emergency construction of "hardstands" for open storage and by military construction of more adequate facilities. Dangerous overstowage existed until February 1966, when construction and many other actions combined to ease the situation.

This was all a part of a bigger problem, that of sufficient ammunition. Rear Admiral Irvin had predicted coming shortages and urged production increases. Although many in Washington appear not to have shared his concern and few believed expenditures would be as high as predicted, shortages would in fact soon develop.

In trying to gain an appreciation for the specifics of the problem, I sought detailed information. The information by my staff was phrased in terms related to Prepositioned War Reserve Stocks, which seemed to make no sense since we were already heavily engaged in a dynamic shooting war. Thus, one of my earliest acts was to initiate and guide a study of requirements approached from the naval logistics point of view. This was most helpful in the months to follow. The resultant forecasts proved valid for over a year, and were used as a basis of monitoring the adequacy of stocks throughout this period.

Logistic requirements in the study took into account the needs for filling the magazine spaces of the ships of the Fleet and for providing Marine "mount–out" stocks. Next, recognition was made of cargoes required in ammunition ships (AE) of the underway replenishment force, whereby adequate ammunition could be delivered to the combatants wherever and whenever needed. Allowance was made of the pipeline needs so that shipments would flow in timely fashion from the West Coast to Subic with allowance for the needs of transshipment there. An additional allowance was added to cover the training needs in the eastern and mid–Pacific areas. Against these logistic requirements, predictions were made using production plans and forecasts of expenditures. For this study, optimistic and pessimistic projections stemmed not from someone's guess but were based on expenditures already experienced. The former used the maximum weekly rate, the latter used the average rate since April.

One surprising result was the discovery that 5"/38 gun ammunition was highly critical. This had been expected of 5"/54 but not 5"/38. Another highlight was that bomb ammunition was critical even when obsolete types were included. Many at the time, and some later, believed that the criticality existed only for preferred weapons such as the "slim bombs" developed by the Navy for high performance aircraft. Actually the shortages extended to other types as well.

In any case, no other area was as challenging and demanding as that of ammunition logistics. None required so much attention and so much time and effort, with hardly a letup. Ammunition was to remain highly critical for the next sixteen months and more, and some items were from time–to–time critical throughout my entire tour. Keeping the combat forces supplied with ammunition required extraordinary operational logistic management and day–by–day attention at all times by Commander Service Force and the Weapons Division at the headquarters. Some of the specific problems encountered will be discussed in a later chapter.

A third set of problems had to do with providing support to combat forces in the critical I Corps Tactical Zone of the Republic of Vietnam.

On 17 July 1965, the Secretary of the Navy, Paul Nitze, had approved the establishment of the Naval Support Activity, Danang, under the Chief of Naval Operations and the command of Commander in Chief, U.S. Pacific Fleet, to be exercised through Commander Service Force with the mission "to conduct military logistic operations at ports and beaches for the support of U.S. Forces and attached third country forces in assigned areas." The area as assigned by Commander in Chief, Pacific, Admiral U. S. G. Sharp, soon stretched from the Demilitarized Zone in the north to Quang Ngai in the south.

Rear Admiral Irvin asked me to review the sound plan he had put together for personnel, craft, equipment, and facilities—a plan based on the "Advanced Base Functional Component System," a concept which had been kept alive since World War II. This system set forth "components" and combinations of "components" which could readily be tailored to carry out tasks at advanced bases. Included were personnel by grade and qualifications, equipment, craft, vehicles, consumables, construction materials, designs, and instructions for establishing the "component." Also included were plans for assembling and shipping the "components," and calling them forward by the Service Force Commander.

On 21 July, after I had expressed concurrence in the preliminary plan and given assurances to Vice Admiral Clarey that we could get the Activity established as soon as personnel were available, the Commander in Chief,

U.S. Pacific Fleet, concurred in principle with the plan, and promulgated the mission and tasks. On my recommendation activation was set for 15 October. Much had to be done in organizing the effort. Personnel, craft, vehicles, and facilities, had to be acquired and deployed and many other necessary steps had to be taken.

The need for daily actions on the part of COMSERVPAC and his staff would continue as long as the Naval Support Activity was in being. With memories of SERVPAC's Advanced Base Section in World War II, I initiated action to establish an Advanced Base and Shore Activity Division of six officers, including individuals specially qualified in personnel, supply, logistics, craft, and civil engineering. This division would not do the whole job, but would draw upon and coordinate the efforts of the other staff divisions. Prior to the arrival of Captain W. C. Dozier, Jr., to head the Division, an ad hoc group was formed from other staff sections. In addition to the Naval Support Activity, the Division would later act as the focal point for other Support Activities, Naval Stations, and Fleet Activities under the Service Force.

A fourth series of problems had to do with support of the expanding Coastal Surveillance Force, called "Market Time," which had been activated and placed under the command of the Chief of Naval Advisory Group, Rear Admiral N. G. Ward. A number of actions had already been taken to provide repairs and other logistic support. These actions had been formulated in a sense of expediency and were understandably somewhat fragmented. A more comprehensive and more complete plan would be required for adequate and efficient support as operations expanded.

In view of the responsibilities of COMSERVPAC as Principal Logistic Agent for "supervision and coordination of the planning, conduct, and administration of logistic services and supply of material," I discussed my intention to come up with an overall logistic support plan for Market Time. This was discouraged until problems to do with the concept had been resolved, including matters to do with relationships between the Fleet and Commander U.S. Military Assistance Command, Vietnam. Development of the plan will be discussed later. Meanwhile, staff actions continued, and a conference in Subic, chaired by Commander Service Group Three, Rear Admiral Joseph W. Williams, Jr., helped resolve immediate logistic problems.

The fifth problem area requiring immediate and special attention had to do with salvage, one of the specific areas of COMSERVPAC responsibilities.

At 0235, on the night of 18 July (19 July, West Longitude time), destroyer USS *Frank Knox* (DDR–742), proceeding north toward Hong Kong at sixteen knots, had run hard aground on Pratas Reef. From the evidence that came in during the first few hours, survival of the ship was in doubt. Not only would every possible effort have to be made on the scene, but they would need all the advice and help we in Pearl Harbor and in the Bureau of Ships could give them. The story will be told in a later chapter of the ingenuity, hard work, perseverance, and bravery by which success was finally achieved in what some considered to be the most difficult single ship salvage job in history.

The urgent problems facing Commander Service Force in the summer of 1965 did not end here, but these were the most prominent ones. Clearly this was going to be a busy job.

# CHAPTER VI

# The Seventh Fleet in Action

The Vietnam Conflict saw many examples of the use of mobile naval power. Guarding the interests of the United States throughout the Western Pacific and in readiness for combat there or elsewhere, the Seventh Fleet was able to move suitably configured task forces immediately into the troubled area; to apply military force by air attack and surface gunfire without waiting for the establishment of security ashore, or for the building of airfields, ports and other facilities; to project forces ashore by amphibious means; to guard against attack from the sea; to secure the sea lines of communication; to restrict the enemy's use of the sea; and to be ready to cut off the flow of his supplies by ocean–going vessels, if the strategy so directed.

For maximum effectiveness it was necessary to sustain these task forces at sea for as long as required to accomplish their missions, maximize their fighting power, and take advantage of their mobility. This was the primary role of the Service Force.

Operations in the South China Sea were not new. In addition to visits by naval units to Indochina in the years preceding Pearl Harbor, Halsey's Third Fleet had made a foray into the area in January 1945, striking at Tourane (later known as Danang), Qui Nhon, and Cam Ranh Bay and sinking Japanese ships along the coast. U.S. submarines had found this a profitable World War II hunting ground. The activities of the Seventh Fleet toward the end of the Viet Minh War and up until the winter of 1965 has already received brief mention.

The author's own acquaintanceship with the Indochina area had grown as a result of a tour in the Western Pacific when in command of Amphibious Group One. In addition to following the daily course of events in the area and planning for contingencies as Commander Amphibious Force, Seventh Fleet, I had been assigned responsibilities as Exercise Director over SEATO Exercise Tulungan in the spring of 1962, and exercised operational command over the forces involved. The plan, as we developed it, involved landings by two amphibious groups, one near each end of the west coast of the island of Mindoro, preceded by a movement to the objective area with

113666

*Bridges at Haiphong severed by Task Force 77 air strikes.*

submarine and antisubmarine actions, and followed by antiguerrilla action ashore. Our plan produced a constructive land mass as a mirror image of the southeast part of the continent of Asia with Mindoro the equivalent of the northern part of the Republic of Vietnam.

Further experience with the area was gained in May of that year, when Communist forces threatening Laos approached the Thailand border. As result of information received one Friday evening while proceeding out of the channel at Inchon, Korea, I had all the amphibious ships underway by 0800 the next morning and heading for points where they could pick up Marines. Subsequently, 1,800 Marines were put ashore on 16 May 1962 in Thailand from the Amphibious Ready Group, commanded by Captain Henry S. Jackson, in USS *Valley Forge.*

Almost three years later, the Amphibious Task Force of the Seventh Fleet and subordinate task groups were to place the first organized ground forces ashore at Danang and Chu Lai in the spring of 1965 and engage in numerous amphibious actions along the coast of Vietnam for many months to come.

On 12 March 1965 the Fleet initiated air and surface patrols off the coast to counter enemy infiltrations by sea. The first non–retaliatory strike against North Vietnam occurred three days later when carrier pilots from *Hancock* and *Ranger* struck an ammunition depot at Phu Qui. A month later *Coral Sea* and *Midway* planes conducted the first carrier strikes against the Viet Cong within the Republic of Vietnam. In addition to a carrier at Yankee Station in the Tonkin Gulf, Dixie Station was established off South Vietnam in May on a part time basis, to become full time in July. The operations of carriers, both north and south, proved of immense value during the long time required to build airfields ashore for the Air Force. Carrier aircraft continued to carry a major portion of the load after the fields had been established, particularly in the north.

Demands for gunfire in support of U.S. and allied forces ashore, which started with the bombardments of destroyer USS *Henry W. Tucker* on 16 May 1965, rapidly expanded and became crucial during periods of intensified enemy efforts such as offensives across the Demilitarized Zone. Cruisers and activated battleship *New Jersey* were to add their weight and longer ranges later. On 25 October 1966 Operation Sea Dragon started with the objective of destroying waterborne logistic craft and coastal lines of communication by ship gunfire along the panhandle region of North Vietnam, the first mission being conducted by destroyers *Mansfield* and *Hanson.*

*Recommissioned battleship* New Jersey *added the fire power and range of 16–inch guns to the Vietnam War.*

Basically the Fleet and its logistic support system were well prepared for these diverse types of operations, although there would be many complicating factors and special problems to be solved. Herein, we are concerned primarily with the Service Force's part of the overall role.

Maximizing the effectiveness, mobility, and endurance of the operating forces of the Fleet, and enhancing their readiness for emergencies and contingencies elsewhere required supreme effort on the part of many units and activities. The services and logistic support required were extensive and varied. They encompassed such diverse areas as repairs, ammunition, petroleum products, provisions, consumables, repair parts, fleet freight, towing, salvage, stockage and issue of aeronautical material, communications relay, technical research services, mail, movies, medical support, and port services. Support was provided not only for units of the Fleet and their weapon systems, but for the personnel who manned these units and systems. The latter support extended to the spirit as well as the body—as dedicated "circuit riders," chaplains of the Service Force, highlining from ship to ship tended to spiritual needs, and advised and consoled those who had personal or family problems.

These many tasks demanded an integrated effort on the part of the entire Service Force. They required overall coordination by the headquarters in Pearl Harbor and, in particular, direction and coordination of the specific efforts in the Western Pacific. The latter was a role of Commander Service Group Three, who exercised command over SERVPAC ships, craft, and mobile support units homeported in the area, who exercised operational control under Commander Seventh Fleet of most of the deployed SERVPAC ships and units, and who coordinated the combined efforts of the mobile force and shore activities in support of the Fleet. Rear Admiral J. W. Williams, Jr., had this assignment in the early days. He was relieved by Rear Admiral F. E. Janney on 13 November 1965, who in turn was relieved by Rear Admiral N. G. Ward in June 1967.

Repairs to ships of the Fleet were provided by repair ships and tenders; by Mobile Technical Units 3, 7, and 13; by the Ship Repair Facilities, Subic, Yokosuka, and Guam; by the Ship Repair Department, Fleet Activity, Sasebo; and in some cases by Service Force ships, craft, and activities under the Naval Support Activities, Danang and Saigon. Material support for the repairs was provided by the Service Force supply system. Some contract repair support was provided by the Headquarters Support Activity, Taipei. The communication relay ships, USS *Annapolis* (AGMR–1) and USS *Arlington* (AGMR–2) provided specialized communications and electronics repair support.

Ammunition was provided by ammunition ships (AE) and fast combat support ships (AOE); by Naval Magazines, Subic and Guam; by Naval Ordnance Facilities, Yokosuka and Sasebo; and by Naval Support Facility, Cam Ranh Bay. Under Commander Service Force, Commander Service Group Three was charged with supervising and directing the distribution of ammunition in the Western Pacific.

Petroleum products were provided by fleet oilers (AO) and fast combat support ships (AOE), and by Naval Supply Depots, Subic, Yokosuka, and Guam.

Provisions were provided by provisions ships (AF), combat stores ships (AFS), and fast combat support ships (AOE); by the Headquarters Support Activity, Taipei; and by the Naval Supply Depots.

Fleet freight was delivered via Naval Supply Depots and underway replenishment ships.

Aeronautical material was stocked and issued by Naval Supply Depots, Subic and Yokosuka.

Consumables and repair parts were provided by stores issue ships (AKS) and combat stores ships (AFS), by the Naval Supply Depots, and by the Supply Department, Fleet Activities, Sasebo.

Towing and salvage were undertaken by salvage ships (ARS), by ocean tugs (ATF and ATA), by Harbor Clearance Unit One, and by other Service Force units and experts. The fleet [ocean] tugs (ATF) and salvage ships (ARS) also provided almost continuous "blocking services" against Soviet intelligence ships to prevent interference with Fleet operations.

Hydrographic surveys were provided by survey ships.

Mail and movies were delivered by underway replenishment ships.

Port services and other support were provided by the Naval Stations and Fleet Activities.

The mobile support concepts developed in World War II had been further refined and made standard operating procedures in the Western Pacific. Although the magnitude of these operations under normal operating conditions would fall far short of what would be required in similar operations under combat situations, the crews of underway replenishment ships and the ships they supported were continually trained in the basic arts. The load lists of the stores issue ships (AKS) and the new combat stores ships (AFS) emphasized items in high demand and were periodically updated to take care of not only the normal operating needs but also to ensure that in case of combat these needs too would be met. Whenever an AKS or AFS was in port, other ships were required to go to them before placing a request on a naval supply depot. Repair ships and tenders were deployed to the Seventh Fleet to accomplish repairs and maintenance beyond the capabilities of the ships themselves. Floating drydocks and supporting craft augmented the capabilities established ashore, although their readiness for independent operations had declined after long periods of satelliting on ship repair facilities and steps would be required to enhance this readiness.

## SUSTAINING OPERATIONS

The location and nature of Seventh Fleet operations in the Vietnam Conflict were such as to place special requirements on logistic support. In the first place, the ships to be supported were scattered along a band stretching 1,100 miles from the Tonkin Gulf all the way around to An Thoi in the

Gulf of Siam. Compared with the Korean War, where supply lines to the nearest fleet base, Sasebo, were about 5,200 miles from the continental United States, with an additional 140 miles to Pusan, the supply lines to the Fleet off Vietnam extended 6,300 miles to the fleet base at Subic, and an additional 700 to 1,300 miles to Yankee, Dixie, and Market Time stations.

In the second place, never before had carriers and other ships been so continuously engaged in high tempo combat operations for such long periods of time. This was particularly true of the carriers who launched strikes around the clock. Now and then they would "stand-down" for a day of recuperation and catching up with maintenance tasks, but these days were rare. The sustaining of these types of operations placed special demands on the mobile support force so that underway replenishment would not be the limiting factor.

The situation with regard to destroyers and cruisers engaged in gunfire support or Sea Dragon operations was similar, as the Mobile Support Force sought to minimize the time of these combatants off the line. Likewise, surveillance against infiltration along the long coast of the Republic required the continuous patrolling of ships on station. Although their endurance was somewhat greater, amphibious task groups also had to be continuously poised off Vietnam in readiness for prompt action.

This was far different from the wartime support operations for which we had normally trained. These involved the World War II practice of combat task groups retiring to rendezvous with replenishment task groups for a day or portion of a day. But the procedures were not rigid and our mobile support forces were adaptable.

Other requirements stemmed from the continuous high tempo of operations. They stemmed also from the nature of the war and from advances that had been made in naval weapon systems. One result was extraordinarily high consumption rates of certain commodities. For example, jet airplanes had gluttonous appetites for fuel. These modern aircraft carried extraordinary bomb loads and, with their speeds and the efficiency of large carrier operations, were able to deliver them on the enemy at unprecedented rates. To cite an extreme measure, nuclear powered USS *Enterprise* reached expenditures of air to ground munitions as high as 4,478 tons in one month. Statistics on World War II indicate that her predecessor dropped only 2,000 tons of bombs in the entire war. Even with allowance for the amount of effort expended in air–to–air actions, the contrast was startling.

As the deployed fleet doubled in size, the number of support ships remained relatively few, considering the mammoth job to be done, and most were reaching the end of their useful life.

The operations of the Seventh Fleet off Southeast Asia could only be sustained by making the most efficient use possible of the ships that were available, including the few additional that would be provided from the Eastern Pacific, the Atlantic, and the inactive fleet. This was particularly true in the case of the underway replenishment ships.

## UNDERWAY REPLENISHMENT

Much of that which would have been transferred at anchor in a protected location in World War II was accomplished at sea in this conflict. In Fiscal Year 1967, a typical year, over 70 percent of the ship fuel, 95 percent of the jet fuel, virtually all of the aviation gasoline, over 95 percent of the ammunition, 97 percent of the provisions, and over 70 percent of the stores were transferred at sea. Based on statistics of World War II from the book *Beans, Bullets and Black Oil* for the peak of the Okinawan campaign, one arrives at the following monthly underway replenishment comparisons with Fiscal Year 1967 when far fewer ships were involved: ammunition—World War II, 7,000 short tons; VN, 15,000; aviation fuel—World War II, 221,000 barrels; VN, 450,000; provisions—World War II, 2,800; VN, 2,699; mail—World War II, 1,005,000 pounds; VN, 3,400,000. In the case of stores, the line items available for supply at sea were 100 in World War II; in 1967 they were 21,215.

The underway replenishment ships that contacted all the naval units in the South China Sea on a regular basis, provided lift for a multitude of other items. Transportation and delivery of mail, fleet freight, and personnel were carried out on a daily basis. Surface mail was carried from Subic to ships on Yankee and Dixie stations, ships operating in the Tonkin Gulf, gunfire support ships, the amphibious groups, and Market Time units. Some of the airmail brought out to the carriers from Cubi Point and Danang by COD aircraft was delivered to nearby units by helicopters. Most of the remainder was delivered by underway replenishment ships. Over 95 percent of the personnel received at Subic for transfer to fleet units were transported by ships by the Service Force, and personnel were returned in the same manner. Hundreds of thousands of gallons of fresh water were provided to ships at sea, to ships ranging in size from carriers to ocean minesweepers.

Special consideration had to be given to scheduling, coordinating, and controlling these operations. This was the mission of Commander Mobile Logistics Support Group (CTG 73.5). The Commanders of Service Squadrons Five and Seven were deployed alternately from Pearl Harbor and San Francisco, accompanied by some members of their staffs, and in rotation with the Assistant Chief of Staff for Readiness of COMSERV-GRUTHREE. Initial deployment periods of two months were extended to three.

From time to time consideration was given to making this a permanent command. Although there would have been accompanying advantages, I always ended up favoring the existing situation. Rotation meant that squadron commanders brought back experience and know–how which gave them valuable perspective in training and otherwise preparing their ships for deployment. It gave these commanders operational command experience. The major disadvantages were lack of continuity and absences from their squadrons. My relief, Rear Admiral Walter V. Combs, later requested the change. As a result, Commander Service Squadron Nine was established in January 1969 and assigned on a one year unaccompanied tour.

Major replenishments were normally planned two weeks in advance and a schedule was promulgated every three days, showing areas in which the underway replenishment ships would be operating in the South China Sea. Each such ship transiting along the coast promulgated its own position and intended movements to naval ships in the area and then guarded the appropriate operational circuits for the area through which it was transiting. Fifteen minutes notice of a ship appearing and speeding alongside for replenishment was a normal way of life.

To impart a feeling for the nature of these operations and the control of them, a review will be made of the critical fuel and ammunition replenishment operations, with brief mention of provisions and the impact of new ships.

### FUEL

A typical cycle of fleet oilers (AO) in Fiscal Year 1966 went something like this. An oiler from Subic would rendezvous at Yankee Station where she would replenish the carrier task groups on the first day. The second and third day she would swing clockwise through the northern Market Time stations and into the Tonkin Gulf, return to Yankee Station to replenish

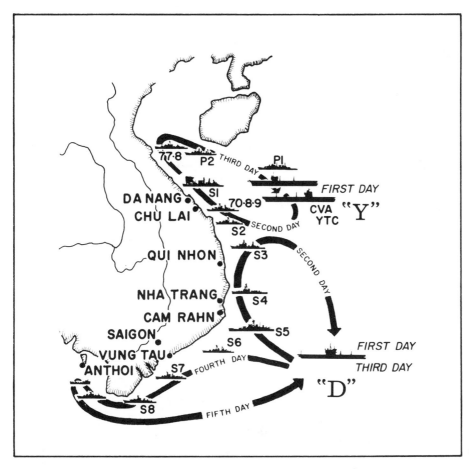

NH–74350

*Replenishment cycles in 1965 and early 1966.*

once more the units there, and perhaps consolidate with an incoming oiler before returning to Subic. Another oiler would go from Subic to Dixie Station. She would replenish the carrier task group there on the first day, steam along the Market Time areas off the middle section of the Republic on the second day, return to replenish Dixie Station on the third, swing south along the coast to An Thoi on the fourth day, and return to Dixie Station on the fifth day.

In the summer of 1966, the pattern of underway replenishment was changed when all the carrier striking power was shifted north to concentrate on North Vietnam. By then airfields ashore had developed to the point where the Air Force and Marines could handle the vast majority of the support missions within the Republic itself.  USS *Intrepid*, the last of the southern carriers, departed for Yankee Station on 5 August 1966 and Dixie Station was disestablished three days later.  With three, and some times four or five, of the attack carriers of the Task Force 77 operating from Yankee Station, where they were joined for long periods of time by an ASW Group providing surface and sub–surface surveillance, the basic replenishment cycles were modified accordingly.

The typical cycle became 3,300 miles in length (more than the distance across the Atlantic) and typically took twenty–one days.  Starting in Subic, the first stop was Yankee Station.  While in this area, replenishment ships would go approximately 200 miles to the north in Tonkin Gulf to replenish ships at the northern and southern Sea–Air Rescue stations, in the Positive Identification Radar Zone ("PIRAZ") ships whose tasks had to do with conducting air surveillance and control, and ships on Sea Dragon operations.

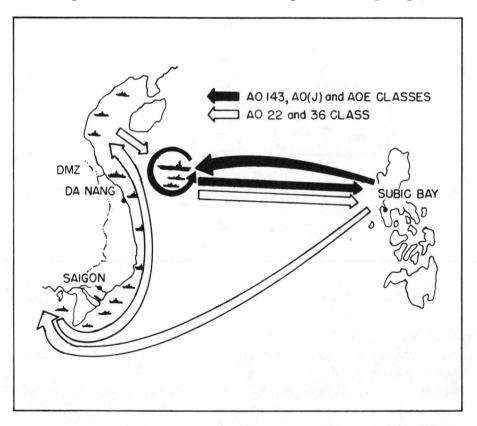

NH–74349

*Oiler underway replenishment cycle after June 1967.*

After leaving Yankee Station the ship would proceed south along 1,000 miles of coastline replenishing naval gunfire support, amphibious, and Market Time ships, and then return 1,300 miles back to Subic for resupply. Cycles were varied to adjust to the operations being supported.

The low jet fuel (JP–5) capacity and low pumping rates of the older oilers created problems. This meant long times alongside the carriers. In June 1967, Commander Service Group Three implemented a revised oiler rotation plan to improve the utilization of the greater pumping capabilities of the AO–143 class and the AO–105 (*Jumbo*) class oilers. These larger oilers remained in the vicinity of Yankee Station for their entire replenishment cycle. Under the new plan the smaller AO–22 class oilers left Subic and transited to the southernmost Market Time area, and from there proceeded north replenishing ships along the coast and up in the Tonkin Gulf. Then they went to Yankee Station to transfer remaining fuel to the larger oilers, and returned to Subic for resupply. An additional benefit was that replenishment of the smaller ships was less affected by late or unscheduled changes in CVA underway fuelings. The result was improved regularity of

K–72293

*Oiler* Hassayampa *with destroyer* Lynam K. Swenson *leaving from the starboard side. The fueling of carrier* Ranger *(foreground) is completed except for one station.*

mail, passengers and fleet freight deliveries to ships along the coast of the Republic.

Another change instituted later in the year was to load 5-inch ammunition on the deck of oilers going south to reduce the demands on the critical ammunition ships (AE), as had been done on occasion during World War II. In December 1967, the oilers started delivering fresh produce to the naval gunfire support ships.

In an eight month deployment, USS *Ponchatoula* (AO–148) conducted 484 underway replenishments to 503 ships, transferring 50,000,000 gallons of fuel and 69 tons of freight. One day in November she conducted twenty underway replenishments and one consolidation with another oiler, transferring 2,680,000 gallons of fuel oil and 653,000 gallons of jet fuel during a 24–hour period.

These records would later be broken several times. For instance, in a seven month deployment in 1967, USS *Mispillion* (AO–105) transferred over 70,000,000 gallons of fuel.

The impact of increased petroleum requirements was particularly severe

USN–1127887

*Crewmen steady a crate of 8–inch powder casings highlined from ammunition ship* Pyro.

at the Naval Supply Depot, Subic, where there was capacity only for about twenty days supply each of Navy Special Fuel Oil and jet fuel. Tight scheduling was required to avoid critical shortages. My staff closely monitored the resupply of POL products for all Pacific Fleet ships and bases, working directly with the CINCPAC's Joint Petroleum Office to alter delivery schedules and tailor tanker cargoes to insure sufficient POL was maintained for uninterrupted operations.

In order to align storage to requirements and improve facilities, COMSERVPAC sponsored several military construction projects in 1965. These included a project at Subic to increase stowage of Navy Special Fuel Oil (NSFO) by 100 percent, and jet fuel (JP–5) by 50 percent; a project to provide an offshore loading/unloading POL terminal to handle deep–draft MSTS tankers resupply at Subic in order to free the congested fuel lines to Alava Wharf adjacent to the Ship Repair Facility and at the freight terminal pier; and to lay a line for NSFO to accompany an existing JP–5 line to the Cubi Point carrier pier. The peacetime military construction procedures were such that it was not until two years later that these projects were completed.

## AMMUNITION

On each trip the ammunition ships (AE) normally conducted about six carrier replenishments in the Yankee area, catching Sea Dragon forces in between CVAs, and then transiting Market Time areas. The schedule permitted rearming gunfire support ships every three days.

The record of *Pyro* (AE–24) was particularly outstanding on a ten and a half month tour, for which she was awarded the Navy Unit Commendation. Her record of 227 underway replenishments totaling over 10,000 tons with a peak rate of 193 tons per hour seemed unbreakable. Not only did she shatter these records on her next deployment of over eleven months, but other AEs, the old as well as the newer ones, even broke those records. When one of the most ancient, *Mount Katmai*, sustained an average of 7.3 tons per minute for 56 minutes in a transfer to *Oriskany* (CVA–34), I felt obliged to put a damper on record setting for fear that safety might be compromised.

We needed help, so one Atlantic Fleet AE was kept in the Western Pacific starting in November 1965, when *Wrangell* (AE–12) joined the SERVPAC units. Two World War II cargo ships *Virgo* and *Chara* were activated and converted to ammunition ships. It was not until 1967 that we were able to reach a deployment schedule reasonable from the point of view of the men manning these important ships.

## PROVISIONS

In the early days one stores ship (AF) would depart from San Francisco every 35 days. This was later compressed to 28 days as demands increased. Then in 1967, I increased the efficiency of utilization of these ships by adjusting to the differing capacities of the ships involved. After one of the two large stores ships would depart San Francisco, there would be a 42–day interval before the next one. An interval of 35 days would follow departure of the medium capacity ship, with a 28–day interval for the others.

The critical items were chilled produce, which easily spoiled. Improved service in the case of these fresh provisions was achieved by the purchase of fresh fruits and vegetables from Taiwan through SERVPAC's Headquarters Support Activity, Taipei.

## NEW TYPES

Two new ships, the fast combat support ship (AOE) and the combat stores ships (AFS) proved extremely valuable. Each had a new capability, that of vertical replenishment by the two helicopters embarked in each ship. More than one–third of the stores and ammunition transferred by these ships would be by helicopter, day and night, both augmenting the alongside methods and replenishing at distances up to seventy miles. At times, transfers would be made to carriers during the cycle of landing and launching aircraft and to destroyers on screening stations. These UNREP ships would proceed along the coast and up into the Tonkin Gulf at high speed, transferring cargoes without stopping or going alongside.

In Fiscal Year 1967, excluding one month when the UH–46 operations were suspended following a crash of a Marine CH–46 helicopter, about 70 percent of *Mars* (AFS–1) replenishments were by VERTREP. This included about two–thirds of the tonnage transferred to carrier task groups. Vertical replenishment accounted for about 36 percent of the USS *Sacramento* (AOE–1) replenishments—including 27 percent of the ammunition, 48 percent of the provisions, 80 percent of the stores, fleet freight and mail, and 56 percent of the passengers. In the case of *Sacramento*, even when

K–36498

*Aircraft fuel tanks being delivered by vertical replenishment during topping off of fuel for carrier Hancock from fast combat support ship Sacramento.*

carriers were alongside for fueling and were receiving ammunition provisions and stores to the hanger deck from her multiple alongside replenishment stations, helicopters continued deliveries to the flight decks. When receiving stations became saturated, deliveries were made by helicopters to other ships of the force.

Vertical replenishments were made to destroyers when wind and sea precluded alongside replenishment. On one occasion, urgently needed supplies were delivered to cruiser *Canberra* while she was engaged in a gunfire support mission at night. Vertical replenishment at sea was here to stay.

There has been previous mention of records being set by ammunition ships. On one seven–month deployment, *Sacramento* conducted 583 underway replenishments, 213 by VERTREP, providing Seventh Fleet ships with over 67 million gallons of fuel; over 14,000 tons of ordnance; over 1,800 tons of provisions; 1,624,000 pounds of stores, fleet freight and mail; and 930 passengers.

It is of interest that the AOE was conceived for a different type of operation, that of dashing forward with fast carrier task groups and remaining as long as practicable, with the help of fuel consolidations. Her charac-

1109952

*The first of the combat stores ships,* Mars *(AFS–1).*

teristics proved ideal in the case of the unique Vietnam operations as well, a typical case of flexible use of Navy ships.

The large AOE was blessed with a 27–knot speed, and would make one–stop replenishments of ship and aviation fuel, stores, provisions and ammunition at high transfer rates. The AFS, alternating with stores issue ships (AKS), transferred stores, provisions and repair parts.

For a long time we had only two of these new type ships, *Sacramento* and *Mars*. Their tremendous capabilities proved what could be done by modern ships designed for the job. In other warfare situations their value would be even higher.

## MOBILITY, SUPPORT, ENDURANCE

The fighting power of the Seventh Fleet reached new heights in the Vietnam War. This was made possible by levels of achievements of the underway replenishment ships beyond that ever before thought remotely possible. Had this flexible application of mobile fleet operational logistics not reached these levels, the effectiveness of the Fleet as a whole would have been but a fraction of that actually achieved.

As the war intensified, replenishment to these ships and those at Yankee and Dixie Stations was normally provided every three to five days on demand. Replenishments grew from less than 4,000 in Fiscal Year 1965 to more than 8,139 in Fiscal Year 1967, or almost one every hour, day and night, throughout the year. From about 100 in 1965, night replenishments reached 2,529 in 1967.

Some measure of progress may be sensed from increases over the peak month of the Tonkin Gulf incident, August 1964. Oilers deployed to the Western Pacific increased from six to ten; underway replenishment increased more than threefold. Provision ships increased from three to four; their issues went up by a factor of almost five. Stores ships remained at three; their issues increased by a factor of ten. Ammunition ships went from three to six, one of which was from the Atlantic; their transfers at sea multiplied more than twenty–five times.

## HARD, UNGLAMOROUS WORK

Increased demands on underway replenishment required long deployments and many extensions of these deployments as delays were encountered in ship overhauls and ship activations, those hardest hit being the fleet oilers and ammunition ships. An added difficulty was the age of these ships and the toll time had taken on their hulls and equipment. In 1966, 93 percent of the SERVPAC ships were twenty or more years old.

The underway time of these ships in the Western Pacific increased 46 percent in the first two years of the conflict, but this is not the full story, because on their return to port they would work around the clock taking on cargo and preparing for the next trip. In the case of ammunition ships this meant four to five days of backbreaking and dangerous work. Then, back at sea, their work was never done. Keeping obsolescent equipment operating at this high tempo was itself a challenge.

To reflect the tempo more accurately we adopted a "percentage of utilization" figure within SERVPAC. In the case of underway replenishment this was the time on replenishment station, en route, loading inport and—when applicable—engaged in inport replenishment. In the case of others ships the measures were adjusted to their support missions. In Fiscal Year 1967, the "percentage of utilization" of Service Force ships in the Western Pacific varied from a low of 70.5 percent (survey ships) to 91 percent (light cargo ships), averaged over the year. Underway replenishment ships varied from a low of 73.5 percent to 81.5 percent. The remaining time was spent in such functions as inport maintenance, casualty repairs, and rest and recreation.

The morale of officers and men of the replenishment ships under these circumstances was truly inspiring, as their dedication to service achieved remarkable heights. The harder they worked the higher their spirits seemed to be. This was all the more remarkable in view of the fact that the work they were engaged in lacked the glamour of that of the combatants they supported. At the same time their "can do" attitude earned the respect of the Fleet as never before.

The high performance of the underway replenishment ships stemmed in part from the leadership of their commanding officers, some regular line officers, others aviators. Normally aviators assigned to command Service Force ships would alternate with their more experienced counterparts—a wise policy. Whereas the aviators usually were lacking in shipboard experience, they were all highly selected and brought fresh points of view to the Force. It was gratifying to see the enthusiasm of "tail–hook pilots" commanding these auxiliaries. With few exceptions their performances were such as to challenge the regular line officers to match or excel in their own commands. Many of these aviators went on to command carriers, carrying with them invaluable experience.

# CHAPTER VII

# Country–Wide Support

As noted in Chapter II, the Navy had been assigned logistic responsibilities as "Administrative Agent" to support the Military Assistance and Advisory Group (MAAG) in Vietnam, and the Headquarters Support Activity, Saigon, had been established as the focal point for this support.

When established in 1962, the Headquarters Support Activity, Saigon, was assigned such diverse common support tasks as operating the military port at Saigon, warehousing in Saigon, motor transportation, industrial relations, housing and messing, security, public works and housekeeping services, transportation within the capabilities of assigned aircraft (a C–47, a C–45, and an HU–16 amphibian), common supply items, and coordinating or arranging for support of MAAG field advisors. Provisions were supplied to all Services and were delivered directly to the units concerned. Common supplies were issued to the COMUSMACV Staff and to the senior advisor in the four tactical zones.

By this time, the job had become far more than a routine MAAG support assignment. More and more advisors appeared in Vietnam. Not only did the population in Saigon expand, but more and more were deployed to scattered locations throughout the country. At the end of 1964, U.S. military personnel had reached a total of 23,310. Each of the Services provided its own service–peculiar items, but reliance was placed on the Navy for common support and services, and for many tasks for which provision had not otherwise been made. And, in addition to the growing U.S. military population, support was also provided to third country forces, and in varying degrees, to some 2,700 U.S. Government civilian employees and dependents.

Of the 23,310, 14,697 were Army advisors. They had established an Army Support Command in Vietnam to provide for maintenance of Army aircraft and service–peculiar items, but were heavily dependent on the Headquarters Support Activity for other support and services.

At this time there were 900 Marines, including a helicopter squadron in the Danang area. The latter received service–peculiar items through normal Marine and naval aviation channels.

Including two A–1 squadrons, four C–123 squadrons, a temporary duty fighter squadron, and a B–57 bomber detachment, the Air Force personnel totaled 6,604. Although receiving provisions from the Navy, most other supplies were flown in from the "Main Operating Base" at Clark Field in the Philippines.

Of the 1,109 Navy personnel, 610 were in the Headquarters Support Activity.

With deployment of combat units to Vietnam, starting in March 1965, the forces to be supported expanded rapidly.

In February 1965 the Secretary of Defense had approved in principle an Army Logistical Command and the deployment on 1 April of a small planning nucleus. On 2 April the full 2,100–man Logistical Command was approved. Complicated by the fact that the Army logistic units required were in the Reserves and there was no call–up of Reserves, it would be several months before the First Logistical Command could be effective. Meanwhile, the Navy's job would have to increase in magnitude and scope to ensure that the expanding forces were adequately supported. By the time I arrived in Pearl Harbor, the support operation had grown into big business. United States forces had already grown to 168,000 and other Free World Military Assistance Forces and U.S. Government agencies in Vietnam were expanding as well.

The achievements of the Headquarters Support Activity, Saigon, in meeting the explosive growth of requirements were outstanding in every respect. Noted for the high standards and responsiveness of its services from the start, the superior performance of the Activity was maintained despite the rapidly increasing and constantly changing requirements.

Captain Archie C. Kuntze, its commander at the time, was well qualified for the job. Never inhibited by red tape, never bashful, but always energetic, imaginative, aggressive and ambitious, he had a good sense of the comforts of those being supported. Every effort was made to see that individuals, from Ambassador Lodge and General Westmoreland on down, received personalized treatment. Captain Kuntze was proud of being called the "American Mayor of Saigon." His responsibilities were extended to military police and explosive ordnance disposal. Incidents of Viet Cong using explosives or grenades seemed to peak during my visits. Several times I was riding in his car when word of an incident came in. The car radio served to ensure the right actions were underway. Usually he went to the scene and took charge himself.

Others who manned the Activity were competent and dedicated. Few in number, they made the best possible use of indigenous help and local labor.

On 1 September 1965 the First Logistical Command took over support of Army advisors and organized units in the field, while HEDSUPPACT continued to provide common support. From the start it had been envisaged that, when capable, the Logistical Command would take over certain common support functions. Admiral Sharp, CINCPAC, weighed the pros and cons carefully. After receiving a recommendation of Admiral Johnson, CINCPACFLT, that a shift be made, he decided that common support responsibilities in II, III, and IV Corps zones would be phased over to the Army and so advised the Joint Chiefs of Staff. This coincided with my own recommendations which were based on the fact that the preponderance of forces in these zones was Army. It had already been decided that the Navy would continue to be responsible for I Corps where Marines were in the majority.

With the help of Rear Admiral Henry S. Monroe, COMNAVPHIL and the Navy Area Coordinator, a plan was evolved whereby Army personnel would work alongside their Navy counterparts and step–by–step take over functions, completing the shift on 1 July 1966.

Responsibilities for port operations in Saigon were transferred in October 1965. This was followed by translation, dental, and port operations in November; exchange services at the low point of 26 December; chaplain services in January 1966; purchasing, contracting, and civilian administration in February; medical, maintenance, supply and engineering, clubs and messes, special services, billeting, provost marshal operations, and installation coordination in April; and motor transportation, troop education, and funding in May.

Meanwhile, the Naval Support Activity, Danang, had assumed responsibilities for common support functions in I Corps on 15 October 1965.

The period of transition in the other zones would be accompanied by mushrooming activity on the part of HEDSUPPACT. The increasing needs had to be met, additional facilities had to be acquired, and the build–up of stocks had to continue—so that the Army would not be caught short.

HEDSUPPACT reached a peak in the operation of the military port operations in Saigon when, in October 1965, more than 330,000 measurement tons of military cargo were offloaded from some ninety–six ships. From Saigon over 40,000 measurement tons of military cargo were transshipped by Military Sea Transportation Service ships to other ports in

*Entrance to Headquarters Support Activity, Saigon, housed at the former Cofat ciga-
rette factory.*

Vietnam.  The requirements for shipments by air made HEDSUPPACT's
"Air Cofat" (then one DC–3 and two twin–engined Beechcraft) a very
busy little airline.*

One of the most critical operations was that of supplying all the forces
with provisions, particularly those requiring refrigeration.  A crisis in regard
to the latter, requiring special actions at my headquarters, was reached on
28 October 1965.  We called it "Operation Opu," but never used the code
name in messages for fear that some would consider it stretching humor a
bit too far.

On that date HEDSUPPACT noted that consumption was less than half
of what the Army had requested and that storage had not yet been completed to accommodate perishables requested for Cam Ranh Bay and Qui
Nhon.  It was predicted that at the present rate of consumption November
deliveries would exceed storage capacity by 600,000 cubic feet.  In a

---

* The aircraft detachment was locally named after the former French cigarette factory, called
Cofat, which now housed HEDSUPPACT Saigon.

matter of hours SERVPAC's Fleet and Force Supply Office took steps to hold in abeyance further procurement of frozen and chill provisions by all Navy Activities in the Western Pacific, arranged with the Military Sea Transportation Service (MSTS) to divert shipments en route from Vietnam to these activities and to schedule ships to hold in Cam Ranh Bay and Qui Nhon at the end of their swings, and established procedures with the Army and Air Force for a monthly revalidation of requirements.

Whereas this solved the immediate problem there was little margin for error. Thus in December 1965 COMSERVPAC initiated action with MSTS to ensure regular deliveries on a fifteen day basis. Later this was reduced to nine or ten days.

In addition to provisions, HEDSUPPACT was responsible for 3,500 items of supplies common to more than one military Service. Supplies were stored in over a dozen separate areas throughout the Saigon and Cholon area, where 2,730,000 cubic feet of warehouse space were acquired for general stores, dry provisions, freezer and chill stowage items.

The Navy Exchange directly and indirectly served all United States and other Free World Military Assistance Forces in Vietnam. In addition to the main retail store in the Headquarters Support Activity compound, the Exchange operated branch stores in a downtown Saigon Bachelor Enlisted Quarters, the Bien Hoa Air Base, the Danang Air Base, Tan Son Nhut Airport, the Saigon Naval Hospital and the U.S. Army Third Field Hospital. Besides the Exchange branch stores, there were more than one hundred field exchanges managed by United States troop units and detachments. "Customers" of the Navy exchange system, these field exchanges were providing bar sales items to more than three hundred clubs and messes in the field.

By November 1965, the Billeting Division was operating fifty–four Bachelor Officer and Bachelor Enlisted Quarters and four transient hotels in the Saigon–Cholon area. Over 6,460 military personnel and government civilians were housed in these billets. The hotels for officers and civilians were either leased from private individuals or corporations, or were new construction. Sales for all clubs and messes totaled $498,000 monthly, at cut–rate prices. By the end of 1965, HEDSUPPACT operated over 5,400 rooms.

The annual budget of the Service Division, which programmed welfare and recreation projects for all U.S. forces in Vietnam, exceeded two million dollars. One of the most significant recreation projects was the Rest and

Recreation program involving Hong Kong, Bangkok, Taiwan, the Philippines, and Japan. Special Services operated a motion picture circuit which provided a daily change of film for innumerable locations throughout Vietnam, some manned by as few as a half dozen advisors.

A 20,000 volume Special Services library in Saigon served as a feeder for branch libraries in six of the areas of heaviest U.S. troop concentrations. The library also shipped consignments of magazines, newspapers, and paperbound books totaling over 60,000 to some 750 units in the field.

For the academic calendar year of 1965–1966 the Educational Services Office had a total of 287 Army, Navy, Air Force, and American Government civilian employee students in courses under the University of Maryland. The United States Armed Forces Institute had 255 military students enrolled in courses varying from high school English to second year college geometry, through the Headquarters Support Activity Educational Office. This same office gave ninety–eight USAFI General Educational Development Tests, many of which provided an equivalency of a high school diploma for military personnel who had not finished high school. Also, USAFI "end of course" testing was administered to more than seventy–five military personnel.

In December 1965, Public Works was supervising construction and maintenance projects throughout Vietnam, ranging from construction of a new chapel and recreation building in the north at Hue, to building a tower for the Air Force at Ca Mau, south of the Mekong River in the southernmost province of the Republic. In Saigon, Public Works had under lease 201 separate enlisted and officer quarters and industrial sites.

Distributed throughout Vietnam was a fleet of more than 1,900 U.S. Navy vehicles—including jeeps, heavy trucks, buses, material handling equipment, and construction machinery. In Saigon alone, the traffic statistics reached more than 786,000 passenger miles and more than 55 million pounds of cargo a month. Electric generators, ranging from 1,000 to 300,000 watts, were placed by Public Works in over 700 locations throughout the Republic. Teams of Seabees were assigned to each of the four Corps Areas for maintenance of all vehicles and power equipment (generators, refrigerators, etc.).

Real estate leases were worth nearly $9 million. In December 1965, 318 construction contracts were underway at a cost of almost $4 million.

To carry out its duties of safeguarding U.S. installations in Saigon and Cholon, HEDSUPPACT's command security forces consisted of the Provost

Marshal Department and the U.S. Army's 716th Military Police Battalion, working with Vietnamese police. The military police provided anti–terrorist security for 190 U.S. manned structures and hotels. Some were assigned to the U.S. Embassy. A standby force was kept continuously on the alert for swift reaction to terrorist activity and other emergencies. A six–man U.S. Navy Explosive Ordnance Disposal Team inspected buildings and areas for Viet Cong bombs and explosive devices. The Provost Marshal Department made security checks on all Vietnamese nationals hired by U.S. Forces in Vietnam.

The Medical Department provided medical care and services for thousands of U.S. military and civilian officials living in Saigon and the southern portion of Vietnam. The hospital had 107 beds and was staffed with nine doctors, sixteen nurses, and eighty–four hospital corpsmen. Except for three U.S. and five Thai nurses, all were U.S. Navy personnel. Helicopters bringing in casualties from battle zones landed in a soccer field where they were transferred to Navy ambulances.

Dental cases rose to more than 12,000 cases by October 1965.

All elements of the Headquarters Support Activity were voluntarily involved in civic action programs. The Dental Department sent out volunteer teams on weekends to villages and hamlets, where they performed minor surgery to relieve oral suffering and halt infections. In a typical ten–hour day, two dentists would pull as many as 600 teeth. Maxillo–facial devices and artificial eyes would be made for wounded soldiers at the Vietnamese Military Hospital at Cong Hoa during off–duty hours. Children from as far away as Danang and Rach Gia were brought into the Saigon Navy Hospital with congenital defects such as cleft lip. Their mothers or other family members were boarded at the hospital during the pre–operative and post–operative period.

These are samples of the Navy's unusual logistic tasks in the Republic. HEDSUPPACT Saigon was disestablished on 17 May 1966. It was awarded a well deserved Navy Unit Commendation.

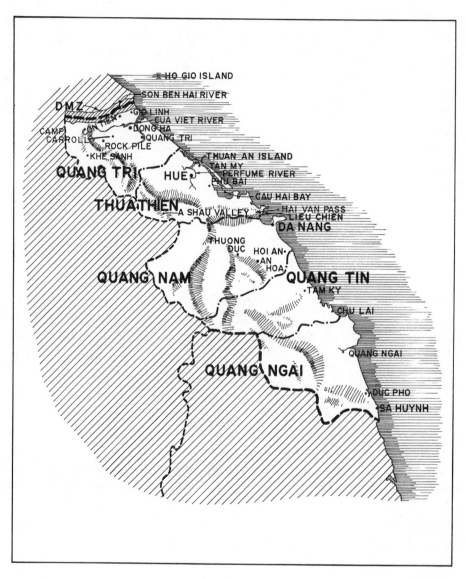

*I Corps Tactical Zone.*

NH–74353

# CHAPTER VIII

# I Corps Tactical Zone

As might be expected due to its proximity to North Vietnam, the most critical area of the Republic and the scene of what were undoubtedly the most determined efforts on the part of the enemy was I Corps. Turning back these efforts was to require extraordinary actions on the part of the Marines and other United States combat forces as well as the forces of the Republic of Vietnam. Success or failure of these U.S. forces depended on the wide variety of logistic support provided by the Navy, not only at the ports, beaches and main base areas, but elsewhere as well. Confronted by a lack of port development, a hostile climate and enemy efforts at disruption, ways had to be found of overcoming seemingly insurmountable obstacles.

The story of this phase of operational logistics is primarily that of two Service Force commands, the Naval Support Activity, Danang, and the Naval Mobile Construction Battalions. The whole story is, however, much more. As has been mentioned previously, the provision of extensive, effective and timely support was made possible by the direct and indirect contributions of many parts of the Service Force logistic system, afloat and ashore; from assistance by ships of the Seventh Fleet; from attention up the chain of command at the Service Force headquarters and through the Commander in Chief, U.S. Pacific Fleet, to the Chief of Naval Operations and the Secretary of the Navy; and from the support of the bureaus, systems commands, and officers of the Navy Department. Had this not been the case, combat operations in I Corps would have been seriously limited.

The I Corps Tactical Zone, consisting of the northernmost five provinces of the Republic of Vietnam, ran from the Ben Hai River, which marked the center of the Demilitarized Zone, down some 225 miles to Sa Huynh south of Quang Ngai. Only thirty to seventy miles wide, I Corps was bordered on the west by the heavily jungled Annamite mountains and beyond them by Laos. One spur of the mountains formed the Hai Van Mountains, a barrier on the northern side of the Bay of Danang. Route One made a tortuous and narrow passage through Hai Van Pass, roughly paralleled by the winding railroad. Another spur of the Annamites formed the southern border of the I Corps zone.

To the seaward of the mountains the land was flat, and much of it covered by rice paddies. Often vast stretches were under water during the rainy season. Rivers and streams coursed their winding ways down from the mountains to the seas. The huts, crowded together in hamlets and villages under the trees, gave no hint of the large numbers of people they housed.

Danang was the only port in the zone, and with a population of some 250,000, many of whom were refugees, the city was second in size only to Saigon.

## AMPHIBIOUS LANDINGS

Danang was not new to amphibious warfare. USS *Constitution*, "Old Ironsides," had called at Danang (then "Tourin" or "Tourane") in 1845 during her cruise around the world. Having been informed that the Apostolic Vicar of Cochin China, Bishop Lefevre, was being held at "Rue" (presumably Hue) where he was reportedly being slowly tortured to death, Captain "Mad Jack" Percival returned the call of the civil and military governors promptly with 300 armed men, and escorted the governors back to the ship where they were held until suitable promises had been extracted that led to the Bishop's release. French warships had attacked the Vietnamese Fleet at Danang in 1847, and in 1858 a Franco–Spanish expedition, commanded by a French admiral, had seized the port of Danang.

With continuing strife in the area, it is not surprising that a century later Danang had been selected as the scene for the Amphibious Warfare Study of the Marine Corps School. I recall having seen the school's excellent "dog and pony show" on the study on two different occasions, in 1960 and 1961.

As evidence mounted of the presence of twelve enemy battalions threatening Danang, a decision had been made to place ground troops in the area. Starting 8 March 1965, only hours after the decision, the Amphibious Force of the Seventh Fleet landed the Ninth Marine Expeditionary Brigade ashore at Red Beach in Danang Bay to reinforce the defenses of the Danang 10,000–foot airfield. In addition, the brigade was given the task of protecting the small Phu Bai Airfield and communication facility seven miles south of Hue to which a Marine contingent moved on 12 April 1965.

Reminiscent of World War II, the full role the Navy was to play in resupply had not been foreseen in advance. The amphibious phase was an established responsibility for which the Fleet was organized and prepared. The Military Sea Transportation Service was in being to ship cargoes for all the Services. But there had been no comprehensive preparation or planning for the Navy advanced base operations which would ensue.

The Marines were initially self–sustaining with their organic supplies, but resupply was another matter. There was no port at Chu Lai. At Danang there was an open roadstead exposed to seas from the northeast. The one pier up the Tourane River was small and could accommodate only shallow draft vessels. Off–loading capabilities, in the form of untrained labor and a few available barges, were totally inadequate.

Port operations were initially supervised by an Army advisor, off–loading being accomplished by Vietnamese under contract to the Headquarters Support Activity, Saigon. It was soon clear that this would not suffice. The Service Force's Cargo Battalion Two was deployed from Subic, but much more was needed.

USN–1113736A

*The only pier in Danang prior to port development accommodated nothing larger than shallow–draft craft and coastal steamers.*

Planning for major combat operations in Vietnam had envisaged the Army assuming responsibility for common logistic support after a six–month period. This was in recognition of the fact that time would be required for obtaining requirements information, for organizing the common support effort, and for developing the capabilities necessary for effective support. It soon became apparent that without the call–up of Reserves the Army would be hard pressed to provide for its own support, much less provide country–wide support.

Admiral Sharp made a basic decision whereby "Logistics Support work-loads were assigned to adapt to Service needs and capabilities." Primary logistic functions in the northernmost Combat Tactical Zone in South Vietnam, for example, were given to the Commander in Chief of the Pacific Fleet because "the combat forces in that zone were predominantly Marines."[1]

Following a conference with top officers of Commander in Chief, U.S. Army Pacific (USARPA); of Commander in Chief, U.S. Pacific Fleet (CINCPACFLT); and the Commanding General, Fleet Marine Force, U.S. Pacific Fleet, Admiral Sharp directed on 24 April 1965 that military logistic operations at ports and beaches for the support of U.S. forces and attached "third country forces" in the Danang–Chu Lai area would be accomplished using Navy resources. This was related to the fact that the Marines were to be in that area of RVN contiguous to the ports and beaches from Chu Lai to the DMZ. In the summer, the area of responsibility would expand to encompass the entire I Corps Tactical Zone. The initial tasks encompassed conducting U.S. Military port operations, to include: development of required military port and beach facilities; establishment and operation of necessary base supply depots at water terminals; provide for loading and unloading of ships in–transit, port clearance to base supply depot areas, common–item support, and the carrying out of harbor improvement projects of military necessity. These tasks were to be accomplished by CINCPAC-FLT's Navy/Marine resources and from other Services by inter–Service support agreements.

The Navy was reluctant to assume continuing responsibilities beyond the water's edge and, on 14 May 1965, the Chief of Naval Operations raised the question of ultimate primary logistic responsibility in I Corps with the Chief of Staff, Army. The Department of the Army reply on 15 June concurred in CINCPAC's decision in view of the fact that Navy/Marines were the

---

[1] Admiral U. S. G. Sharp, USN, and General W. C. Westmoreland, USA, *Report on the War in Vietnam* (Washington, D.C.: Government Printing Office, 1969), p. 55.

dominant forces in the area and were capable of providing their own support. The decision would prove to be sound, not only because of the existing capabilities at the time, but also because of the essential role sea lines of logistics would assume in the operations in the zone.

In May, Rear Admiral Irvin had recommended establishment of a Naval Support Activity. Although not approved at the time, the Naval Support Activity, Danang, would later be established, as related in Chapter V.

As an interim measure Vice Admiral Paul B. Blackburn, Jr., USN, Commander Seventh Fleet, through his Amphibious Task Force Commander, Rear Admiral Don W. Wulzen, had organized and tasked Commander Amphibious Logistic Support Group (CTG 76.4)—initially Captain (later Rear Admiral) W. R. McKinney (Commander Amphibious Squadron Seven)—to conduct logistics over-the-shore to the III Marine Expeditionary Force at Danang and Chu Lai. Composed of amphibious units, this force was gradually augmented by units of the Service Force—including Nucleus Port Crew Two from New York, and ships and craft of Mobile Support Unit Three from Sasebo—and by Mobile Inshore Underseas Warfare Surveillance Unit 13 and Explosive Ordnance Disposal detachments from the Mine Force. SERVPAC's Cargo Handling Battalion Two was sent to assist the Marines, along with a detachment from Cargo Handling Battalion One from the Atlantic.

The movement of Marines into Danang was followed on 7 May by an amphibious landing of Marines across the incredibly soft sand of the beach at Chu Lai. Navy Mobile Construction Battalion Ten (NMCB–10) from the Service Force, U.S. Pacific Fleet, went ashore with the Marines. This "Ready Battalion" deployed from Okinawa was followed by NMCB–3, which went to Danang on 27 May from Guam, and by NMCB–9 to Danang East on 3 June from Port Hueneme. The three construction battalions were organized into the 30th Naval Construction Regiment, established for this purpose, and placed under the operational control of Major General Lewis W. Walt, USMC, who had become Commanding General, III Marine Amphibious Force, on 4 June.

In July 1965, twenty-three days after construction started, an expeditionary airfield was built to relieve the congestion at the Danang field and placed in operation by the Seabees at Chu Lai. This presented a new role for a SERVPAC gasoline oiler, USS *Genesee* (AOG–8), which pumped vast quantities of water ashore to help stabilize the foundation. On the scene day–in and day–out from May to late September, *Genesee* was a work horse at Chu Lai and Danang, keeping ship–to–shore fuel lines in operation under hazardous conditions and, shuttling from Danang, delivering ten million gallons of fuel to the forces ashore. Under the command of Commander Donald Gurke, *Genesee* was the first of a number of SERVPAC ships and units to receive the Navy Unit Commendation. Her sister ships would continue to play key parts in supplying critical fuel to outlying bases in the I Corps zone in the months to follow.

Here and at Danang and other parts of the zone, the Marines, whose strength continued to increase, carried out their combat duties with the usual high professionalism of these elite troops. They were superbly led by Major General Walt, a big, barrel–chested former football lineman, who was promoted to the rank of Lieutenant General on 10 February 1966. Sound of judgment and firm, of calm demeanor and well versed in the fundamentals of warfare, he inspired confidence in everyone. The high intelligence and drive of Lieutenant General Victor Krulak, Commanding General, Fleet Marine Force Pacific, a very frequent visitor, also made significant contributions to morale and strategy.

USN–1144542

*Small oilers such as Genesee (AOG–8) kept ship–to–shore lines in operation at outlying posts and made deliveries of fuel essential to operations ashore.*

Operations were closely coordinated locally with those of the Vietnamese. It was interesting to watch changes, from one visit to the next, the expansion of the Tactical Areas of Responsibility (TAORs) at Danang and Chu Lai and the increasing patrol actions. Whereas defense of the base areas remained first priority, the Marines' strategy was expanded to included support of the Vietnamese, the conduct of offensive operations and, from time–to–time, amphibious actions in other areas of Vietnam.

## NAVAL SUPPORT ACTIVITY, DANANG

There was much to be done before the Naval Support Activity would be ready to take over its duties. Intensive actions were required of the Service Force headquarters to acquire essential resources and get them deployed to do the job. Control had to be exercised over the assembly and shipment of materials and equipments which made up the tailored Advanced Base Functional Components (ABFC). Tugs, lighterage, and a wide variety of craft had to be provided. Some required reactivation or conversion.

During World War II, one of the greatest problems was the transition from the amphibious to the resupply phase, a transition complicated by getting the advanced base organization on the scene and functioning. In this case, the transition was eased by designating as Prospective Commanding Officer of the Naval Support Activity the officer who was in command of the "over–the–beach" operations. On 28 July, Commander Task Group 76.4, then Captain K. P. Huff, USNR, reported to Commander Service Force in this capacity while continuing to carry out his task group responsibilities. The organization under his command started phasing into the expanded role. Responsibility for provisions in support of the Marines was taken over from the Headquarters Support Activity, Saigon, in September before the Naval Support Activity was fully activated.

The secret of early success was the use of ships and craft deployed to the scene, as we had to depend almost entirely on afloat means in the early months. Despite subsequent construction of facilities ashore, the need for afloat capabilities continued as more and more activities were required to meet the forever expanding requirements. In the fall of 1965, 35 craft of 12 different types were at Danang. By the summer of 1966 the number had grown to 131 craft of 21 types. These included: a small auxiliary floating drydock and its companion craft; 11 LCM–3 (landing craft, medium); 11 LCM–6s; 29 LCM–8s; 8 large personnel landing craft; 25 LCUs (landing craft, utility); 8 open lighters; a floating crane; 3 large covered lighters; 3 refrigerated covered lighters; a self–propelled fuel oil barge; a floating work-shop; a large harbor tug; 5 small harbor tugs; 2 self–propelled water barges; 4 picket boats; 8 skimmers, and four 50–foot utility boats.  Still more would be required later.

There were three barracks craft (APL), of World War II vintage, each accommodating 680, which first had to be overhauled and reactivated to provide for personnel berthing and messing.  After reactivation, APL–5 arrived on 5 October 1965, APL–30 in December 1965, and APL–25 in March 1966.  First one, and then two, attack transports (APA) from the Amphibious Task Force of the Seventh Fleet were required to provide these services prior to the arrival of the APLs and the building of barracks ashore. One APA served as the initial flagship and provided the necessary communi-cations.  Later the headquarters was to be established in the so–called "White Elephant" in downtown Danang on the Tourane River, a building which combined offices and warehouse space.

KN–12676D

*The White Elephant, headquarters of Commander Naval Support Activity, Danang, after the move ashore.*

Initially a landing ship dock (LSD) acted as mother ship, providing a means of boat and craft repair until the floating drydock and repair barge could be made ready and deployed. Maintenance support had to be provided Market Time coastal surveillance units, as well as activity craft. Plans included a small craft repair activity ashore, but when this was finally constructed, many months later, the build–up of craft was such that both ashore and afloat resources were needed.

Two refrigerated lighters were provided, and these were augmented by a commercial refrigerator ship, chartered by the Military Sea Transportation Service. The latter was needed until 11 June 1966 when construction ashore in Danang finally was able to provide adequate "reefer" space.

## MEDICAL

The first Advance Base Functional Component to be ordered forward was for a 400 bed Navy base hospital. By the time I took command of the Service Force, the Seabees had started its construction in Danang East. The hospital consisted of Quonset buildings and walkways built from Functional Component material, much of which had been left over from World War II. It resembled the Navy advance base hospitals of that war, although a considerable amount of new equipment was added. After much debate in Pearl Harbor and Washington, the decision was reached in August to make this a part of the Naval Support Activity rather than a separate command.

A Viet Cong night attack against the Marble Mountain helicopter air facility on 28 October 1965 also targeted the hospital and nearby Seebee camp. Well placed satchel charges did serious damage to the first 200 bed increment which was well under construction by Navy Mobile Construction Battalion Nine. Mortar and rifle fire killed two and wounded ninety–three of NMCB–9 that night, but the battalion was back at work the next day.

Although the Marines provided area defense, local defense was not supplied until the hospital neared completion. On every visit I would find the senior medical officer, the competent and dedicated Captain Bruce L. Canaga, Jr., there. Armed with carbine and pistol, he spent every night on the site. His personal efforts in getting the hospital established and in providing the best possible medical service to the wounded were prodigious. The hospital received its first patient on 10 January 1966 and was officially opened by Admiral Johnson during a visit on 17 January.

1114736E

*Naval Base Hospital in Danang East, 1966.*

Continuing steps were taken to improve the quantity and quality of Navy medical support in the I Corps zone, as it was increased in size. A preventive medicine building was added. The effective beds for intensive care were increased by establishing a medical holding company for ambulatory patients. Twenty Navy nurses were added in the summer of 1967. I foresaw potential difficulties as a result of the imbalance of sexes, but as far as I could determine they never appeared. A dispensary was set up at Camp Tien Sha. Medical support for Navy personnel at Chu Lai, Phu Bai, and Dong Ha was increased.

Following one of my trips, special communications were set up so that the Danang hospital could coordinate the distribution of patients between I Corps medical facilities, the Danang hospital and the hospital ships, both for efficiency and to make the best use of specialized capabilities.

By August 1967 the capacity of the Danang hospital had been increased to 467 beds, with construction underway for twenty more. The next month 1,312 patients were admitted. The next peak was in January 1968, when 1,357 were admitted. A daily record was established on 31 January with the start of the Tet offensive. One hundred thirty–nine were admitted that day, and an additional 140 were received and regulated to other medical facilities. The next day, 163 patients were admitted with 181 regulated elsewhere. Altogether there were a total of 2,175 admissions that February.

The hospital ships spent most of their time off the coast north of Danang. The reactivated USS *Repose* (AH–16), with hospital equipment rivaling that of the best hospitals in the United States, had arrived on 16 February 1966. The remainder of that fiscal year saw an average daily bed occupancy of 222.8, 52 percent of the patients being returned to duty. The high count the next year was 639 patients. As many as ninety–eight were brought aboard by helicopter in one day.

The reactivation of USS *Sanctuary* (AH–17) and her deployment in April 1967 meant that at least one hospital ship could be maintained on station all the time. It also provided flexibility for emergencies elsewhere. As *Sanctuary* arrived off Vietnam she received her first casualties, four from the USS *Bigelow* (DD–942) who had been wounded in a gun mount explosion. These were on board one hour after the request for assistance. *Sanctuary* had 634 patients the first month.

In addition to work on the AHs and the heroic Navy officers and corpsmen assigned to the Marines, surgical teams, normally four doctors and ten hospitalmen, were sent to amphibious ships during assault operations.

## ESTABLISHMENT OF THE NAVAL SUPPORT ACTIVITY

Commencing in August, materials, equipment, and other supplies for the Advanced Base Functional Components, specially tailored for the job, were ordered forward by COMSERVPAC in controlled fashion.  The construction items were assembled and shipped from the Naval Construction Battalion Center, Port Hueneme.  Generally, all other portions of the ABFCs were assembled and shipped from the Naval Supply Center, Oakland.

Acquiring the necessary personnel for the Naval Support Activity presented problems.  To the extent the capacity of the Amphibious Training Command permitted, these personnel were given a two weeks course in counterinsurgency training before proceeding west—a change from World War II when the Service Force had conducted its own training of personnel for advanced bases.

There being neither full nor partial mobilization, the entire Navy was drawn down to provide the officers and men needed to carry out the Navy's new Vietnam tasks and to take care of expanding forces.  At the start, top priority was given to filling Danang needs and all looked encouraging.  But the lead time to get qualified individuals ordered from all over the world, trained, and transported normally took a month or two, and progress was hard to monitor.  Usually the first warning of a short–fall was lagging arrivals in Vietnam.  With many other claimants for Navy personnel and shifting priorities, constant effort was required to keep stimulating the flow.

The amount of manpower required for off–loading cargoes, including that for around–the–clock operation of service craft and lighterage, exceeded what was envisaged in the original plan, and personnel desired for other functions had to be diverted for this essential job.  In the months to come augmentations were requested as the needs expanded in Danang and elsewhere in I CTZ.  Meager as these requests were, the justification–acquisition processes were frustrating in the detailed peacetime procedures and in the long delays encountered.

By mid–October, 39 percent of the initial allowance of 170 officers and 3,477 enlisted men had reported.  Despite the shortage of personnel, and the scarcity of lighterage, the Naval Support Activity, Danang, was activated on 15 October 1965 under the command of Commander Service Force, U.S. Pacific Fleet, under the operational control of the Naval Component Commander, then the Commanding General, III Marine Expeditionary Force, and under the area coordination of Commander Naval Forces, Philippines.

At this time the tasking of the Naval Support Activity included: providing of common item support to the U.S. and other Free World forces in I CTZ; operating of ports and beaches; conducting off–loading operations; delivering cargo to terminals and providing in–transit stowage; consolidating fuel (POL) requirements; receiving, stowing and issuing bulk and packaged petroleum products; off–loading ammunition; operating a main supply depot in Danang; providing harbor defense; and operating the hospital. Whereas area defense was provided by the Marines, the Navy had to provide the defense of its own scattered facilities which were to become more and more numerous.

It would be necessary to keep temporary duty personnel on the scene for several months until NAVSUPPACT's manning level could catch up to the workload.

The most valuable of all the temporary units was Cargo Handling Battalion Two, a Service Force unit of two officers and eighty men, mostly petty officers, first commanded by Lieutenant Commander H. Luoto and then by Lieutenant Commander C. V. Bosco. Highly skilled and with their own equipment, they rarely operated in Danang as teams, being more productive as individuals training and supervising others, and working as parts of many teams. We had reason to be thankful to those in the Bureau of Supplies and Accounts who had sponsored these teams over the years.

I finally ordered the battalion to its home port, Subic, in June 1966. Its next job in the combat area was to train and help the Army Terminal Service Companies in Cam Ranh Bay from 19 September 1966 to mid–February 1967. Later the battalion was sent to Guam where difficulties were being encountered due to shortages of stevedores there at the time. In Guam, the Navy was responsible for handling all military cargoes. This included the off–loading of increasingly large quantities of bombs for B–52 strikes. The bombs were then delivered by the Naval Magazine to Andersen Air Force Base, at the other end of the island from Apra Harbor. On COMSERVPAC's initiative, CHB–2 was returned again to Danang on 12 June 1967 in anticipation of a massive turnover of personnel that summer.

Among the temporary duty units were the Nucleus Port Crews. They were comprised of officers who normally were engaged in other primary duties in port areas of the United States. Complaints were received from time to time from the Commandant of the Third Naval District that the team from New York was being improperly employed in Danang, since the officers of the team were not used as a unit. Their concept had to do with coordinating the operations of established port facilities, rather than being advanced base oriented. Furthermore, these operations were a primary function of COMNAVSUPPACT himself. I was of no mind to overrule the decision of the commander on the scene. He was so strapped for personnel that all had to be used in working jobs where needed.

When the necessary work had been accomplished and an Advanced Base Functional Component galley installed, Camp Tien Sha, a former Vietnamese barracks area, was opened on January 1966 for 1,000 people. Eight hundred fifty more moved in after additional renovations and the installation of a second galley. In Danang proper, twenty–three housing units were rented for 288 officers and enlisted men who worked at or near the headquarters.

Initial planning had been on the basis of an estimated military population of 48,000. By the end of the year, more than 100,000 were being supported. The number was to double again by the spring of 1968.

NH–74201

*Rear Admiral Thomas R. Weschler assumes command of Naval Support Activity, Danang, 6 February 1966. Left to right: the author, Captain Huff, Rear Admiral Weschler, and Lieutenant General Walt, USMC.*

Meanwhile, in January 1966, the Commander in Chief, U.S. Pacific Fleet, had established a requirement for a flag officer to be assigned as Commander Naval Support Activity, Danang, and on 6 February Rear Admiral Thomas A. Weschler had assumed command of the Activity. Captain Huff stayed on as Chief of Staff, a wise move from the point of view of continuity. His experience, expertise, and drive proved of tremendous value in carrying out the expanding tasks.

An outstanding leader, Rear Admiral Weschler proved an ideal commander. His intelligence and personality were such as to earn him the respect and confidence of everyone, regardless of Service, both in I Corps and in Saigon.

Rear Admiral Weschler was to be relieved one year later, on 5 February 1967, by another extremely competent commander, Rear Admiral Paul L. Lacy. Admiral Lacy's fine sense of command, good relationships with the other Services, management ability, intelligence and sound judgment made him especially qualified for the expanding challenges which lay ahead. He would be followed a year later by Rear Admiral James B. Osborn, in February 1968. After my tour, their successors would be Rear Admirals Emmet P. Bonner and Robert E. Adamson, Jr.

With added responsibilities, growing numbers to support, and additional detachments, the command was to grow to over 10,000 men by 1968.

## PORT AND TERMINAL OPERATIONS

The most urgent tasks of the Naval Support Activity were those to do with port and terminal operations. Large quantities of vital ammunition, provisions and supplies had to be off-loaded in Danang despite the absence of deep-draft piers. Except for what arrived in LSTs, the cargo could only be off-loaded in the open roadstead exposed to the north, and brought by ramp craft and lighterage.

Up until April 1966, when partial use of the new Bridge Cargo Facility up the Tourane River was possible, locations where the landing craft and lighterage could get cargoes ashore were very limited. One site was Tien Sha ramp, bulldozed on the shallow side of the bay next to Monkey Mountain, a ramp capable of accommodating two LSTs or four LCUs. Another was the Museum ramp in the river, which could handle one LST or LCU. The third was a small, broken-down "T" pier nearby. The fourth was the shallow-draft commercial pier which could handle two LCUs or barges.

*Tien Sha ramp on the east side of the Bay of Danang, October 1965.*

With the exception of minor shed stowage at the commercial pier, there were no in–transit stowage buildings or staging areas. Later, full use of the commercial pier was required by the Vietnamese for their own cargoes and for those of AID.

I had received some of the records on advanced base operations in World War II as a result of a request to retired Rear Admiral Eccles. It was interesting to read that one of the "lessons" was that an airfield should never be constructed until there was a deep–water pier!

The necessity for backloading cargo destined for Chu Lai, and later elsewhere, added to the load of the limited personnel and scarce lighterage. The job to be done was further complicated by a lack of off–loading sites and staging areas.

Fall and early winter were extremely difficult times. This was the result of a combination of factors, foremost of which was the weather.

The northeast monsoon starts in October and lasts until April. During this period, cooling of the land mass of the massive continent of Asia produces a deep high pressure area, with air pouring out from this area and circulating clockwise around the continent. The winds drive across the full reach of the South China Seas, waves build up to pound the coast of Vietnam from the east and northeast. In addition to the seas, the warm moist air piles up layer after layer of cloud on hitting the coast. There are long periods of torrential rains which produce deep mud everywhere, flood vast areas, and change quiet streams into torrents. Then, from time to time, conditions are worsened by the surges of cold fronts from the continental land mass down through the latitude of Danang, and sometimes further. In addition to producing heavy rains, the pressure gradient tightens as the front approaches, and the winds intensify.

Off–loading from the cargo holds of the merchantmen to landing craft and lighterage was difficult and hazardous. There were times when ships had to abandon the roadstead for as long as five days at a stretch.

Working in the heat and high humidity was tiring. Yet the normal working day was twelve hours on and twelve hours off ("watch and watch"). Normally the days off were only one in ten.

The laterite covering roads and staging areas became a gooey mass. The product of the one rock crusher in the area was needed to enlarge the airfield and build a second runway. The remaining source, that provided by women who quarried rock from the side of Monkey Mountain, crushing it by hand hammers and gathering it in baskets, could satisfy but a small fraction of the needs. Here and at Chu Lai, the Seabees were hard pressed to keep the roads passable. I recall, on one of my visits, a muddy hole in a road near the Danang airfield so deep and extensive that a jeep would disappear almost out of sight. It was nearly a year before the most essential roads were paved.

It took a long time to get more rock crushers. The problem was solved in Danang and Chu Lai during the next twelve months, but, as the needs farther north increased, the demand for crushed rock continued to tax the supply as late as 1968.

Even in the first month, cargo arrivals exceeded the requirements stated as a basis for planning. Matters were further complicated by the fact that delays of the few ships available to the Military Sea Transportation Service were prolonged by the custom of loading ships for a number of destinations, in Vietnam and elsewhere.

Poor packaging was a serious problem in the fall of 1965. In addition to cartons dissolving in heavy rains, thin cans of asphalt burst during handling in hot weather. Many items were loose, unwieldy and hard to off–load.

To help alleviate port congestion, COMSERVPAC initiated a number of actions in November. These included: instituting a program for all–weather packaging, heavy duty strapping and loading onto pallets of all cargoes destined for Danang or Chu Lai; requesting, in early December, Commander Western Sea Frontier to place an embargo on any cargo so destined that had not been "unitized"; requesting the Military Transportation Management Terminal Service (MTMTS) in San Francisco to assemble full ship loads for direct sail to Danang—a practice later adopted for other ports in Vietnam; requesting MTMTS to segregate and block stow continental U.S. cargo for Chu Lai to expedite discharge and handling at Danang; and requesting all ordering agents to reduce peaks and valleys as much as possible.

During this critical period, a limited program was instituted by COMSERVPAC whereby some cargo was off–loaded in Subic from deep–draft ships for transshipment to Danang and Chu Lai by LST. Four fleet LSTs were assigned the Subic to Danang and Chu Lai shuttle. These were later phased out as the situation eased. The possibilities of transshipments from Taiwan ports and Point Poro on Luzon were investigated but were not implemented since other steps proved adequate. Complaints on the use of LSTs were made by the Transportation Management Agency, recently established under COMUSMACV in Saigon, which stated that any LST engaged in such operations should be only under their control. But, by then, the emergency was over.

All these steps, plus the magnificent performance of those on the scene, paid off. The highest port congestion reached in Danang that year was 72,634 measurement tons, in early December 1965, and this was down to about 25,000 tons by the end of the month. The ratio between a measurement ton (42 cubic feet) and the more familiar short ton (2,000 pounds) varies greatly depending on the density of the cargo. In Danang the average usually ran about 1.7 measurement tons to one short ton.

Despite my weekly status reports, Washington's concern over the situation mounted after the peak was past. Complaints of delays in Vietnam filtered back from merchant seamen, and a major share of the blame was placed unjustly on Danang. *Life* magazine, in late December, stated that the average delay in Danang was over forty days. Only two ships ever reached that point, in fact, and these were as a result of the need to get more urgent cargoes ashore. The highest average delay was less than eighteen days. By February 1966, Danang had run out of cargoes to off–load for about four days. From there on in, no other port in Vietnam ever matched the performance of Danang.

As a result of the alarm expressed by one distinguished visitor, I took staff members out in late December 1965, on twelve hours' notice, to review the situation. The situation was found to be under control. There was a useful by–product, as the team used the visit to put together a specific port development program from many pieces. This assisted in focusing more in–country attention on this subject. Major General Walt, CG III MAF, was particularly cooperative—as always. I briefed him and key staff officers after dinner at his quarters then on a hill west of Danang. He offered the help of his troops whenever needed, and took steps to improve the flow of trucks during peak periods. The Marine Shore Party did its part until the last remnant at Danang was relieved on 11 March 1966.

In January 1966 a meeting was held at Camp Smith, Admiral Sharp's headquarters overlooking Pearl Harbor, to plan the further build-up of the U.S. forces in Vietnam. One day my representative at the meeting informed me of the conclusion that the desired increase in the I Corps zone had been judged to be logistically infeasible because of limited port capacity. A personal review convinced me the job could be done and I so stated in a message. The judgment was accepted and later proved correct.

In this case, the initial conclusion had been reached by using standard rated capacities for the various off–loading sites. Added weight to these resulted from the estimates emanating from Danang itself. The practice, which took months to correct, was to underestimate the capacities—even when they had already been exceeded in practice. It took little imagination to see that these were understated. Bottlenecks were often not the sites themselves but how rapidly cargoes could move if an adequate flow of trucks could be maintained around the clock and if sufficient manpower could be made available, including troop augmentation when necessary.

A common practice is to carry the planning for combatant operations to an advanced stage, and only then ask whether or not it will be logistically feasible. One cannot argue with the need for determining whether or not an operation can be supported, but the normal approach, drawing upon standard measures of capability, seems often to focus more on limitations than on possibilities. Concurrent logistic planning is far preferable, employing an imaginative approach to see how one can overcome the obstacles to provide the desired support. This may finally be determined to be seriously limited, but such a conclusion should only be reached after all conceivable approaches have been thoroughly explored, and then reluctantly.

The underestimating and understating of port throughput capacity by Danang almost had other adverse effects. Admiral Sharp established a new organization, PAMPA (Pacific Area Movements Priority Agency), in the winter of 1966 in Oakland, California, to set priorities for shipments to Vietnam. One of their early conclusions was that Danang could not handle the planned cargoes. It took much convincing, including my personal visit, to keep them from withholding Danang cargoes. Later they once did hold back shipments on advice from Saigon. MACV's Transportation Management Agency had acted on its own. Not only could these shipments be accommodated but it was clear to us in Pearl that they would reach Danang during a lull in ship arrivals. I learned of the action five days after action was taken, and soon had it reversed.

## PORT DEVELOPMENT

Parts of the port development were handled by the contractor, Raymond, Morrison–Knudsen (RMK), through the Officer in Charge of Construction, Bureau of Yards and Docks, and in competition with many other country–wide projects. Other parts were accomplished by the highly responsive Navy Mobile Construction Battalions, the Seabees. One of the most frustrating problems in those days was getting the necessary dredges, the acquisition of which encountered unpredicted delays after delays. Pile drivers were also hard to come by.

A COMUSMACV directive had assigned first priority for construction to those projects in support of jet–capable airfields with port development far down on the list.

By February 1966, General Westmoreland had recognized the seriousness of the situation and placed first priority for construction on port development for a period of forty–five days. Progress accelerated and critically needed off–loading sites were placed in operation over the next six months. The Bridge Cargo Facility for the off–loading of two LSTs, two LCUs and barges was built by the Seabees on the west bank of the Tourane River just north of the bridge. The first use was in April 1966, earlier use being delayed by dredging. The LST/LCU ramp area and ABFC pier was completed 1 July 1966, along with some of the quay wall.

By 1 August the Museum ramp was capable of handling two LSTs. By

NH–74197

*Site of the future Bridge Cargo Complex, October 1965.*

NH–74196

*Bridge Cargo Complex, 1968.*

15 August 1966 an Advanced Base Functional Component pier had been constructed on the east side of the river, together with LST ramps.

On 1 October the 1,600–foot quay wall at the Bridge Cargo Facility, and the swampy area alongside had been filled to form a staging area. In October dredging of the Tourane River was completed.

Finally, on 15 October 1966, the first anniversary of NAVSUPPACT Danang, we dedicated two deep–draft piers. For the first time, military cargoes were no longer so fully dependent on "logistics over–the–shore" operations. By then the monthly throughput in Danang had reached 240,000 measurement tons, four times the original "requirement." Nevertheless, with new facilities, the next monsoon season proved far more manageable. This does not mean the job was an easy one. For instance, in November 1966, lighterage services in Danang were secured for 169 hours as a result of the weather; the piers had to be abandoned on four occasions; coastal resupply was suspended eleven times, with ninety–six shuttle trips delayed from twenty–four to ninety–six hours.

One of these piers, a DeLong type, which used installed jacks to set the steel piles, had been acquired from the Army to gain an early capability, but was not ready until 1 January 1967. The two contractor–built ones were ready two and a half months earlier, despite troubles with boulders on the bottom of the harbor. This remarkable job was made possible by a unique design and the building of sections in the Philippines. The design was an adaptation of one used in oil platforms off Texas in the Gulf of Mexico, whereby piles were driven through steel tubes which were a part of the pier sections.

It was possible to conduct cargo operations at the piers most of the time, although from time to time seas or swells refracted around the point required ships to leave them. In addition to their immediate value, the piers would, as I pointed out in my speech at the dedication, be of lasting value to Danang and the surrounding area for years to come.

By January 1967, the throughput capability of Danang was calculated to be 10,000 short tons per day, or 300,000 short tons per month, as against the original "requirement" of 60,000 measurement tons (about 35,000 short tons). Informal criticism was understood to be made, from time to time, by some in Washington, that the port had been over–developed. The individuals concerned apparently had no real appreciation of the peaks to be encountered. This capacity, and more, would soon be needed. That year Danang set increasingly higher records in January, February, June, August,

NH–74194

*Observation Point 1965.*

October, and November. The first containerized operations in Vietnam were started at the Observation Point piers on 1 August. Starting in October, Danang was consistently surpassing the entire military cargo performance of the Saigon area. From time to time the daily amount handled would exceed 12,000 short tons.

From the start we had been anxious to relieve the bluejacket from as much of the cargo handling operation as possible. Contract negotiations with Korean Express finally produced a small cargo handling capability by August 1966, although their guaranteed throughput of 70,000 measurement tons was not achieved until February. The training of Vietnamese hatch teams was intensified. This further eased, but never eliminated, the load on the U.S. sailor. It was necessary to keep a nucleus engaged in cargo operations. These personnel permitted continued operations during critical situations, such as during the Tet offensive of 1968 when restrictions of the local authorities and security considerations kept local nationals off the job.

Despite the heavy load on the Naval Support Activity, Danang, which never let up, all hands were proud of the fact that their help in other areas

NH–74344

*Observation Point after construction of piers.*

was requested by the Army. Even though Cam Ranh Bay had the advantage of piers much earlier, had a large logistic force, and was a well sheltered harbor, the port ran into difficulty. NAVSUPPACT Danang sent an officer and ninety–eight men south in the summer of 1966 to help the Army. As has been noted previously, the Army asked for Cargo Handling Battalion Two in October to teach their personnel. The battalion stayed for four and a half months. The Army wanted the team to stay on even longer, but this was vetoed by Admiral Sharp, as was the request that they leave their equipment. Help was also requested in December as the result of a strike in Saigon. Twenty–four hours after the start of the strike ninety–five Navy cargo personnel were there with equipment.

## HARBOR DEFENSE

One of the most enthusiastic groups I encountered on my first visit, in August 1965, was the one engaged in surveillance at the harbor defense post up on Observation Point at the eastern boundary of the Bay of Danang, on the side of Monkey Mountain. A four–wheel–drive vehicle could, in those days, barely make it up the jungle–lined, deep–rutted one lane road from the south, past the sentry and a sign marked "Monkey Crossing."

The remnants of an old lighthouse served as the control post and radar operating station. The lieutenant (j.g.) in charge was particularly proud of the signal bridge complete with yard arms and halyards he had built on the roof. Two Marine tanks served as coastal artillery.

Until the Naval Support Activity could be provided with adequate craft for harbor defense, a Seventh Fleet destroyer normally conducted a night patrol to seaward off the entrance. Ships in the roadstead not being off–loaded would often put to sea during darkness.

Craft entering the harbor after dark were intercepted and turned over to the Vietnamese.

In the months that followed, craft patrolling the anchorage and the river frustrated a number of attempts to attack ships, the Tourane River bridge and, on one occasion, the deep–draft piers.

## CIVIC DISTURBANCES

Added complications had appeared in the spring of 1966 when events led to what could have been a major uprising against the Government, fighting between two different factions of Vietnamese armed forces, and U.S. military involvement.

There were natural differences between former Annam, in the north, and former Cochin China, in the south. Other differences arose from control largely in the hands of Buddhists in I Corps and Catholics in Saigon, but this was far from a simple matter, there being such a wide variety of religions and combinations of religions throughout the entire Republic.

Matters were brought to a head when on 10 March 1966, the military junta under Premier Ky relieved Lieutenant General Nguyen Chanh Thi, the strong Buddhist commander of Vietnam forces in I Corps and the governor of the region. Always aggressive in his operation against the Viet Cong, he and General Walt got along well together, each respecting the other as a true fighting man. On the other hand, Thi tended at times to act independently of Saigon and there were indications that Ky may have viewed him as a rival. Following the relieving of Thi, there was an anti–government demonstration in Danang and a student strike at Hue, followed by a general strike on 15 March.

What started as a popular movement to gain the reinstatement of Thi soon was used by those who desired to overthrow the government of the Republic. Foremost among them was Trich Tri Quang, leader of the militant Buddhists. Signs of Communist efforts to gain control were clearly evident, such as when "The Military–Civilian Struggle Committee" became "Popular Forces to Struggle for the Revolution."

The loyalty of segments of the Vietnamese Army in the zone remained questionable for some time. As a result, in early April, Ky airlifted Vietnamese Marines to Danang and took an increasingly strong stand, as many of the Western press predicted the direst consequences. Things would have been truly serious if Thi had joined the struggle forces, but he did not. Nevertheless, he was subsequently exiled to the United States.

The situation became extremely critical when, on 9 April, an armed column from Hoi An marched north toward Danang. Combat action would undoubtedly have been necessary by the Marines to ensure security of the base at Danang had not an emissary from General Walt been able to

NH–74192

*Tourane River Bridge, 1965.*

convince the column's leader that if he continued his forces would be destroyed.

An even more serious confrontation with United States forces occurred at the old Eiffel bridge across the Tourane River. Although confined to single lane traffic and limited loads, the bridge, a pontoon ferry, and other water craft of the Naval Support Activity were the only means of transferring cargoes from Danang East. It would not be until 25 June 1967 that a new bridge would be built paralleling the old one. With ARVN (Army of the Republic of Vietnam) troops on the east side ready to resist the Vietnamese Marines, troops sent by Ky, preparations were made to blow up the bridge. General Walt personally negotiated on the bridge while a U.S. Marine officer, out of sight, cut the electrical cable to explosive charges placed by the anti–government forces. The plunger was pushed as the discussion on the bridge continued. When no explosion resulted, the confrontation was won and U.S. Marines took over the guarding of the critical bridge. Later, for safety reasons, the U.S. Marines took over the Vietnamese ammunition depot in Danang East until the situation cleared. This too had been rigged with mines for destruction.

The period of 31 May to 6 June was particularly serious in Hue, but Ky's show of strength and the anti–Communist sentiments of the vast majority finally established order.

After several changes of command, Lieutenant General Hoang Xuan Lam, a resolute airborne soldier, was given the job. As a Brigadier General, Lam had performed well in command of forces in the southern two provinces of the zone, Quang Tin and Quang Ngai.

I was one of the few visitors allowed in Danang in April, presumably because of my responsibilities and the essentiality of continuing logistic support. The disturbances and an imposed curfew meant little or no work for the Naval Support Activity by Vietnamese during this period and the whole job had to be done by the officers and bluejackets. During the most tense period only the most critical cargoes were off–loaded. As a result of exemplary behavior, adverse incidents with the Vietnamese were completely avoided by the U.S. Navy.

From then on no liberty was allowed in Danang. Yet morale remained so high that more than one out of four requested to stay on beyond the strenuous one year tour. The patriotism and dedication of these men was in sharp contrast with the minority of youths then conducting demonstrations back in the United States.

## SMALL CRAFT REPAIR

Small craft repairs were accomplished by YR–70, a repair barge; by AFDL–23, a small auxiliary drydock; and by a YFND companion barge with shops and storage space with the help of a floating crane.

By 1 January 1967, the Naval Support Activity was overhauling craft formerly sent to Subic Bay. Sixty–seven were overhauled that month.

Dredging a channel into the small craft repair site and fill for the facilities ashore did not start until the summer of 1966. The bulkhead was not completed until March 1967, when an internal combustion repair shop was set up ashore. By June the number of craft to be overhauled or repaired each month had reached 173.

## SUPPLIES

The Navy supplied provisions to the Marines who had landed with their own initial 30–day supply. One officer and seven men were deployed north by the Headquarters Support Activity Saigon on 15 April 1965, and construction of storage facilities started.

For supply categories other than provisions, placing full dependence on the Naval Support Activity for common items was a phased process as storage facilities were built and stocks acquired.

The responsibility for common supplies in I CTZ was taken over from HEDSUPPACT Saigon on 15 October 1965. Originally, the required common item list was 3,500, a list that would grow to over 11,000.

Through great effort on the part of the Seabees, the Butler buildings in Danang East began to go up. Initial construction of six groups of warehouses, with eight 40 by 100 foot Butler buildings in each group had commenced in February 1966. Construction of 144,000 cubic feet of refrigerator stowage started in January. With the shortage of crushed rock, the sand and mud posed difficult problems. Only with great effort did the Seabees keep roads in the area passable. However, as Butlers went up stocks were moved in and support of common items increased.

With few exceptions, the Navy resorted to "pull" shipments; that is, shipping only in response to requisitions on the Naval Supply Center, Oakland, to meet actual usage. Well–qualified supply personnel and good management helped avoid the building up of large excesses which became such a problem in the other zones. The mission was extended when on 23 March 1966, the depot took over the stowage and issues of organization equipment, vehicles, construction materials, and machinery common item supplies, with approximately 70 percent of the catalogue item range in stock. By June 1967, Navy stowage at Danang had been expanded to 635,300 square feet of covered stowage, 369,830 cubic feet of refrigerated stowage, and 113 acres of open stowage.

## FUEL

In July 1965, Admiral Sharp had directed that the Navy establish a military fuel supply system in I Corps in augmentation of the commercial system. By November, NAVSUPPACT Danang had assumed responsibility for I Corps zone deliveries of bulk petroleum and pipeline transfers to and from MSTS floating stowage tankers. The situation with regard to jet fuel, aviation gasoline, and diesel fuel, remained critical for many months as a reult of the limitations of stowage ashore.

The sea off–load line at Red Beach, at the western border of the city, connected to the tanks constructed at the main Danang air base. Great difficulty was encountered by the Seabees in constructing the tanks here and in Chu Lai. These, from Advanced Base Functional Components, were of the World War II bolted variety, rather than welded. Much time and effort was expended by the Seabees in making them tight. An Amphibious Assault Bulk Fuel System was installed at the Marble Mountain helicopter field. With the completion of an aviation products pipeline from the Marble Mountain tank farm to MAG–16 in 1967, NAVSUPPACT was managing the largest fuel complex in Vietnam.

Requisitioning channels and support levels were set up for packaged POL. Initial stocks were supplied from the Naval Supply Center, Oakland, while resupply requisitioning channels were established through the Army Logistical Command on Okinawa. When this failed to provide adequate stocks in timely fashion, the more efficient channel direct to Oakland was resumed for resupply.

## PROVISIONS

The Naval Support Activity, Danang, had taken over responsibility for the stowage and issue of provisions from the Headquarters Support Activity, Saigon, utilizing initially the 33,000 square feet of covered storage in Danang Main which had been built for this purpose.

The providing of refrigerated provisions was a particularly difficult problem, complicated by the lack of reefer space and by the shortage of refrigerator ships for charter by MSTS. As had been noted previously, two refrigerated lighters, augmented by an MSTS chartered refrigerator ship in the bay, provided the space in the early months. Meanwhile, MSTS took steps to get more such ships to deliver provisions.

The fifteen–day delivery schedule for such products to Danang and other Vietnam ports had to be stepped up later to provide deliveries every nine to ten days. This was a very tight affair, and MSTS had to fulfill other Pacific needs for refrigerated products as well. Delays, such as those in off–loading at ports other than Danang, caused much concern.

For insurance, Commander Service Force established a reserve stock of twenty days of frozen provisions at the Naval Supply Depot, Subic. This proved a wise move. When stocks neared depletion in Danang in September 1967, arrangements were made for *Aludra,* a refrigerator ship (AF) deployed to the Seventh Fleet for mobile support, to make two deliveries of provisions from Subic. In addition, stores ships (AKS and AFS) were requested to advise NAVSUPPACT Danang of any reserve stocks after Seventh Fleet requirements had been met.


## REAL ESTATE


A particularly vexing problem of the Naval Support Activity was that of procuring real estate. At the close of 1965, the only real estate available for construction was Camp Tien Sha; the sandy East Danang warehouse site, where most of the warehouses and reefer spaces were to be constructed; and the hospital site. Real estate was at a premium and required much red tape through U.S. and Vietnamese offices with final approval in Saigon. Once property was acquired, there often followed additional delays while local settlers and innumerable hand–patted circular graves were relocated. As a result of such considerations the development of NAVSUPPACT Danang had to depend on many scattered locations, thus magnifying the problems of security.

In March 1966, NAVSUPPACT was given the task of operating a Joint Real Estate office for all military services in the I Corps. In May, responsibility was added for the administration of the civilian personnel program, acting for COMUSMACV in the zone.

## PUBLIC WORKS

As the construction of Navy and Marine Corps facilities neared completion, it became necessary to establish arrangements to operate and maintain power plants, utility systems, airfields, roads, waterfront structures, reefers, and transportation equipment. Some provision was also required for maintenance of cantonment areas, particularly mess halls, galleys, heads, and their utility systems. The Marines asked for assistance.

As an interim measure, detachments from Navy Construction Battalions provided some of the more critically needed support. A study by a Service Force and Pacific Division of the Bureau of Yards and Docks team evaluated the situation. The requirements for the total job, as reported in October 1966, were staggering. As a result, I made recommendations which would place limits on the support and emphasize self–help. Upon approval by the Chief of Naval Operations on 30 January 1967, the Naval Support Activity, Danang, was tasked to assume public works responsibility for Navy and Marine units within the advanced base complexes of the I Corps zone to include: maintenance, repair and minor construction of all permanent and semi–permanent facilities; provide, operate and maintain transportation and construction equipment as required; maintain and operate utility systems; acquire real estate; and outfit and replace non–technical plant and minor property for personnel support such as mess halls, barracks, and BOQs. Public works support was later extended to the Advisory Groups of MACV in the zone. Further extensions of this R and U (Repair and Utility) support was later extended to Army units deployed to Chu Lai and Phu Bai, as this became the largest Navy public works activity in the world.

## NEW RESPONSIBILITIES

Responsibilities of the Naval Support Activity continued to expand. One was to develop, operate, and support the China Beach Recreation Facility, with a USO, barber shop, gym, softball field, horseshoe pits, shuffleboard, tennis, volley ball, post exchange, and beach. This accommodated 23,000 on daily R and R passes. The facility was opened on 1 January 1967.

On 1 February the Activity took over delivery of all cargoes to the first point of delivery both in Danang and in Chu Lai. That same month saw assumption of responsibility for maintenance and support of all airfields in I Corps except for the eastern Air Force portion of the main field at Danang.

On 25 July generator and vehicle maintenance was extended to MACV
advisors at Tan My, Hoi An, Quang Tri, Hue, and Quang Ngai.  Trash and
garbage collection responsibilities were assumed in the Danang area in
January 1968.

In addition to NAVSUPPACT personnel augmentations, a contract was
negotiated for a labor service contract with the Philco–Ford Company.
Many of the persons employed were Koreans, who proved to be excellent
mechanics.  Construction Battalion Maintenance Unit 301 was formed and,
in May 1967, deployed and reported to the operational control of Commander Naval Support Activity.  This unit proved particularly valuable in
providing public works support of airfields such as at An Hoa, Dong Ha,
Khe Sanh, and Duc Pho.  Its performance in the critical fall of 1967 at
Khe Sanh was especially noteworthy.  Thirty–five men of the detachment
provided invaluable assistance during the siege when, under daily enemy
artillery, rocket and mortar attack, and despite the heavy rains, they kept
the airstrip in operation, built bunkers and fortifications, and carried out
many other valuable tasks.  During the siege, two of the men were killed
and eleven wounded, as they carried out their important duties.


## SECURITY


The guerrilla type operations of the enemy and the scattered locations of
NAVSUPPACT installations placed heavier demands on the Navy's security
personnel than had originally been expected.  Monthly incidents against
these installations, which only averaged four or less prior to May 1966, rose
to over thirty per month by May of 1967.  The supply complexes were a
special target for the Viet Cong, and there was often harassing fire at Camp
Tien Sha.  The radio transmitter site built in the hazardous area near Marble
Mountain had, as might be expected, its share.  A mortar attack on 9 July
failed to slow its construction.  Then there was a two hour gun fight at this
site with one grenade reaching inside the compound, and the series of
attacks by small arms, mortars, and grenades on 26 and 27 December.
NAVSUPPACT was involved in twenty–five hostile fire incidents that
month, one of the three terrorist attacks in Danang being against NAVSUP-
PACT's Claims Office.

A force of twenty–nine sentry dogs had been established under the Naval
Support Activity in February 1967, after prolonged effort to get Washington

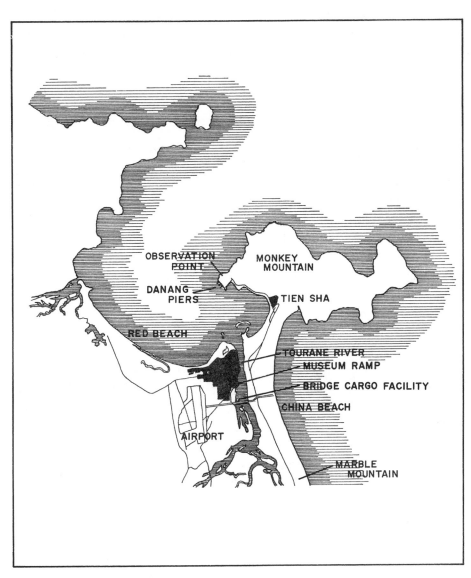

NH–74352

*Danang area.*

approval. On 1 July, a special training course was set up in California and an expert 800–man Guard Force organized, a step set in motion by Admiral Horacio Rivero, Vice Chief of Naval Operations. By then there were twenty–two separate installations to protect in Danang with 27,000 yards of perimeters.

As Marines shifted from the primarily defensive operations around Danang, Chu Lai, and Phu Bai, to seek and destroy operations farther north, Danang was subjected to more attacks. A factor in this was the augmentation of mortars with Soviet rockets in the hands of the North Vietnamese. Sometimes Navy facilities were damaged, such as was the case on 27 February 1967, when a rocket attack on the Danang airfield destroyed five communication vans of the Naval Support Activity. On similar attacks on 17 March, the fuel (POL) system was damaged. NAVSUPPACT accomplished the repairs in fifteen hours.

I was on my way to Danang in an aircraft over the South China Sea when the airfield was hit by a heavy rocket attack in July. At first they said we would have to divert to another field, but finally they let us land on the north end of the runway. In addition to holes on the west runway, the upkeep of which was a Navy responsibility, there was damage to the power supply and POL system. Most damage on that side came from hits in ARVN ammunition stowage just off the field. New stowage was under construction, but the shift had not been yet made. New barracks for personnel of the Navy VQ–1 squadron close by were demolished by the exploding ammunition dump. By the time the dump went up, the Navy men were within sandbag revetments. There being no roof on these, it was miraculous that the only casualty was one man with a slight arm wound. When I arrived, large fragments of bombs could be seen all around the area. The casualties on the Air Force side were numerous, one plane loaded with bombs having exploded. As on so many occasions the Naval Support Activity's hospital handled the casualties rapidly and effectively. The Navy Surgeon General, Vice Admiral Robert Brown (MC), and the Fleet Medical Officer, Rear Admiral John Cowan (MC), were at the hospital that night. The next day they said they had never before seen such superb performance, even in World War II.

As will be recounted later, logistic lines of communications became a prime enemy target in the spring of 1967. In March seven tank cars of a Vietnamese train were destroyed near the Lieu Chien Esso terminal nine miles north of Danang. These had been used to help supply the airfield with fuel. In April the Namo bridge just south of there was dropped, severing the land lines from Danang to Phu Bai.

The frequency of enemy rocket attacks at Danang increased in January 1968. Damaged facilities and utilities were expeditiously repaired by the Naval Support Activity. On 3 January, it was the air base when the west taxiway, MAG–11's hangar, and power lines were hit. The power lines were repaired by 0600, the hangar by 6 January. On 7 January, the Marine Force Logistic Command near Red Beach had four buildings destroyed and thirty damaged. NAVSUPPACT restored twenty–nine of these by the end of the week and the electrical feeder system by 8 January. The water main was replaced by the 9th. The I CTZ Army Headquarters, Marble Mountain air facility, northwest tank farm, and the air base (Air Force) power line were also hit. The latter was connected to NAVSUP-PACT's system by 1000.

The night of 30 January saw the start of the Tet offensive. A harbor security boat thwarted a swimmer attack against the Tourane River bridge. Three enemy sampans were destroyed, four of the enemy being killed and two North Vietnamese captured.

A curfew in Danang meant that once again local labor was not available for port terminal operations. To free Navy men for the job, NAVSUPPACT Danang shut down shops and other activities. The Army augmented the operation with the Navy supervising and training their personnel. As a result the cargo kept moving.

## CIVIC ACTION

Throughout the I Corps zone the Navy carried out many important civic action programs. One officer was given a full time job of supervising this effort. The rest were volunteers.

Naval Support Activity personnel taught in schools. They managed a polytechnic school for the teaching of various skills.

Village action teams were established to rebuild homes in damaged hamlets out of excess dunnage. There were eight teams by June of 1967. They established parks, and taught refuse collection and disposal, mosquito control, and traffic planning.

The medical assistance and training, rendered by volunteers from the hospital, in outlying hamlets were particularly helpful.

## AWARD

The Naval Support Activity, Danang, was awarded the Navy Unit Commendation from 15 October 1965 to August 1966. This was later extended through 1967. They also received the National Defense Transportation award for 1966.

# CHAPTER IX

# Southern I Corps

## CHU LAI

One of the most critical logistic problems faced by the Navy was support of Chu Lai, a problem which remained serious throughout the first year after the initial landing. The landing and resupply were initially across the soft sandy beach exposed to the full sweep of the South China Sea. Even in the summer months the causeway and ship–to–shore fuel lines were wiped out frequently by the seas, and the question of resupply during the coming northeast monsoon became a matter of great concern to us all.

An adequate flow of fuel, ammunition, and other critical supplies to Chu Lai was essential to sustain the operations of aircraft from the newly constructed runway in support of actions throughout the zone. It was needed for the supply of troops providing security to the enclave. It was needed to deliver materials for the building of a major airfield. The concern of Admiral Sharp, Commander in Chief Pacific, was such that he asked Admiral Johnson for a special briefing shortly after I had reported.

In the presentation I gave at Admiral Sharp's Camp Smith Headquarters on 30 July 1965 I outlined the steps being taken (some of which were initiated just that week) and the plans to provide full logistic support to Chu Lai.

At the time, the units being supported consisted of the Fourth Marines, Marine Air Group 12, logistic support units, and Navy Mobile Construction Battalion Ten—totaling 7,200 men. The additional units about to arrive would double the number of personnel ashore.

I identified the key elements of the logistical support concept as: first, Chu Lai would be provided logistic support as a satellite of Danang; second, when appropriate, direct over–the–shore supply would be provided from outside Vietnam; third, an all–weather capability would be developed for over–the–shore support. I noted that "In view of the urgency of acquiring such a capability before the onset of the northeast monsoon, emergency action was underway to gain an interim all–weather capability adequate to meet difficult requirements under adverse conditions." I highlighted the need for dredging and stated my understanding that a clam–shell dredge was being brought down from Danang. I noted the possibility, even with the steps being taken, of restrictions being imposed by the most severe weather conditions, and that a suction–type dredge might be required. We were taking soundings to ascertain the magnitude of the problem.

Chu Lai was clearly dependent on supply by sea. Although only some fifty–five miles separated it from Danang, the railroad was no longer in operation. Route One was crossed by many streams. The road was subject to mines and ambushes, and bridges were often dropped by the enemy. Despite the fact that armed truck convoys were pushed through from time to time and aircraft made high priority deliveries, the bulk of the cargoes, ammunition, food, supplies, construction materials, and fuel had to be brought in by sea lines of logistics to support the troops, the Marine Air Wing, and construction.

Getting the cargoes in was extremely critical during the fall and winter of 1965. The problems of keeping the ship–to–shore fuel lines in operation a reasonable amount of time would never cease.

In addition to shuttling supplies to Danang by LCUs and LSTs, the Naval Support Activity was charged with port control, port services, harbor security, and limited support of Market Time[1] craft at Chu Lai. Up until September 1965, LST cargoes were off–loaded over a single 13–section causeway on the exposed beach, while LCUs entered the Truong River and landed their cargoes at the temporary Cus Ho ramp. On 5 September 1965, the first 542–Class LST crossed the bar off Rosemary Point during high tide and beached at the ramp. Although occasional temporary ground- ings occurred, such LSTs with drafts up to eleven feet continued to make crossings when the weather permitted.

At the end of July, steps had been initiated to have the Seabees hastily bulldoze two temporary LST ramps at Cus Ho just inside the mouth of the Truong River, just inside Rosemary Point. Plans were prepared for a more permanent off–loading area. Repeated requests were made to get a con- tractor–operated dredge to cut a channel through the bar at the river mouth. But, although promised week after week, mishaps and other delays occurred, and then the seas set in. Meanwhile cargoes would have to be delivered from Danang by LCUs and by LSTs, the latter after having to bump over the bar

---

[1] See Chapter IX.

NH–74192

*Rosemary Point, Chu Lai, January 1966.*

at high tide on the swells rolling in from the South China Sea and refracting around the small islands at the river mouth.

After a long delay a 16–inch channel dredge and a small clam–shell dredge arrived on the scene to work on the bar as weather permitted. Little progress was made until an 11–foot deep pass was completed in mid–January 1966. It took until 20 March to get it down to 14 feet. Finally, a more adequate dredge arrived and cleared the total channel to 16 feet in April. USS *Maury* made a survey and provided provisional charts. A Coast Guard tender installed buoys.

## STARLIGHT

As in Danang, the initial job of the Marines was to defend the field and base area while launching air strikes against the VC. Soon Chu Lai was to serve as an important and expanding enclave from which operations would be projected against the enemy. My initial visit there was during "Operation Starlight," the first regimental–sized action involving U.S. forces in Vietnam.

On 15 August 1965, intelligence had been gained that the First Viet Cong Regiment, a force of some two thousand men, was in the area of the Van Tuong Peninsula, fifteen miles south of Chu Lai airstrip. A three–pronged operation against them was launched by the U.S. Marines. Amphibious vehicles brought Chu Lai troops in from the north, helicopters landed forces to the west, and a Seventh Fleet Amphibious Task Group made an assault across the beach to the south of the peninsula.

This was one of the rare cases, in those early months, in which the enemy appears to have been caught completely by surprise. General Walt told me that General Thi asked him not to inform any other Vietnamese of the plan. Finally, it was agreed that General Lam, who commanded the two southern provinces, should be informed twenty–four hours before the battle.

By 24 August the body count of enemy dead reached 964. The result was a complete victory, the effects of this action going well beyond that of the elimination of the threatening force. As the first such major victory, it had an important psychological impact on both friend and enemy.

## BASE DEVELOPMENT

Meanwhile, the logistic tasks grew. High priority was placed on the building of a major airfield by the construction contractor Raymond, Morrison–Knudsen (RMK) to parallel the expeditionary field constructed so rapidly by the Seabees. Most of the remaining base construction was the job of the Seabees. In 1967 the Seabees were also to add the finishing touches to the airfield in the form of a 4,700–foot concrete cross–wind runway and a 5,400 foot taxiway.

While NAVSUPPACT's Detachment at Chu Lai provided effective harbor defense with the help of craft deployed from Danang, there was much concern over security of Cus Ho and Rosemary Point until the Marines had swept the island across the other side of the river. A few cases of sniper fire were experienced, but no serious attack occurred until shortly after the Marines had been replaced during the spring of 1967. Then, one night, mortar rounds hit two LSTs, naval support installations, and the Seabee barracks area. The LSTs sustained minor damage and two crewmen were wounded. One Seabee was killed.

Requirements for personnel in Danang delayed the build–up of the Chu Lai Detachment, but the job got done. Beacons were mounted in pilings to permit night transit, and step–by–step the Seabees extended the ramps and the staging area to the point where four LSTs and three LCUs could be accommodated simultaneously. We were told that the contractor (RMK) stated he would build a barge quay for the off-loading of construction materials. When progress was not made, the Seabees did the job.

Under Commander Naval Support Activity, Danang, a Naval Beach Group Detachment on temporary duty from the Amphibious Force continued to handle cargo for several months. It was not until 15 March 1966 that sufficient NAVSUPPACT permanent duty personnel were available to relieve the Beach Group Detachment. The Marine Division Shore Party continued to function until May when, with 200 personnel and sufficient material handling equipment on the scene, NAVSUPPACT assumed all cargo operations. By June 1966, Chu Lai was handling almost as much cargo as had originally been expected for the entire I Corps zone. From then until March 1967, the average was over 50,000 measurement tons per month.

In March 1966, the Chief of Naval Operations had approved the establishment of a small supply depot as a sub–depot of Danang. Naval Mobile Construction Battalion Three started construction of facilities ashore, including a 10,000–gallon water tank, engine repair shops, mess hall, barracks, warehouses, and later small craft repair facilities to accommodate Market Time craft then stationed there. APL–5 from Danang provided temporary berthing and messing.

By August, 30 days of dry provisions were being stocked for 30,000 troops. Items in the sub–depot ready for issue reached 8,970 in November. By July 1967, 14,518 items in adequate depth for 40,000 men were being carried.

Fuel tanks were constructed ashore by the Seabees to replace the bladder farm, but the tremendous struggle to keep three offshore lines in operation for long periods to deliver adequate quantities of fuel to support the aircraft and vehicles continued.

Meanwhile the detachment assumed an increasing role in logistic support operations. On 1 October 1966, the detachment became responsible for port clearance of all contractor cargo, and in February 1967 all military cargoes were being delivered to secure areas within the Chu Lai enclave. By this time, an electrical system for the area was being operated and maintained, public works support of the airfield had been taken over from the Seabees by the Naval Support Detachment and bus service was being

NH–74346

*Rosemary Point, September 1967.*

provided. Actions such as these freed more and more troops for combat action.

In April 1967, General Westmoreland deployed Army Task Force Oregon to Chu Lai so that Marines could be sent north where trouble was brewing. This was a busy month, as the throughput peaked to 147,787 measurement tons, seven times that of any month in 1965.

## DUC PHO

In April 1967, the Army also took over from the Marines at Duc Pho at the southern boundary of the I Corps Tactical Zone, where the Seabees had built an airstrip for the Marines. Sea lines of logistics were extended to Duc Pho from Chu Lai, other supplies being shipped up from the Army base at Qui Nhon. This was a logistics–over–the–shore operation during the southwest monsoon season with the Navy maintaining a causeway and two offshore fuel lines. Later the Naval Support Activity established a detachment in the area to work with the Army.

While these actions were underway in southern I Corps, things were really picking up in the north.

CHAPTER X

# The Crucial Fight for the
# Northern Provinces

Early in 1966 evidence gradually began to mount that the enemy would make a major effort to gain control of the northern two provinces, Quang Tri and Thua Thien. Defense of these provinces, isolated on land from the rest of I Corps by the Hai Van Mountains, except for the narrow winding mountain road and railroad, would be made possible only by the imaginative and determined effort on the part of Navy logistic forces to deliver supplies by water.

Seizure of these two provinces was a logical objective for the Communists. First of all, Quang Tri was separated from North Vietnam only by the narrow Demilitarized Zone (DMZ). Second, flanking movements around the western end of the DMZ, through Loatian territory, entailed relatively minor problems compared with supply down the Ho Chi Minh trail to the more southerly provinces. Third, the former capital, Hue, in Thua Thien, was of great political and psychological significance to all of Vietnam, north and south.

The first sign of a major effort was the enemy attack on 4 January 1966 against the Special Forces Camp at Khe Sanh in the northwest corner of the Republic of Vietnam. This was followed the next month by evidence of groups from above the seventeenth parallel infiltrating through Laos into Thua Thien and of two North Vietnamese divisions threatening invasion across the DMZ.

Then, in March, the Special Forces in A Shau Valley were attacked and forced to retire. The valley, subsequently held by the Communists for two years, was transformed into a major logistic base with roads constructed in Laos to support it. A Shau Valley was to be the staging point for many attacks, including the seizure of Hue during the 1968 Tet offensive.

The bulk of the Third Marine Division was shifted north to augment the single Marine battalion in northern I Corps and the Vietnamese 1st Division.

Many more forces were to follow. Their logistic support would create extremely serious problems for the next two and a half years.

When evidence was gained of the North Vietnamese 324B Division move across the Demilitarized Zone in July 1966 the Marines and the Vietnamese airborne division launched "Operation Hastings." As the result of many bloody actions contesting high ground, the Communists suffered heavy losses and withdrew into the DMZ. Nowhere has the valor of the Marines been greater than in the intense fighting by which they finally succeeded in capturing the "Rock Pile," an aptly named steeply sloped 700–foot hill located in a commanding position several miles west of Dong Ha.

The enemy soon made other attempts across the DMZ, and "Hastings" was followed by "Operation Neutralize" in which naval gunfire and naval aircraft joined artillery and land–based aircraft in support of the Marines, particularly at their strong point at Con Thien, just south of the DMZ. "Operation Prairie" took a heavy toll of the enemy and was followed by one series of battles after another.

Throughout, naval logistic support was crucial. There seems little doubt but that at least the province of Quang Tri, and perhaps Thua Thien as well, would have been overrun had it not been for the fact that this support surpassed what was thought possible. The weight of effort required to repulse the enemy could only be achieved and sustained by maintaining a constant flow of munitions and other supplies from Danang. Some critical supplies could be delivered to the airstrips, built and maintained by Seabees, but far greater quantities were required than could be moved by air and by trucking over the inferior roads, roads often broken by mining of the multitude of bridges. For the bulk of the requirements the solution was deliveries by landing craft proceeding along the coast and up the difficult Cua Viet River to Dong Ha, or into Tan My and up the Perfume River to Hue.

Seabees performed herculean tasks in building fortifications, bases, and logistic facilities, and helped defend against enemy attacks.

The hospital ship USS *Repose,* offshore, joined on 10 April 1967 by USS *Sanctuary*, provided surgery and medical care for the wounded. These reactivated ships, which had seen service in World War II, were equipped with the most modern heart and kidney machines, frozen blood banks, pressure chambers, and other first class medical and surgical equipment. They were truly life savers, particularly in northern I Corps. In many cases helicopters would deliver wounded to these ships just minutes after they had been hit. The result was a remarkable recovery rate, aided by the

USN-1128510

*Hospital ship* Repose *(AH–16) off Vietnam.*

sympathetic treatment by Navy nurses in the air conditioned wards. On 24 March 1967 *Repose* completed its 2,000th surgical operation off Vietnam. That month alone saw 635 admissions in the ship's hospital.

## HUE, TAN MY AND PHU BAI

Hue, some forty miles north of Danang on the other side of the Hai Van Mountains, was the third largest city in the Republic of Vietnam. As the traditional capital of all of Vietnam and a center of Buddhism and Vietnamese culture, its importance was enhanced. In 1968 Hue would be the scene of prolonged fighting for its control.

Hue sits on both sides of the Perfume River. The newer city with its university is on the southern bank, across from the large moated citadel and the Imperial Palace grounds.

When I first met Lieutenant General Lam at the dedication of the deep–draft piers at Danang in October 1966, he expressed his desire to give me a personal tour of the Imperial Palace. During one of my later trips he made good his promise, with dividends. Prior to a luncheon of special dishes at the governor's mansion, General Lam had a prolonged and intense conference with a number of his officers, which I assumed had to do with some urgent combat situation. Actually the session concerned my coming tour.

The trucks and jeeps full of troops, ahead of and behind our limousine, seemed strange for a trip just across the river bridge. Instead we headed some miles west beyond the city past ornate tombs of lesser officials and into the area of the imperial tombs. Our visit was to the magnificent tomb of the Emperor Tu Doc. Walking through the gate, by the small lake and its pavilion, fishing platform, and wives' quarters, along the winding stream, and up steps, past statues and through bronze doors on the upper level to the tomb itself, the general would—from time to time—give an order upon which a squad or two would spring ahead and fan into the trees on either side of the path.

During the visit to the tomb and later during the tour of the Imperial Palace and its grounds, the thought arose what an interesting spot this would be for tourists when peace was finally restored, but at the time it was known as "VC country."

As has already been noted, the Marines had moved a small force to nearby Phu Bai soon after landing in Danang in the spring of 1965.

Sea lines of logistics would later prove to be a key to success of combat operations in the northern part of the I Corps Tactical Zone but the logistic demands on the Navy were not heavy in those early months. Initially logistic support was by air and by road, with occasional Marine truck convoys, called "rough riders," and Esso tank trucks. There was even some movement by rail from Danang before bridges were dropped.

The truck loads were seriously limited by the road, particularly through the Hai Van Pass, and by the bridges. As they were then loaded it would take some thirty odd trucks on this route to equal the delivery of one landing craft, utility (LCU). In June 1965, a trip up the Perfume River by one LCU and one LCM–6 to the city park alongside the university at Hue gave a hint of future deliveries. The improvised ramp at the city park was to become the primary off–loading site for almost three years. However, that year low water restrained use of the river until the monsoon rains began.

Limited use was made of the Col Co ramp just south of the river mouth in the lagoon at Tan My. This small ramp, from which the Colonial Company dispensed fuel to sampans, was connected to the mainland by a low and narrow causeway.

When the seas were rolling in, navigating a landing craft into the lagoon from the sea through the outer entrance was a difficult feat. The channel scoured by the river ran north for a way paralleling the beach, so that the landing craft had to spend some time in the trough of the waves. Once inside, the craft would go through a small opening in an inner breakwater. After this breakwater had been removed in 1967 to make a channel for an LST port at Col Co, we learned that this was not a breakwater in the true sense, but rather a French–constructed barrier to create a head of pressure of water flowing out and thus keep salt water away from the rice fields.

In the fall of 1965 two LCUs were assigned to transship cargo from Col Co up the river to Hue when conditions were right—usually under escort of helicopter gunships. Other cargo for Hue and Phu Bai was delivered up a narrow low road which went from the Col Co causeway, threading its way tightly between rice fields and dwellings to connect up with Route One near Hue. During the monsoon season the Col Co ramp, the causeway, and much of the road were often under water. I was there when the entire area was submerged for miles around.

Resupply overland from Danang via Route One became increasingly dangerous, particularly through the Hai Van Mountains. Difficulties also resulted from the many bridges on the way north and from enemy minings. In the early part of 1966, as the military population in the Hue/Phu Bai area increased, major dependence had to be placed on supply by water from Danang. By late March when the U.S. military population in the area had reached 5,600, improved means were sought, including the possibility of port development. But it would take a long time before any significant capacity would be constructed. Meanwhile the shuttles of LCUs by sea and up the river increased. With a beam sea, the trip from Danang was a rough one, often requiring the transits to be suspended to prevent disaster. Then, from time to time when the backlog of Hue cargo at Danang rose, a Seventh Fleet amphibious cargo ship (AKA) would take cargo north and send loads up the river by amphibious landing craft.

In April 1966, an Amphibious Assault Buoyant Fuel System was installed whereby an AOG would pump fuel ashore to a bladder farm on Thuan An Island on the south side of the outer river entrance. From there mechanized landing craft (LCM) with fuel bladders made deliveries to tank trucks at the Col Co ramp. Keeping the ship–to–shore line in operation was a continuous chore here as elsewhere in the I Corps Tactical Zone even after a bottom–laid line had been installed.

In early May the Seabees began overhauling the Col Co ramp in anticipation of increased use. On 4 May, one Navy officer and twenty–seven enlisted men arrived at the bladder farm from Danang to form the first increment of the Naval Support Detachment, Hue. Cargo operations continued despite the civil disturbances at Hue, as the cargo throughput in June reached 8,529 measurement tons.

While awaiting a decision by Commander U.S. Military Assistance Command Vietnam concerning the building of port facilities, a number of interim steps were needed. In August 1966, a refrigerated covered lighter was anchored in the Tan My lagoon to provide floating storage for chill and freeze provisions, and from which daily deliveries were made to Hue. In September the bottom–laid offshore fuel line was installed to Thuan An Island. A causeway for mooring and fueling Market Time craft was built on the lagoon side of the camp.

Commencing in February 1967, with still more Marines positioned in the north, with increased ambushes and enemy mining of Route One, and with the destruction of the Namo Bridge just south of the Hai Van Pass, the requirements for delivery by sea lines of logistics tripled. When fuel expenditures at Hue/Phu Bai exceeded the capabilities of trucks to deliver from Tan My, LCMs with bladders made deliveries up the river to Hue, averaging 80,000 gallons per day. A fuel tank was then constructed at Hue and connected by Col Co by pipeline.

On 1 February 1967, as more personnel became available to the Naval Support Activity, Danang, the Hue Detachment became large enough to relieve the Marine shore party at the Hue ramp, the detachment based on Traun An Island becoming the Tan My Detachment. Seabees overhauled the road from Tan My and provided points for passing. The Hue city ramp and its small staging area were improved.

Finally in April 1967 funds were approved to dredge a channel and construct a four–LST off–loading and transshipment site at the location of the Col Co ramp at Tan My. Dredging started 8 May, but it would be months before there would be a usable facility. Dangerous and challenging times lay ahead for the Hue Detachment and for those transiting the Perfume River.

Dredging permitted USS *Meeker County* (LST–980) to enter the mouth of the Perfume River. In November *Patapsco* became the first AOG to enter Tan My lagoon to deliver fuel, and a temporary pontoon causeway was constructed at Tan My to permit LST off–loading. The total throughput

NH-74193

*Hue ramp, June 1967.*

of cargoes in northern I Corps zone reached 102,604 measurement tons (58,000 short tons) that month.

## TET

Then came the famous Tet offensive of 1968.  The lunar New Year, or Tet, a very important holiday for the Vietnamese, was a sentimental time for families to get together.  Large percentages of their armed forces would head for home on this occasion, whether or not they had leave.  Every year there had been a truce for the duration of the holiday, although there had always been scattered violations on the part of the Communists.  This time there were signs of a Communist build–up, and some talk of reduced leaves on the part of ARVN troops, but few seemed really to think that the enemy would strike until after the holidays.  Three months before, General West- moreland had told me that their big offensives would come right after Tet and early in May, as seemed to happen each year.  This turned out to be the case—except for the fact that this time the enemy hit in the early morning hours after the midnight celebration of the start of Tet, in violation of the truce the Communists themselves had declared.  It was an offensive of amazing scope and intensity.  All over the country the cities had been infiltrated by the enemy who struck simultaneously and furiously.  There were indications that the Communists expected large portions of the popula- tion to rise up against the government.  This did not happen.  On the contrary, the treachery was bitterly resented by most of the Vietnamese, particularly in I Corps.

The first day of the lunar New Year was a busy one with coordinated attacks on military installations and population centers throughout the I Corps.  Attacks at Quang Tri City, Danang, Hoi An, Tam Ky, and Quang Ngai City were quickly repulsed with heavy enemy casualties.  Twenty– four rounds of artillery were aimed at the ramp in Dong Ha.

The most serious threat was at Hue where the enemy must have been confident of his ability to seize and hold this traditional capital of all of Vietnam.  As it was, he gained control of the city for a considerable period and ruthlessly killed many citizens loyal to the Republic of Vietnam.  It took several weeks of house–to–house fighting by the Marines to regain control of the city, first on the south side of the river and then to assist the Vietnam Army in eliminating the Communists occupying the north side. It was not until 25 February that the enemy was ejected from the Citadel. More fighting was required to clear him from the outskirts of the city.

Nowhere was the Tet offensive of 1968 as determined as in Hue.   At 0815 on 31 January, the Hue ramp was hit with small arms, mortar and recoilless rifle fire.   Three LCUs were damaged transiting the Perfume River.   All LCUs and YFUs at Tan My cove were ordered to sea.   By 1230 the Viet Cong were within 300 yards of the Hue jet fuel tank.

The Naval Support Detachment insisted on working the ramp all day, until finally ordered to evacuate to the MACV compound.   There was great concern when no word was received of this group of men for two days. Finally we learned that they had survived the attack in the University. Regretfully, there was one casualty, the officer in charge, Lieutenant (jg) Robert W. Moinester, USNR, who had been killed as he tried heroically to join his men from Phu Bai.   Lieutenant (jg) Moinester was awarded the Silver Star Medal posthumously for "conspicuous gallantry and intrepidity in action," "inspiring leadership, courageous actions and selfless devotion to duty."   He and his ramp personnel, proceeding to Hue, came under hostile mortar fire.   The following is quoted in part from his citation:

> Quickly organizing his men into an infantry platoon, composed of United States Navy, Marine Corps and Army personnel, Lieutenant (jg) Moinester repeatedly exposed himself to increasingly intense hostile fire as he led his men in house–to–house clearing operations.   Alertly observing enemy soldiers in a building to his front, he rapidly organized a frontal attack utilizing automatic rifles and grenade launchers as a base of fire and aggressively led the assault against the well entrenched enemy.   Although Lieutenant (jg) Moinester was killed during the attack, the enemy was driven from their reinforced positions and sustained heavy casualties, enabling the column to continue its movement into the city.

Meanwhile, at the mouth of the Perfume River, LCUs provided fire support in the cove, as all civilians at Tan My were evacuated to sea.

On 1 February, the 3,000–barrel JP–4 tank at Hue was hit, and helicopter pads were prepared at Tan My for refueling.

Cargo trips up the river resumed ten days later.   All month long these craft were subjected to small arms, recoilless rifle and mortar fire, requiring suspension of trips for three days.   Forty–four craft were hit, and two LCUs destroyed; five of the crews were killed and thirteen wounded.

On return trips, Vietnamese refugees were transported down the river and to Danang.   All in all 1,461 refugees were transported to Danang from Hue and 140 from Dong Ha.

In four days the Hue ramp was under heavy attack.   When the Hue bridge was destroyed, two pontoon causeway sections were assembled to make a ferry.

By March the main offensive was defeated. Also by this time, plans had been completed for a logistics–over–the–shore operation after the monsoon at a site north of the entrance to the Perfume River. The Navy would deliver the supplies to the beach and take care of a causeway and sea load line. Additional Army troops deployed to this area would operate the site and make deliveries over a road improved by the Seabees to Route One near Quang Tri.

## CUA VIET AND DONG HA

A prerequisite to success in repulsing the North Vietnamese near the DMZ was the delivery of ammunition, supplies and construction materials. Nowhere was the job so difficult. Enemy action and a hazardous river made the transit up the Cua Viet just south of the DMZ to Dong Ha a dangerous undertaking. The shallow mouth of the river was difficult even when the seas were calm. When water was low, there were shifting bars blocking the way further upstream. These were made passable by mounting a crawler crane with a "clam–shell" on a Naval Support Activity LCU for dredging.

The most crucial deliveries by water in August 1966 were ammunition and fuel, the latter carried in drums. These cargoes were delivered to a dirt ramp just downstream from the bridge at Dong Ha.

Intense effort was required to achieve the initial build–up of stocks. This was accomplished in two months by the delivery of 35,000 measurement tons by water despite the fact that weather greatly complicated the job.

By mid–October 1966, a fuel bladder farm had been established at Cua Viet on the south side of the river mouth, from which deliveries would be made by bladders in LCM–8s, fuel having been first pumped ashore by AOGs through a bottom–laid line. Keeping this line in operation a reasonable percentage of the time was a tremendous struggle in itself.

Meanwhile the Seabees were hard at work throughout the area. Improving the small airstrip at Dong Ha was a particularly taxing job, which had to be accomplished with an absolute minimum of interruption of C–130 flights. Then, once the matting was laid, it was found that it had been so manufactured as to leave sharp edges on top which cut aircraft tires. So it had to be replaced, piece by piece.

In November 1966 the Naval Support Activity established the Dong Ha

*The shallow mouth of the Cua Viet River before dredging operations.*

Detachment of one officer and fifty enlisted men. On 15 March the Naval Support Detachment was split into two sections, one officer and thirty–four men remaining at Dong Ha, and one officer and sixty men taking station at Cua Viet. The job of "port clearance" at Dong Ha was the duty of the Marines, who were often hard pressed to provide enough trucks to keep the cargoes moving fast enough.

A bulldozer and the LCU–crane combination cut away the northern side of the river mouth. A regular dredge started work in November but had to abandon the job in December because of the seas. Fortunately there were but two cases of groundings and one of broaching during those two months.

In January 1967, a major redredging job was required to cut through two sand bars in the Cua Viet river.

There were frequent occasions when LCUs were unable to make the transit from Danang, and difficulties continuing into the New Year as the northeast monsoon continued to pound the coast with high seas and heavy rains. In January 1967, for instance, trips from Danang by LCU and

NH–74198

*New cargo lift craft for logistic support in I Corps.*

YFU [1] had to be suspended a total of sixteen times, and the bottom–laid fuel line was out all month necessitating AOGs to transfer fuel directly to bladder boats. It was not until 18 March that the ship–to–shore line could be restored.

Among the more important cargoes delivered were 175–millimeter guns to be set up on a knoll at Camp Carroll west of Dong Ha, which were capable of reaching across the DMZ. Artillery fire from these guns produced heavy aggressive reaction on the part of the North Vietnamese in March. This required the still further build–up of U.S. military personnel in the northern I Corps zone, added to the requirements for supply by sea, and made more work for the Seabees.

By now a ramp had been scraped out of the sand at Cua Viet with a very small staging area covered by Marston matting. Dredging had produced a minimum channel. The first LST, USS *Caroline County* (LST–525), made it inside the river mouth in March and off–loaded supplies for transshipment up river by LCM–8s. Eight LCM–8s were assigned to the Cua Viet–Dong Ha River run, two being fitted out for the handling of fuel. Two 16–foot Boston Whalers were assigned to provide security.

With twenty–six LSTs off–loadings in April 1967 at Cua Viet, Dong Ha's throughput of cargo reached a new high of 36,369 measurement tons. By now the main enemy effort was clearly focused on the I Corps zone.

## ENEMY ACTION

Due to the accumulation of bits of information regarding enemy preparations, I reported a conclusion that sea lines of logistics would soon become a prime enemy target. Additional security measures were taken and chain dragging of the Cua Viet and Perfume Rivers, an anti–mining step, commenced. Harbor security patrols in Danang were increased with the assignment of additional craft and personnel. Underwater lighting was rigged at the piers. Minesweepers were assigned to keep the entrance and anchorage at Danang clear. These preventative actions were soon rewarded when one of the Naval Support Activity's Skimmers at Danang sighted "an object with strings attached" in the water 200 yards from the moored

---

[1] The *Skilak* (YFU), a new craft, hastily built and delivered to the Naval Support Activity proved an important addition. Similar to the LCU but of slightly greater capacity, it was specially designed for logistic operations and was highly efficient.

barracks barges (APLs). A grenade produced a secondary explosion. On another occasion two swimmers with scuba equipment were turned over to the local authorities. On a third occasion investigation of bubbles produced two diving masks; somehow no swimmers could be found.

On 9 May in the new Cua Viet turning basin, dredge *Hyde* was holed by an explosion on the starboard side. Later, after beaching near the sand ramp, another explosion put a hole on the port quarter. A "damage control" party sent up from Danang by Rear Admiral Lacy undertook repairs. *Hyde* was back dredging the next day. Surely this was an unsurpassed record of recovery, one for which the civilian captain, James Bartell, of the dredge deserves a major share of credit.

On 15 May, YFU–59 anchored at Dong Ha was damaged by an explosion under the port bow.

On 17 May, the Explosive Ordnance Disposal Team recovered a 150–pound command detonation mine in the main channel at Danang.

On 12 June, near the Naval Support Detachment at Cua Viet ramp, an underwater explosion blew a three by nine foot hole in the bottom of USS *Coconino* (LST–603) and flooded her engine room. After emergency damage control actions, the LST was towed to Danang. Temporary repairs by the Naval Support Activity permitted her to proceed under her own power to the Naval Ship Repair Facility, Guam.

Despite all these attacks the Naval Support Activity kept the cargoes moving at a record pace to supply the combat forces.

In August, USS *Elkhorn* was the first AOG to enter the Cua Viet turning basin to deliver fuel.

On 27 August heavy rocket and mortar fire hit Dong Ha, destroying thirteen 10,000–gallon fuel bladders. Sporadic artillery attacks were received for three days. Two sailors were wounded.

September 1967 saw a further intensification of combat near the DMZ. Explosion of the ammunition dump at Dong Ha lasted eight hours causing much damage which had to be repaired by the Seabees. For the Naval Support Activity this meant an added load in order to replenish stocks as rapidly as possible. Construction materials added still further to the workload, as deliveries were made to Dong Ha so that the Seabees could construct the defensive line planned south of the DMZ and a new major airfield near Quang Tri being built beyond the range of North Vietnamese artillery fire.

On 2 September, underwater explosions at Dong Ha damaged two LCUs and one YFU. This was followed by sporadic artillery fire on 3, 4, and 5

September.  All in all there were forty–seven attacks in thirteen days.  The runway required repairs on five occasions.  In one attack eleven Seabees were wounded, and in another four were killed and twenty wounded.

By 13 September, the manning of the Naval Support Detachment had been increased to the point where the Marine Shore Party could be completely relieved and around the clock operations were started for the first time to meet the heavy demands, although river passages were still confined to daylight hours.  Then, as the result of heavy rains, silting of the Cua Viet River mouth prevented entrance of LSTs.  Dredge *Davidson* was sent up from Danang, but every daylight pass she would be bracketed by artillery fire.  Shifted to night operations, the channel was reopened 22 September.

## WEATHER

While rushing to get supplies in before the northeast monsoon, the inter-tropical convergence zone with moist winds from north and south hung over the Cua Viet River and the DMZ for a week or more in late September 1967 when heavy rains fell.  Shortly after this, I paid a visit.  The day before my visit a typhoon had passed inland through the I Corps zone adding many inches of rain.  At Dong Ha the river was up seven feet with off–loading operations being conducted over the now submerged ramp and staging area.  River currents reached ten knots so that no craft could make its way up.  The river mouth was impassable, the tremendous outflow being bucked by the seas.  An attack cargo ship (AKA) with cargo from Danang was standing helplessly by waiting to send loads ashore by landing craft.  One empty LCU which had tried to make its way out was caught in white water in the semicircle of heavily breaking seas outside the river mouth.  We watched for a considerable time from a helicopter as this craft was tossed violently about, unable to move in or out.  I have no idea how long it took for the craft to work free, but mere survival seemed miraculous.

When I later called on General Westmoreland in Saigon, he expressed concern over the ability of the logistic system to get supplies in to the heavily engaged troops during the monsoon.  I expressed confidence that the vital supplies would get through, although noting that construction materials would be at times delayed.  The determined efforts of the Naval Support Activity personnel proved this forecast right.  General Westmoreland also discussed plans to deploy the First Cavalry Division into Quang Tri in the spring.  Providing adequate support would depend on construction of the LST off–loading site at Tan My.  This and an over–the–beach operation further north in the spring and summer of 1968 met all the needs.

In October 1967, Cua Viet resupply was particularly critical.  Dong Ha was hit by twenty more artillery and mortar attacks and *Davidson* had to return to Danang because of heavy seas.  Nevertheless, with the help of a barge off–load site constructed by the Seabees, of amphibious ships, and of the deployment north of more LCUs and LCM–8s, a record throughput of 45,592 measurement tons was set at Dong Ha that month.  On the recommendations of COMSERVPAC another AOG was deployed for the duration of the monsoon seas to keep the fuel deliveries flowing.

NMCB–10 did a remarkable job of building the Quang Tri Airfield, the first aircraft landing after only thirty–eight days of work.  One trip was made by an LCM–8 from Cua Viet to the Quang Tri Airfield, but the shoal water deterred further such voyages.

The situation in northern I CTZ remained critical throughout November, but attacks on sea lines of logistics subsided as Marines and ARVN forces gained further control along the river.  Cua Viet sustained only one mortar attack that month, on 7 November, when one man was wounded.  Dong Ha's throughput reached 72,453 measurement tons.

On 6 December, dredge *Davidson*, assisting in a rescue operation, suffered severe damage to rudder posts and screws.  Parts were flown out from the United States and Danang had her repaired by 17 December.

Silting again closed the Cua Viet River to LSTs on 7 December, the channel being opened on the 31st.

Cua Viet received artillery fire once on 11 December and twice on the 16th, with one killed and two wounded.

River patrol craft (PBRs) such as operated in the Delta were deployed north in January 1968 when a mobile base was established in Tan My cove.  Self–propelled "Ammi" fuel barges were towed to the Cua Viet and Perfume Rivers on 22 January.  A second off–loading site with five LCU ramps was established at Dong Ha in February.

In January 1968, enemy efforts to disrupt the Navy's resupply efforts up the Cua Viet River intensified, and hit a peak toward the end of the month.  Craft were ambushed and hit by small arms and recoilless rifle fire on the 7th and 20th.  Mines were exploded in the river on 21, 22, 23, 24, and 27 January.  All in all eight craft were damaged, one LCM–8 was sunk, two Navy men were killed in action, and eighteen wounded.

Action against the Navy's Cua Viet line of logistics continued to be intense in February when the ramp areas at Dong Ha and Cua Viet were hit by twenty–six separate artillery and rocket attacks.  Logistic craft transiting the river were subject to frequent attacks by small arms, recoilless rifle and mortar fire, twenty–seven craft being hit with seven Navy men killed and forty–two wounded.  But still the supplies got through.

Craft going up the river had been given escorts following a COMSERV-PAC recommendation.  On 24 February Task Force Clearwater was established to coordinate movements and protect craft on the Cua Viet and Perfume Rivers.  The Task Force Commander coordinated helicopter gunships, naval gunfire, and other fire when convoys were attacked.

The foreign civilian crews of USNS LSTs voiced objections to off–loading at Cua Viet on 19 January.  On 23 January these MSTS LSTs refused to beach, and fleet LSTs took over the entire job thereafter.  On 19, 21, and 24 February LSTs at Cua Viet had to be ordered to sea, three having received shrapnel damage from the artillery fire.


## KHE SANH

Nowhere in Vietnam was the fighting as heavy for such a prolonged period of time as at Khe Sanh.  Close to the Laos border on Route 9, this was initially an outpost of the Special Forces.  General Westmoreland had the Marines take over its defense, along with ARVN troops, when the seriousness of enemy efforts to launch a combined offensive from Laos and across the DMZ was clear.  Many questioned the wisdom of staying in Khe Sanh. In many respects the location resembled Dien Bien Phu, the scene of the decisive defeat of the French.  Khe Sanh was surrounded by jungle covered hills and by mountains overlooking the valley, which provided high ground for mortars, rockets and artillery.  The enemy obviously had high hopes of a victory there, one which would have had great propaganda value in Vietnam and throughout the world.

The Navy played key roles here as well.  In January 1967, the Naval Support Activity, Danang, had been assigned responsibility for maintenance of airfields at An Hoa, Dong Ha, Khe Sanh, and later Duc Pho.  The 307 officers and men of Seabee Maintenance Unit 301 were divided into details and given the assignments.  In September extensive repairs were required at Khe Sanh, including 2,300 feet of subgrade and weather proofing, which essentially amounted to building a new airfield.  Yet the field had to be kept in operation a large percentage of the time since this was the only way of delivering the vital supplies. As if frequent enemy gunfire was not enough, the crash of a C–130 at a critical point in construction did much damage and destroyed 500 barrels of asphalt by fire. But finally the runway was completed and then extended to 2,900 feet to accommodate C–123s. The job was completed by 2 December, truly a heroic achievement under fire.

Defensive actions by Marines and ARVN troops and air attacks inflicted tremendous casualties on the North Vietnamese. When Army troops moved in from the east in April 1968, the enemy precipitously abandoned the scene, leaving large caches of materials, arms and munitions.

Regretfully Saigon and the press described the move as "lifting the siege." When somewhat later COMUSMACV decided to level the base and pull out the Marines and Vietnamese Rangers, North Vietnam pulled out all the propaganda stops in claiming a Communist victory. This actually was their worst defeat, they having abandoned the area after sustaining massive casualties.

## MAJOR MILITARY FEAT

General Westmoreland summarized it well when he observed that: "The fact that we were able to meet this formidable threat of five to six divisions in the far north without giving up any positions of real value further south is, to me, the major military feat of the war." He also emphasized that "we were utterly dependent upon the sea logistical line." [2]

------

[2] Sharp and Westmoreland, *Report on the War in Vietnam*, pp. 116 and 172.

# CHAPTER XI

# Inshore and Inland Waterways

Throughout the history of the United States, there have been many occasions when the Navy has been called upon to engage in combat on inland waters or in shallow coastal regions. In the Revolution, Benedict Arnold's "Navy" fought an action on Lake Champlain causing the crucial postponement of British efforts to cut the colonies in two. Then in the War of 1812, naval actions were conducted on such inland waters as the Great Lakes, again on Lake Champlain, the Patuxent River, and in the approaches to New Orleans. Later, naval operations against pirates in the Caribbean and Gulf of Mexico ranged into inlets, lagoons, and small rivers. It was in the Florida Everglades that the Navy assisted in inland operations during the Seminole and Creek Wars. Ships and craft in the Mississippi were a determining factor in winning victories for the North in that theater during the Civil War. Then, in the twentieth century, riverine type operations were conducted in the Philippines. For 75 years the U.S. gunboats of the Yangtze Patrol ranged far inland in China. Still more recently, Navy craft played an important role in the crossing of the Rhine during World War II.

On each occasion, the need for inland naval operations had not been anticipated by planning or advance preparations. Instead the means and tactics were innovations—tailored at the time to meet special requirements posed by the particular situation and the specific operating conditions. The Vietnam Conflict was no exception to the rule. The wide variety of operations in shallow coastal regions and on inland waterways were for the most part unanticipated. Specialized combat craft were designed and other craft were altered to carry out unusual assignments in restricted waters.

As always, the effectiveness of the combat forces depended on timely and adequate logistic support convenient to the widespread operating areas. Appropriate operational logistic forces had to be created as a part of the overall naval logistic system, and tailored for the jobs to be done and the difficult operating environments.

The first of shallow–draft operations to be organized in the Vietnam Conflict was that designed to stem the flow of enemy supplies by sea.

The importance to the enemy of bringing supplies into coastal areas by the sea route has been mentioned in Chapter I. The Viet Cong could live off the land insofar as food was concerned, but most weapons, ammunition and medical supplies had to be provided from outside the Republic. By far the easiest way to furnish these supplies from North Vietnam was by water. Consequently one of the more important tasks faced by the forces of the Republic of Vietnam and the United States was to cut off, or severely reduce, the flow of logistics by this means.

The Sea Force of the Vietnam Navy was extremely limited in its capabilities to seal the long coastline. A "Junk Force" had been added in May 1961, initially as a paramilitary organization, for the conduct of coastal patrols and operations in inlets and rivers. Armed with 50–caliber machine guns and small arms, the vessels of this force operated out of twenty–eight tiny bases along the coast.

When movements from North Vietnam stepped up in the fall of 1964 and the succeeding winter, it became clear that the Vietnamese Navy could not handle the anti–infiltration job along the coast by itself. Matters came to a head on 16 February 1965 after a camouflaged steel–hulled trawler had been sighted in Vung Ro Bay by an Army helicopter engaged on a medical mission. Notification of the local U.S. Naval advisor resulted in actions which destroyed the ship. Much contraband, including arms and munitions, was recovered.

## MARKET TIME

In answer to a Vietnamese Government request for surveillance assistance, U.S. destroyers and destroyer escorts were subsequently deployed along the coast to detect and track all suspicious vessels, the latter being reported to the Vietnamese. The U.S. counterinfiltration effort initiated on 12 March 1965 was given the designation "Market Time," with naval aircraft patrols complementing the efforts of the surface ships. In that same month, joint surveillance centers were established along the coast to help coordinate the efforts of the U.S. and Vietnamese navies.

The next month, following a U.S. Navy study, a decision was made to extend the U.S. effort to shallow waters. Seventeen Coast Guard cutters

(WPBs) were transported to the scene from the United States and procurement of 50–foot aluminum–hulled boats, Swifts (PCF), was commenced by the Navy. On 30 April the decision was reached to shift operational control of Market Time from Commander Seventh Fleet to the Chief Naval Advisory Group, the latter acting as the agent of Commander U.S. Military Assistance Command, Vietnam.

On 11 May, the government of Vietnam authorized the United States to stop, search, and seize vessels within the territorial waters of Vietnam.

The introduction of shallow–draft coastal patrol types into the operation meant new and different logistic problems. The operating range of the Swifts, in particular, was limited; their sea–keeping capabilities were marginal in heavy weather; and their repair capabilities were such as to require extensive in–port assistance. Unlike the destroyer escorts, which could be kept on station for prolonged periods with the help of underway replenishment and occasional trips to Subic Bay, effective operation of the inshore patrol units required nearby basing in sheltered waters.

To support the first inshore patrol units, two bases were planned, one in the north at Danang and the other in the Gulf of Siam at An Thoi. Steps were initiated in May to outfit a repair barge (YR) at the Ship Repair Facility, Subic, for deployment to Danang, and to send a small repair ship (ARL) to An Thoi. As will be described later, the original two bases would subsequently be augmented by the establishment of bases ashore in Qui Nhon, Cam Ranh Bay and Cat Lo in 1966.

Admiral Johnson tasked Commander Seventh Fleet, Vice Admiral Blackburn, with the responsibility of providing direct support to Market Time forces through Commander Task Force 73 (Commander Service Group 3).

On 30 July 1965, the Coastal Surveillance Force (Task Force 115) was established under the command of the Chief of the Naval Advisory Group, Rear Admiral N. G. Ward. The Vietnamese junk force was integrated into the Vietnamese Navy that same month. With the activation of Task Force 115, the Chief of the Naval Advisory Group assumed operational control of 7 destroyer escorts (DER), the 17 Coast Guard Cutters, 2 minesweepers (MSO), 2 LSTs (which were to provide interim support at Danang and An Thoi until repair ships and craft were on the scene), and 5 patrol aircraft (SP–2H) operating out of Tan Son Nhut, Saigon. Commander Coast Guard Squadron One headed the Gulf of Thailand Support Group with 9 WPBs at An Thoi, and Commander Coast Guard Squadron 12 the Danang Support Group of 8 WPBs. In addition to the P–2 aircraft, higher performance P–3As of Task Force 72 based at Sangley in the Philippines flew supporting patrols.

During a visit to Vietnam, Secretary McNamara approved an increase in the Swifts from 20 to 54—the number originally requested by the Navy. This was to expand the number of craft available for inshore operations to the point where, in combination with the Vietnamese, they could establish an effective patrol along the entire coast of the Republic.

As planned in May a landing craft repair ship, USS *Krishna* (ARL–38), was transferred in July 1965 to Commander Service Force, U.S. Pacific Fleet, from the Amphibious Force of the Atlantic. Two small cargo ships, which had initially been built for the Army in World War II, were also transferred to the Service Force—USS *Mark* (AKL–12) from Commander Naval Forces, Marianas, and USS *Brule* (AKL–28) from Commander Naval Forces, Philippines. These two ships were fitted out by the Ship Repair Facility, Subic, for the job of resupply to Vietnam. A repair barge and supply barge were also activated to provide in–country support.

The roles of the Service Force in the early stages were confined to limited actions in the areas of supply and repair, and to the providing of logistic support ships. In August 1965, Vice Admiral Bernard F. Roeder, Commander Amphibious Force, U.S. Pacific Fleet, urged that COMSERV-PAC be tasked with the overall responsibilities for Market Time support. I proposed to prepare a comprehensive plan, but on the advice of Vice Admiral Clarey, Deputy CINCPACFLT, waited until arrangements had been completed concerning operating concepts and command relationships.

Early in October, Commander in Chief, U.S. Pacific Fleet announced the intention of having COMSERVPAC plan, provide or arrange, and conduct logistic support of Market Time operations in Vietnam when the concept became firm. The first two Swifts arrived at An Thoi at the end of the month to augment the WPBs already there. Then on 22 November, Admiral Johnson assigned me the responsibility for "supervision and coordination of planning, and for the conduct and administration of services and supply of material" for Market Time support. Shortly thereafter, COM-SERVPAC's tentative plan was issued, setting forth the logistic support to be provided by the various commands and the coordination of such support.

The plan was a comprehensive one based on making maximum use of the existing Service Force logistic system. It provided for continuing support to Market Time ships by the Mobile Support Force. It set forth the specific responsibilities of Service Force activities, afloat and ashore, for the support of craft in–country, including their repairs and supply of fuel, ammunition and other items. Activities at Subic Bay were tasked with providing backup support. Except in I Corps, "common supply support" was to be the responsibility of the Headquarters Support Activity, Saigon.

As in the case of ships of the Seventh Fleet, logistic responsibilities beyond the capabilities of the combatant units themselves were assigned to Service Force commands, along with the other support responsibilities of these commands. At An Thoi almost all of these responsibilities were assigned to the Commanding Officer *Krishna,* which was later augmented by a specially outfitted barracks craft, APL–55.

At Danang the logistic support responsibilities for Market Time were added to those already held by the Commander of the Naval Support Activity. The repair and supply craft there were assigned to the Activity, as were repair personnel not required in the PCFs themselves. With the addition of a floating drydock, a floating crane, and later, repair facilities ashore, the Naval Support Activity had the means of utilizing the personnel and resources most efficiently in combination with its other capabilities for the repair of both Market Time craft and its own numerous craft. Initially, provision was made for returning craft to Subic Bay for overhaul by the Ship Repair Facility there. Later Danang gained the capability to accomplish many of the overhauls in–country. In addition to the more routine jobs, the resultant repair organizations proved highly responsive to emergencies, accomplishing major work on dredges, LSTs, and craft damaged by enemy action or groundings. A fragmented organization would have been far less effective, and would have required more resources.

Some associated with the Swifts would have preferred to have responsibilities for all repairs of Swifts, ashore and afloat, but the amphibious force commander, Vice Admiral B. F. Roeder, and later Vice Admiral F. J. Blouin, concurred in the SERVPAC plan.

Immediate steps were taken to implement the plan while it was still under review. After concurrence had been received from the Type Commander, Commander Seventh Fleet, and CINCPACFLT, the final logistics support plan (SERVPAC's Operation Plan 10–66) was issued in January 1966.

With the logistic support provided, the Market Time units started patrols as soon as the craft arrived. Their effectiveness, in combination with the other U.S. Navy ships and aircraft and units, was attested to by the fact that only sporadic attempts were made to deliver supplies to the Viet Cong by steel–hulled vessels in 1966. It was estimated that such deliveries by trawlers of about 100 tons had been at the rate of two per month the previous year.

The Communists resumed attempts to deliver supplies by sea the next year. On 1 January 1967, a steel–hulled trawler, found off–loading into sampans off the Delta province of An Xuyen, was engaged by PCFs, set on fire and exploded. Engaged by a DER, Coast Guard cutters, and PCF it beached at Phu Thien, 60 miles southeast of Danang where it was destroyed by its own crew. This trawler was carrying guns, ammunition, food and medicine. On 23 May a group of junks were engaged off Ho Gio Island. These were loaded with rice, ammunition and arms. Another trawler was detected moving in during July. This one retreated to the Paracels and then made a second attempt. Taken under fire on entering Vietnam territorial waters, it beached near Balangan Peninsula, 15 miles northeast of Quang Ngai. Rigged for self–destruction, the charges had not been exploded. This particular trawler had come from Hainan Island.

Next year there was a flurry of effort on the part of the enemy to get supplies in following the Tet offensive of 1968. One trawler was turned back on 21 February. On 1 March another was turned back, and three others were destroyed or captured.

## GAME WARDEN

One of the most critical areas in Vietnam was that of the vast Delta area which comprised the IV Corps Tactical Zone. The entire region south of Saigon is a complex mass of waterways, some natural, some man–made. Most of the remaining area consists of rice paddies. The Mekong River, which starts on the distant Tibetan plateau beyond the Himalaya Mountains, together with its innumerable tributaries, drains a large percentage of Thailand and most of Laos and Cambodia.

In the summer months, the southwest monsoon brings moist air in from the Indian Ocean and the Gulf of Siam, the resultant tropical deluges causing tremendous outpourings of water saturated with fine silt. At times, the entire countryside in the Delta is inundated except for small scattered tree–covered hamlets. But for vehicles on a few major roads, hardly anything moves other than by water.

The Viet Cong had base areas at several locations throughout the Delta, and had long controlled many sections. Key to control of this large area was control of the waterways, which were used extensively by the VC for the movement of troops, for transportation of food, supplies and munitions, for the collection of "taxes," for intercepting rice being shipped to market, and for many other purposes.

In addition to regions of the Mekong Delta a particularly critical area was the Rung Sat Special Zone, a mangrove covered area, mostly under water and laced with narrow waterways—strategically placed astride the waterway to Saigon. A Viet Cong base area, it was also a key route of the VC in their north–south movements.

First with the French and then later alone, the Vietnamese Navy had established a River Force, operating craft which fought in the waterways and conducted joint assault operations with their Army. But this was only a small percent of what was really required to cover the extensive maze of rivers and canals.

From the needs of the Delta and those of the river approaches to Saigon arose the plan for a U.S. Navy river patrol force. The boat to be used, a river patrol boat (PBR), was, as I understood it, based on a prototype proposed, designed, and built by a contractor in something like two weeks. Of glass fiber construction, and with water jet propulsion, these were fast, highly maneuverable craft. A machine gun mount forward, and an over–and–under combined machine gun–mortar mount aft, gave them the fire-power they needed.

The U.S. Navy River Patrol Force (Game Warden) was conceived to police these waterways and Commander River Patrol Force (CTF 116) was established under Rear Admiral Ward, with headquarters initially in Saigon. The force was tasked with enforcing curfews established on the waterways; interdicting Viet Cong infiltration, movement and resupply efforts; participating with other allied forces in eliminating VC insurgency; and maintaining the Long Tau River open to ocean–going traffic and clear of mines.

The small PBRs required bases in each operating area. As originally conceived, it was planned to base PBR operations at eight sites—at Cat Lo and Nha Be at either end of the Rung Sat Zone; and at Can Tho, Vinh Long, My Tho, Sa Dec, Chau Doc, and Tan Chau along the Mekong and Bassac. Long Xuyen was chosen as an interim base for Chau Doc and Tan Chau. From bases at these locations and from the locations of three fleet LSTs in river mouths, 120 patrol boats were programmed to carry out operations against the enemy.

A team from Hawaii, headed by Captain Sol Neman from SERVPAC's

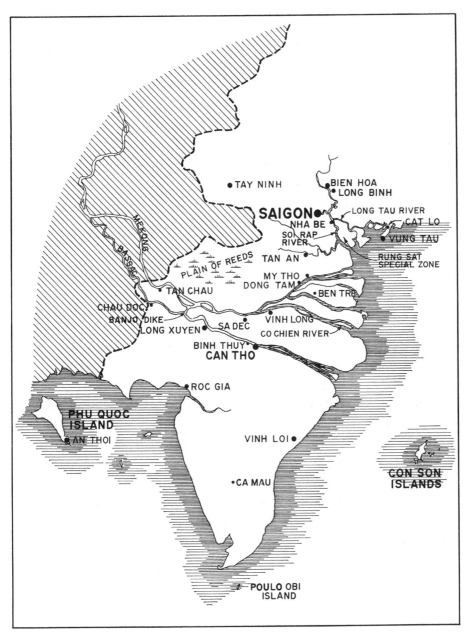

*Saigon and the Delta areas.*

NH–74356

Fleet Maintenance Office, was assembled on 15 March 1966 to conduct a thorough, base–by–base review of maintenance requirements in Vietnam for both Market Time and Game Warden craft. A review was made of programs at bases already in being and those in the formative stage. The report was comprehensive and thorough—although, as I noted in my endorsement, it focused only on facilities ashore and did not include the all–important maintenance resources afloat.

## NAVAL SUPPORT ACTIVITY, SAIGON

The increasing Market Time forces, the plans for Game Warden, Admiral Ward's concern about his logistic support after HEDSUPPACT was disestablished, the plans for additional units for minesweeping and harbor defense, and other considerations were now making desirable a re–examination of Navy logistic support in II, III and IV Corps zones. The providing of this support was the subject of a number of discussions between CINCPACFLT, COMSERVPAC and the Chief of the Naval Advisory Group during the winter of 1966.

The concept subsequently adopted was one proposed to me by Captain Robert B. Poage, my Plans Officer. It envisaged consolidation of all support not necessarily organic to the units supported. Rather than each force having its own bases, these bases would be operated as satellites of a single Service Force command headquartered in Saigon. This command, backed up by the rest of the SERVPAC system, would provide support to all the Navy forces in Vietnam outside of I Corps, and have the flexibility to refocus effort from one force to another as the situation changed. All the key commands, having agreed informally with the basic concept, I asked Captain Kuntze, HEDSUPPACT, to initiate planning for the in–country support effort.

Meanwhile, Admiral Johnson, CINCPACFLT, had recommended the establishment of a Naval Component Command in Saigon. The Joint Chief of Staff publication, *Unified Action Armed Forces*, provided that "the senior officer of each Service assigned to a unified or subordinate unified command and qualified for command by the regulations of his own Service is the commander of the component of his Service unless another officer is so designated by competent authority." As the result of seniority, the Commanding General, III Marine Expeditionary (later Amphibious) Force had been acting as MACV's Naval Component Commander, remotely from Danang where his efforts had of necessity to be concentrated primarily on command of U.S. and other Free World Military Assistance Forces in I Corps.

In March 1966, the Secretary of the Navy approved the establishment of U.S. Naval Forces, Vietnam (COMNAVFORV), as a major naval command in Saigon, and the principal naval advisor to COMUSMACV. Rear Admiral N. G. Ward was to assume these additional duties on 1 April 1966. He would be succeeded by Rear Admiral Kenneth L. Veth on 27 April 1967, who in turn would be followed by Vice Admirals Elmo R. Zumwalt and Jerome H. King.

On 5 March, CINCPACFLT had tasked COMSERVPAC "to initiate plans, programs and directions" for the purpose of:

> (a) Providing or arranging for required Navy support to enable COMNAVFORV to perform all anticipated shore based support functions and responsibilities.
> (b) Enabling the prospective NAVSUPPACT Saigon and possible detachments to fulfill the proposed mission and anticipated tasking.
> (c) Enabling NAVSUPPACT Danang to fulfill the proposed expanded mission.

In response, COMSERVPAC proposed a concept for logistic support along the lines discussed previously, "with the goal of the simplest and most efficient system which would be fully responsive to COMNAVFORV," and "with the fundamental principle that support functions for all the various commands would be consolidated to the maximum extent practicable." The concept included establishing detachments of NAVSUPPACT Saigon to operate the various bases in support of Market Time, Game Warden and other Naval forces in II, III and IV CTZ. This concept was approved by CINCPACFLT on 4 April.

The question was as to how to implement the concept in the earliest possible fashion. This was discussed during my trip to Vietnam in April 1966. Captain Herbert King, the prospective commanding officer of the new activity, having been given accelerated orders, was already on the scene. In–country planning had not progressed very far, but it was decided with Rear Admiral Ward to establish the Naval Support Activity on that same day and to transfer all remaining HEDSUPPACT personnel to the new command along with others then engaged in support operations.

So it was that the Naval Support Activity, Saigon, was activated on 17 May 1966, under the command of COMSERVPAC, and under the operational control and area coordination of COMNAVFORV. The activity

USN-1119058

*The author inspecting the Naval Support Detachment, Qui Nhon, with Captain Herbert King.*

was assigned the mission of supporting all U.S. Naval forces and bases in the II, III and IV Corps areas of Vietnam, and of providing emergency support to other operating forces of the U.S. Navy. Similar support in the I Corps zone was to be provided by the Naval Support Activity, Danang.

To fulfill the new responsibilities, I promulgated a new Logistic Support Plan 11–66, to cover support in II, III and IV Corps zones. The previous Market Time Logistic Support Plan was changed to cover the enlarged scope of support in I Corps.

Operational control of Service Force ships *Mark* and *Brule*, as well as *Krishna*, was transferred to COMNAVFORV. I was going to recommend delegation of operational control of these ships to COMNAVSUPPACT Saigon, along with that for the various service craft involved, but Rear Admiral Ward took this sound step on his own initiative. Thus, along with the bases, and the transfer of HEDSUPPACT's Air Cofat, Captain King had control of the repair, supply, berthing and messing, and resupply means ashore and afloat. After a year in–country, Captain King was relieved by

Captain Burns W. Spore on 21 April 1967, and he in turn was relieved by Captain Max Duncan a year later.

The initial allowance of the new activity was for 58 officers and 1,018 men for the activity and its twelve detachments, including support personnel previously assigned directly to Market Time and Game Warden. In spite of the fact that requests for personnel were extremely modest in respect to the number of jobs to be done, difficulties were encountered at every step along the way in getting approval for the allowance and for the required in–country ceiling increase. Arrival of support personnel was slower than the build–up of American forces to be supported. Washington's requirements for the justification of procedures approximated those of peacetime and approvals were long delayed.

A further complication was that in later build–ups NAVSUPPACT Saigon tended to underestimate its personnel needs in the expanding situation. A year and a half after the original request, an officer from Washington told me that they had not realized or appreciated the size of the job to be done. By April 1967, the allowance had been increased in three steps to 112 officers and 1,751 enlisted. NAVSUPPACT Saigon finally reached the approved manning level in the summer of 1967.

Another source of difficulty faced was that of warehouse and office space in Saigon. The Army's First Logistical Command needed stowage facilities to carry on the efforts inherited from HEDSUPPACT. Understandably, they preempted the best warehouses in Saigon and provided NAVSUPPACT with only old, inadequate warehouses at scattered locations throughout the city. Most of the headquarters at the Cofat compound were taken over by the Army along with Captain Kuntze's quarters, as Captain King moved to a room in one of the bachelor officers' hotels. For office space, he and the bulk of his staff were moved into a building near COMNAVFORV's Headquarters.

What the Naval Support Activity accomplished with inadequate personnel and scanty resources was truly remarkable. A key factor in carrying out the required tasks was the ever increasing number of Vietnamese civilians hired. Five hundred were on board by June 1967. They performed many of the clerical and housekeeping chores at the headquarters and at the detachments, thus freeing military personnel for other duties.

Responsibilities were assumed rapidly. By the end of June 1966, temporary bases at Qui Nhon, Cam Ranh Bay, My Tho, Cat Lo, Nha Be and Can Tho, in addition to the one at An Thoi, were operational, although it would be a year and more before the semi—permanent construction would provide the desired capabilities ashore. Preparatory work had commenced in varying degrees at Sa Dec, Vinh Long, and Long Xuyen. Base sites were under study at Chau Doc, Tan Chau and Nha Trang.

In the summer of 1966 the flood waters of the Mekong were particularly high. I was at My Tho when crews of our river patrol boats returned from a two week operation away from the river, having roamed over the "Plain of Reeds" area assisting RVN forces to surround and attack the enemy isolated on patches of the higher ground.

NAVSUPPACT, with headquarters in Saigon and planning underway for twelve base detachments, was tasked with providing support for COM-NAVFORV headquarters and all ships and craft under his operational control—including Task Force 115 (Market Time), Task Force 116 (Game Warden), Harbor Defense Forces (Stable Door), Harbor Clearance Units, and Mine Countermeasure Forces in II, III and IV CTZ. The responsibilities encompassed direction and control of logistic lift; acting as Navy cargo coordinator; procurement, distribution, control and accounting for material in support of NAVFORV forces; provision of in—country base support for NAVFORV forces and establishment of the in—country base support structure; negotiation and consummation of inter—Service support agreements for these forces (which took many months); coordination of construction requirements; boat maintenance, personnel support; expendable ordnance support; and support and services for visiting fleet units.

COMSERVPAC Logistic Support Plan 11–66 provided also for the repair and overhaul of ships, boats and craft under the operational control of COMNAVFORV by Ship Repair Facilities, Subic, Guam, and Yokosuka, and by Fleet Activities, Sasebo; supply support by Naval Supply Depot, Subic; stock allowance and issue of expendable ordnance by Naval Magazine, Subic; technical support by SERVPAC's Naval Shore Electronics Engineering Activity, Pacific; and additional services and support by other Navy activities in the Western Pacific. It assigned Commander Service Group Three with type command responsibilities, under COMSERVPAC, for Service Force ships under the operational control of COMNAVFORV, with responsibility for ammunition support, and—as CTF 73 and subject to direction by COMSEVENTHFLT—with responsibility for underway replenishment ship support.

In addition to the permanent harbor defense unit established at Danang, Mobile Inshore Undersea Warfare Surveillance Units (MIUWS) were first deployed to Vung Tau and Cam Ranh Bay. Harbor Defense requirements were increasing, the total Harbor Defense Program being still in the planning stage. NAVSUPPACT Saigon was responsible for supporting this effort, including logistics for the 782 personnel, and repair and supply support of 24 LCPLs and 12 Skimmers. This required additional support means over those initially planned at the bases used by Market Time. A new activity was planned to support the unit at Nha Trang. Because of the small size of this unit, a decision was made not to establish a NAVSUPPACT detachment there as originally planned, but to assign NAVSUPPACT individuals to assist in the base operations.


## SUPPLY


In August 1967 after review of NAVSUPPACT Saigon's capabilities, determination was made that the boat repair parts held at Naval Supply Depot, Subic, could be more effectively handled in Saigon. As a result the Naval Support Activity assumed the total depot level support function for Market Time, Game Warden, Stable Door and mine countermeasures craft in October. By establishing a single WESTPAC backup stock and distribution point in–country, supply responsiveness to the bases and operating units was improved. Requisition lead times were reduced to a minimum, and efficiency and economy were promoted by the elimination of one echelon of backup support material. From July 1966 to April 1967 the number of items carried quadrupled to over 26,000.

Extraordinary difficulties were encountered in the supply of repair parts for PBRs. These arose from a number of considerations. The initial allowance of these parts was inadequate, as is often the case with new equipment. False economy should not govern in the initial purchase of spares; it may be better to over–buy initially and adjust procurement downward later. Initially quantity estimates had been on the basis of engine overhauls every 2,000 operating hours. Under the conditions of Vietnam combat in the Delta, it was found necessary to overhaul every 900 operating hours. The need for replacement parts skyrocketed. For a while the situation was so critical that I was reviewing the situation and corrective actions in detail at the headquarters at Pearl Harbor each week.

The corrective action involved a three–step program. The first was to obtain the parts as rapidly as possible, and then ship them immediately to

Saigon by air. The second was to build up the NAVSUPPACT stocks, and the third was to monitor the actions of the Continental Inventory Control Points by the SERVPAC headquarters. A related action was centralized control of the parts at the detachments as well as in Saigon, and to redistribute these parts as needed by air. Intense actions were taken by SERVPAC's Fleet and Force Supply Office, the Naval Supply Systems Command and others—as the entire Navy's logistic system went to work on the problem. As a result the critical PBR items had been reduced from 213 to 16 by October 1967, and the remainder were soon taken off the critical list.

Difficulties were also encountered in the obtaining of common supply support from the Army, whose First Logistical Command had relieved the Navy's Headquarters Support Activity, Saigon, of the responsibility for 3,500 items of common supply to all forces in II, III and IV Corps zones on 1 April 1966. More than a year later, I found the support to be unsatisfactory. The problems were explored with the Army, who without a call–up of reserves was having tremendous problems in regard to supply activities. Captain Spore was told to do all he could to help the Army, to assist in pinpointing problem areas and to seek mutual solutions. One result was that the Naval Support Activity, Saigon, was placed on a "fill–kill" basis, whereby if the Army could not fill a requisition the activity would obtain it through Navy channels. Whereas common supply under the right circumstances is desirable, this does not relieve a Service of the responsibility of providing support to its own forces. If the prescribed way won't work, other means must be found.

## MAINTENANCE

The maintenance concept in support of NAVFORV forces was influenced by several factors, including changing operational requirements, scarcity of suitable real estate, insufficient dredging services, time consuming land reclamation, cutbacks and reprogramming of the military construction program, and the steadily increasing tempo of operations. Construction of facilities ashore for craft maintenance and repair was dependent on the availability of real estate, including that which could be filled by dredging.

As a result of such considerations, stopgap measures were taken initially, such as co–locating at Vietnamese River Assault Group (RAG) bases and selecting temporary sites. Covered lighters, YFNBs 9 and 16, were provided with cranes and machine shop equipment from Advanced Base Functional Components. The latter had been ordered forward to provide capabilities ashore. These craft, converted at Nha Be, provided interim support at Can Tho and Nha Be.

The fact that an extraordinarily high percentage of the PBRs was kept operating was a tribute to the combined ingenuity and hard work of the maintenance personnel in the boats and at the bases.

During the next two years, the PBRs to be supported were to grow from 120 to 250. The number of personnel to be supported more than doubled from June 1966 to February 1967 when it approached 6,000.

## NEW TASKS

As time went on, additional Naval Support Activity tasks were added.

For instance, in May 1967, the Activity was assigned responsibility for support of the construction and resupply of radar sites on Poulo Obi and Con Son Islands off the southern tip of Vietnam. This was to pose many interesting problems later, such as delivery of materials to a site high on a hill by Air Cofat helicopters. Roads were repaired and the helicopter pad high on Poulo Obi was built by NAVSUPPACT public works personnel.

NAVSUPPACT took over the operation and maintenance of the airstrip at An Thoi.

A decision was reached to supply a quantity of surface ship ammunition at Cam Ranh Bay for Seventh Fleet resupply. This came to be the regular rearming point of the rocket ships (LSMR and IFS), these ships having no underway replenishment capabilities. The trip to Subic at slow speed was long and wasteful of time.

Cryptographic, electronic, and teletype repairs were undertaken for all forces supported. A registered publication library was established. The Oceanographic Office in Saigon was added to the list of those supported. A bi-weekly Navy newspaper, *The Jackstaff*, was published. Navy Post Offices were operated at Cat Lo, Nha Be and Cam Ranh Bay.

Another dimension was added to the River Patrol Force in the form of Helicopter Attack (Light) Squadron Three (HAL–3), which flew helicopters known as "Sea Wolves." COMNAVSUPPACT assumed responsibility for support of the Squadron at Vung Tau, Vinh Long, Can Tho (Binh Thuy airfield), and those LSTs operating in river mouths.

## PUBLIC WORKS

The Army was tasked by an inter-Service support agreement to provide public works support for the Naval Support Activity, Saigon, and its outlying detachments.   This support provided through a contractor, Pacific Architects and Engineers, left much to be desired, competing as it was with the massive Army requirements.   Organic support was obviously needed.   To provide this support, it was found necessary to deploy a Seabee detachment south from I Corps.   Then, on 20 September 1967, Seabee Maintenance Unit 302 was deployed to Vietnam and placed under COMNAVSUPPACT Saigon.   It was stationed at Cam Ranh Bay with units being deployed wherever needed.

## RESUPPLY BY WATER AND AIR

One of the keys to the success of support by scattered Navy bases, ashore and afloat in II, III and IV Corps zones, was the organic lift by water and by air under the operational control of Commander Naval Support Activity, Saigon.

Initially, *Mark* and *Brule* spent much of their time delivering supplies from Subic.   Later these light cargo ships were deployed almost continuously in–country, where they made deliveries from Saigon to bases along the coast and up the treacherous waterways of the Mekong Delta.

These original waterlift assets of NAVSUPPACT Saigon were later augmented by self–propelled refrigeration craft, YFRs 889, 890, and 866, by a small oiler (YOG) and a self–propelled water barge (YW), by an LST for resupply of the Mobile Riverine Force, and by a fleet of 41 LCMs (39 LCM 3s and 6s, and 2 refuelers).   As more detachments and the Game Warden LSTs became operational at dispersed locations, the demands for waterlift resupply increased significantly.   The tonnage delivered by this means passed 400 short tons in December in 1966 and was up to 1,800 short tons by April 1967.

On a number of occasions the resupply ships and craft were engaged by the enemy as they transited the Long Tau and branches of the Mekong.   On one such occasion, 15 February 1967, *Mark* en route to Saigon from Vung Tau came under heavy automatic rifle fire and mortar attack from both sides of the Long Tau River.   A running battle continued for approximately 45 minutes.   *Mark* engaged in return fire and suffered no casualties.

On 23 July 1966, *Mark* escorted by the Vietnamese Navy LSIL–331, became the first cargo ship in approximately ten years to transit the Bassac River from Can Tho to the open sea. The trip was particularly hazardous because of the shifting and unmarked channel and the dangers of VC attack. However, this route reduced the resupply cycle to detachments in the Delta by two days. The normal river run would be down the Long Tau from Saigon and then up the Mekong, traveling only by day. The ships would cross over into the Bassac through the often rapidly flowing "Banjo Dike" northeast of Long Xuyen, down the Bassac, and then make the reverse trip.

Other Service Force ships made the Mekong–Bassac run under operational control of the Military Sea Transportation Service. Landing Ship Squadron Two (operating 11 LSTs) had been transferred to SERVPAC from the Atlantic. In the Far East these ships operated under MSTS instead of the Seventh Fleet. For reasons of cost it was then decided to transfer them entirely to MSTS and man them with Korean crews. When this was well underway, signals were changed because of the dangers of the river runs and the desire to have guns manned. As a result, five were restored to Navy manning and remained under COMSERVPAC's command, although still under the operational control of COMSTS.

*Mark* and *Brule*, in their numerous transits of the Mekong Delta, com-

1117682

*AKL* Mark *and her sister ship continuously engaged in resupply of the Naval Support Detachments along the coast and in the Delta.*

piled valuable information for incorporation in a Mekong Delta Pilot Guide, published late in 1967 by the U.S. Navy Oceanographic Office.

In a first, YFR–889 in March 1967, replenished one of the river mouth LSTs, USS *Harnett County* (LST–821), in the mouth of the Co Chien River. In October, NAVSUPPACT's YFR–890 made the first transit of the Co Chien River by a U.S. craft larger than a PBR.

Starting in June 1967, an Amphibious Force LST under the operational control of Commander Naval Support Activity, Saigon, commenced resupply runs to the Mobile Riverine Force on a seven–day cycle.

The movement of high priority cargoes and passengers by air was extremely important in view of the small size of the bases and the many emergency needs. The meeting of these needs in a highly responsive fashion was made possible by Air Cofat, which NAVSUPPACT had inherited from HEDSUPPACT. This "airline" then consisted of four C–47 and one TC–45J aircraft. Later, two H–46 helicopters were added.

Passengers carried were about 800 in June 1966 and over 4,000 in January 1967. Cargo rose from about 30,000 pounds in June 1966 to about 340,000 pounds in November and 397,081 pounds in April 1967. The growth was accomplished without any increase in aircraft assigned, despite the fact that one or more of the aircraft was down during a portion of the time. This outstanding performance was made possible by support and prompt replacements by Commander Fleet Air, Western Pacific.

Operational accidents were few, but in March 1967, one of NAVSUP-PACT's C–47s lost a wing after leaving Cam Ranh Bay and crashed with no survivors among the 28 on board. In May a US–2C aircraft, on loan to NAVSUPPACT, crashed four miles east of the An Thoi airstrip, killing the pilot and co–pilot.

The "airline" usually kept one aircraft on alert. In addition to many flights on short notice, a regular flight schedule was established. Three days a week trips were made on the northern route of Qui Nhon and Cam Ranh Bay to Danang and return. Two days a week the run was made by NAVSUPPACT Danang's aircraft. Three days a week Air Cofat made the southern trip to An Thoi, stopping at Vung Tau, Binh Thuy and Roc Gia (for U.S. advisors). Special flights were made to Con Son Island.

This organic airline made many vital contributions. By transporting personnel, repair parts and other cargoes, it deserves a considerable share of the credit for the notable support job of NAVSUPPACT Saigon and its scattered bases. When backlogs arose, help was obtained from the Air

Force through MACV's Transportation Management Agency, but with many competing requirements this did not have the same quick reaction to Navy needs.

Aided by the logistic support of the Naval Support Activity, Danang, and its detachments, the operations of the river patrol boats rapidly increased in their effectiveness in exercising control of the waterways. Originally they patrolled only sections of the Mekong and Bassac Rivers. Step by step the operations were expanded to the point where they patrolled other key waterways as well.

The value of the Navy's concept of logistic support became even more strongly evident when the decision was reached to form the Mekong Delta Mobile Assault Force, later called the Mobile Riverine Force. With a minimum of additional resources, the Naval Support Activity, Saigon, was able to extend logistic support and services to this large new force in addition to the others being supported.

## MOBILE RIVERINE FORCE

Control, such as provided by the river patrol boats (PBR), was necessary to minimize the enemy's use of the numerous waterways south of Saigon, and to furnish security for friendly use for both civilian and military purposes.

The waterways also presented a major opportunity for offensive actions against the enemy strongholds ashore, through the extension of the amphibious concepts of seapower into the riverine and restricted water environment.

The initial plan for U.S. Naval operations of this nature, which was developed in 1966, drew upon the experiences of the French "Dinassaut" squadrons and the Vietnamese River Force, but went a step further by providing major mobile bases for the troops and equipment in joint operations, as well as for the naval forces involved.

During the French Viet Minh War, the French had organized "Divisions Naval D'assaut" (Dinassaut). In addition to providing security to the ports and their approaches, the Dinassauts operated on the inland waterways. Under the control of their navy, they furnished naval support in close coordination with the Army. The Dinassauts had 12 to 20 landing craft (LCM, LSSL, LSIL, LCVP, LCU, and LCT) specially modified for the river work. Most were heavily armored, one being an armor–clad monitor built from an LCM and armed with 40 mm., 20 mm., and 50–caliber machine guns, and

an 81 mm. mortar.    Another was a small steel–hulled river gunboat, the
*St. Can.*   The largest Dinassaut included an integral landing force of Army
commandos with their own reconaissance aircraft and armored vehicles.
These same craft were later used by the Vietnamese Navy when they
formed the River Force in 1961, organized into the River Assault Groups
(RAGS), the River Escort Group, and the Transport Group.   Commander
Amphibious Force, U.S. Pacific Fleet, took the lead in planning for the
Mobile Assault Force, Commander Service Force, Pacific, having the usual
responsibilities for planning logistic support.   Craft converted for the Force
were refinements of the earlier French modifications.

In addition to landing craft conversions to provide 2 command craft
(CCB), 5 monitors, 26 armored troop carriers (ATC), and one refueler to
each river assault squadron, a new type of "assault support patrol boat"
(ASPB) was developed.   Sixteen ASPBs were assigned each squadron.
The supporting ships and craft were to be 2 self-propelled barracks ships
(APBs) converted from LSTs, 2 LSTs (one to deploy with the mobile base,
the other to be used in resupply), 2 tugs (YTB), a non-propelled barracks
craft (ARL), and a barge (YFNB) outfitted for repairs.   The last four
types were assigned to the Service Force.

The assault squadrons were organized into two River Assault Groups,
one to operate from the ships and craft forming the mobile base, the other
from a fixed base, Dong Tam, just west of My Tho on the Mekong.

Since the Marines were heavily engaged in the crucial I Corps Tactical
Zone, the Army was teamed with the Navy in the joint riverine assault
operations.   The Ninth Infantry Division started training for the operation
in late 1966.

January 1967 saw the first Navy units which would form the Riverine
Assault Force arrive in Vung Tau, with *Tutuila* assisting in the preparation of the ASPBs and other craft for operations.   As an interim solution,
USS *Askari* (ARL–30) was diverted from the planned support of Market
Time and Game Warden craft.   *Askari*, which departed Pearl Harbor on
14 January for Vung Tau, constituted the major repair and maintenance
asset for the Mobile Riverine Assault Force, functioning as an afloat advance
base tender.   Prior to departure from the continental United States, *Askari's*
shop spaces and tooling had been reconfigured to provide a broad range of
diesel, hull–ordnance, electronic and specialized repair, maintenance and
overhaul capabilities.   Shop spaces were also fitted for repair and maintenance of Army equipment, and Army personnel were assigned for the

task. When not deployed with the Mobile Force the plan was for *Askari* to provide repair support at the Dong Tam base.

Barracks ship APL–26 departed Pearl Harbor on 16 January en route to Vung Tau via Subic Bay. Its crew had been ordered and trained and was en route to Saigon to meet the craft.

SERVPAC's Ship Repair Facility, Yokosuka, converted a large covered lighter to a repair, berthing and messing barge (YRBM–17) to provide support at Dong Tam, arriving there in June 1967.

In February 1967, Commander Service Force promulgated a revised support plan (number 11–67A) for the II, III, and IV Corps areas. Logistic support of the new force was to be provided through the existing channels. The plan, an extension of the concepts already in existence for support of other U.S. Navy forces in the II, III, and IV Corps Tactical Zones, coordinated overall support and set forth responsibilities for all Service Force units in the Western Pacific and Vietnam.

Responsibilities of the Naval Support Activity, Saigon, were extensive. They included operating the naval portion of the base to be built at Dong Tam, command of repair craft, resupply via LST, and establishment of a naval support detachment at Vung Tau. The Naval Support Activity, Saigon, was responsible for support of Navy peculiar items. The U.S. Army Support Command, Vietnam, was responsible for supplying common support and Army peculiar items.

Two Amphibious Force LSTs were provided. One was assigned to the Riverine Force as a floating supply point for all classes of supply except POL. The other was turned over to the operational control of COMNAV-SUPPACT for resupply from Vung Tau, where a NAVSUPPACT Liaison Detachment, augmented by Army troops, was established for the purpose of processing requisitions, handling transit cargo and coordinating load–outs of the resupply LST.

The highly competent and energetic Captain Wade Wells, who was to command the Mobile Riverine Force (MRF), strongly felt that all ships and craft for his force and its support should be organic to the MRF and assigned at all times to his operational control, including units of Harbor Clearance Unit One, which will be discussed later. The latter had been augmented so as to take care of the additional salvage tasks to be expected. My stand, supported by COMNAVFORV, COMPHIBPAC, and CINCPACFLT, was that only those ships and craft operating with the MRF should be "chopped" to Captain Wells, and that COMNAVFORV should have operational control and delegate this control as he saw fit. As a result of this, resupply ships and craft when not operating as an integral part of the force were "chopped" to Commander Naval Support Activity, Saigon, in the same fashion as similar units providing logistic support and services to other U.S. Navy Forces in II, III, and IV Corps zones. By this means these units were more fully employed, and could be pooled to provide support to whatever force needed them most at the time.

The Riverine Assault Force (TF 117), the Navy element of the Mekong Delta Mobile Assault Force, was established 28 February 1967. It was fully operational by June.

One of the surprises was when the CNO directive, establishing the force, assigned to the Commander of Task Force 117 additional duty under COMSERVPAC as Commander River Support Squadron Seven. Those clearing the directive in Washington thought I concurred in the concept. However, the need for such a designation was not apparent, since the Naval Support Activity, Saigon, could provide the necessary support. I debated asking for a change, but decided to let things ride as they stood.

NH–67468

Benewah *(APB–35), acting as tender for armored troop carriers and monitors of the Mobile Riverine Force.*

Vung Tau was used as the training area for the Mobile Riverine Force, the first detachment moving to Dong Tam on 10 April 1967. Sixty new craft arrived in–country in May and were put in operating condition by *Askari.*

One notable repair job for the Force was that of diesel generators in *Benewah* (APB–35) and *Colleton* (APB–36), which had histories of casualties. *Colleton* had her generators replaced at the Ship Repair Facility, Subic, when medical spaces were installed. *Tutuila* did the difficult job on *Benewah* in a mere five days.

In March 1967 the newly formed Riverine Assault Force conducted joint operations with the Ninth Infantry Division in the Rung Sat Special Zone. The immediate result was a marked decrease in Viet Cong activity in the zone toward the end of the month.

In June 1967, a floating crane, YD–220, was moved from Cat Lo to Dong Tam. Two large harbor tugs of the Service Force, YTBs 784 and 785, arrived at Cat Lo on 10 June. They were outfitted and "chopped" to the operational control of Commander Mobile Riverine Force. *Askari* and APL–26 also deployed in support of the Mobile Riverine Force.

The first combat operations by the Mobile Riverine Force in the Mekong were conducted in June. In September the Mobile Riverine Force, in "Operation Coronado V," defeated a VC battalion—as anchorage location of the mobile base was shifted three times. These early successes resulted in a recommendation to expand the operation and provide another group with supporting craft so that by August 1968 there would be two brigades afloat and one based ashore at Dong Tam.

In November 1967, Commander Service Force specified that maintenance support was to be provided by the Naval Support Activity for follow–on armored troop carriers (ATC) and riverine command craft (CCB). Training was established for gas turbine repairs and a rotatable pool was established for these turbines. Hull repairs were to be accomplished ashore. The plan and associated supply actions were initiated accordingly. Meanwhile, the Service Force was branching into other areas.

## PERSONAL RESPONSE PROJECT

At the request of COMSERVPAC, and with the enthusiastic assistance of the Chief of Chaplains, Rear Admiral James W. Kelly, a "Personal Response Project" was initiated for the IV Corps Tactical Zone, a project to which the Fleet and Force Chaplain, Captain Joseph J. Tubbs, contributed much.

The program stemmed from the success of lesson plans which had been prepared by a Navy Chaplain on the customs of the many religious sects of the Vietnamese and Montagnards in I Corps. These had proven of great value to the Marines, Navy personnel and others in that zone in their relations with indigenous personnel. Comparable information was not available for the variations of religious attitudes of those in the Delta.

After service as Marine Personal Response Officer in I Corps from June 1965 to August 1966, Commander R. L. Mole had returned to the United States for graduate work. Then in September 1967 he was ordered to the Naval Support Activity, Saigon, as I had requested.

Objectives for the Personal Response project were:

a. Assemble, organize and evaluate information pertaining to the religious belief and value systems of indigenous citizens with special emphasis given to the Mekong Delta region.

b. Formulate, validate and administer questionnaires to military personnel and indigenous citizens to identify positive and negative cross–cultural attitudes, and favorable and unfavorable cross–cultural interactions, and devise a program and communications strategy for the project.

c. Prepare and distribute programs and presentation materials, background information and training aids to assist personnel in understanding why the peoples of the Delta think, feel and act as they do.

On arrival in Saigon, Commander Mole's project was received with such enthusiasm by the staff of COMUSMACV that much effort was needed to keep members of the staff from diverting too much of his enthusiastic efforts from his primary mission.

# CHAPTER XII

# Bases for the Support of Naval Craft in Vietnam

The interfaces of naval logistics with combat units operating in restricted waters were at outlying bases manned by detachments from the Naval Support Activities, and at Service Force ships and craft deployed to Vietnam for mobile support. The problems of each base and mobile support unit varied according to its tasking and location. Each deserves a share of the credit for the success of naval combat in the coastal and river environment of Vietnam.

As mentioned before, it was the establishment of bases, ashore and afloat, at Danang, An Thoi, Qui Nhon, Cam Ranh Bay, and Cat Lo that permitted establishment and maintenance of a reasonably dense surveillance zone in shallow waters adjacent to the coast, in augmentation of the Vietnamese Navy's own efforts. Together with the patrols of destroyer escorts and minesweepers of the Seventh Fleet and the naval aircraft patrols in still greater depth, the establishment of the inshore operations had a major impact on enemy logistic operations. A measure of the success achieved was General Westmoreland's estimate that, whereas about 70 percent of the enemy's supplies had come by sea before 1965, not more than 10 percent of the requirements were being delivered by that route once the inshore patrol had become fully effective.[1]

## I CORPS

Extensive coverage has already been given to logistic operations by the Navy in I Corps. In addition to the base at Danang, the "Swifts" and Coast Guard cutters received I Corps support from the secondary base at Chu Lai at a small pontoon pier just inside Rosemary Point. Logistic support provided by the Naval Support Detachment, Chu Lai, included

---

[1] Sharp and Westmoreland, *Report on the War in Vietnam*, p. 128.

153

limited repairs, as a maintenance shop was constructed nearby to replace a small shack first set up on the pier.   North of Danang limited support was provided just inside the mouths of the Perfume and Cua Viet Rivers by the small detachments at those locations.

Originally the river patrol forces of Game Warden operated only in III and IV Corps, but the Commanding General, III Marine Amphibious Force, had long requested a force that would interrupt the movement of the enemy on inland waterways in I Corps.   One of the areas of particular concern to the Marines was Cau Hai Bay east of Phu Bai, an area of continuing VC activity obviously supported by movements across the bay.   In a test operation, an LST mother ship and ten PBRs deployed north to operate in this area in September 1967.   The operation of these craft in Cau Hai Bay enjoyed but marginal success because of the very shallow water and innumerable fish weirs.   The unit ended the operation on 7 October.

The Naval Facilities Engineering Command proposed building two mobile support bases, each consisting of four units which could be married together to provide berthing, messing, supply, repairs, and a helicopter landing platform.   Two such floating bases were built in a remarkably short time, using Ammi pontoons [2] and unique construction procedures.   The units which would form Mobile Support Base I were deployed in an LST via Pearl Harbor to Danang, arriving on 2 December 1967.   At my insistence,

---

[2] See p. 163.

NH–74206

*A Mobile Support Base constructed from Ammi pontoons.*

the units had a "shakedown cruise" at Danang before being transported to the Perfume River and nearby waterways. The second base was deployed to the Naval Support Activity, Saigon.

In 1968, the Cau Hai Bay area provided a relatively favorable operating area for Patrol Air Cushion Vehicle (PACV). Three PACVs had first been deployed to Cat Lo along with contractor maintenance personnel. Operations of the PACVs in that zone and later at Dong Tam were of questionable value, so the opportunity to move north was a welcome one. Reports of their operations in Cau Hai Bay and the Tan My area, where they were based, were far more favorable.

Another requirement developed for river patrol forces in northern I Corps. Intensified enemy operations against the resupply operations on the Cua Viet River (see Chapter X) resulted in my sending a message to COMNAV-FORV in the fall of 1967 recommending that such forces be deployed north to provide protection to the logistic craft plying the river. When there was further intensification of actions on both the Cua Viet and the Perfume Rivers, "Operation Clearwater" was established to prevent enemy disruption of the river transits—with the detachments at Cua Viet and Tan My providing the necessary logistic support.

## QUI NHON

The northernmost base in II Corps in support of Market Time was at Qui Nhon—on the north side of the entrance to the bay, across from the city and the large Army support complex.

A Naval Support Detachment was established in Qui Nhon in June 1966, initially under very austere conditions. Improvements were slow, competition for contractor construction priorities being especially difficult in view of the large Army demands in the local area. For instance, I was told on one trip that a pile driver arrived on the scene several times to put in pier supports, only to be withdrawn for major harbor development projects before the small job could be accomplished. Another delay was encountered when the contractor lost the pipe for the fuel farm for several months.

Under difficult conditions, the job done by the Qui Nhon Detachment of the Naval Support Activity, Saigon, was notable. The first repair officer struck me as being particularly outstanding. Although the plan for Qui Nhon contemplated only intermediate repairs to Market Time craft, he and his small shop claimed they could do anything, and did. The supply department, although also small, had its stocks under complete control and was highly responsive.

After frustrating delays in base development, some initial progress was made by means of a Seabee detachment sent down from I Corps to accomplish high priority construction. By January 1967, an interim fuel system, an ammunition magazine and bachelor officers' quarters had been constructed. In July Seabees constructed barracks, a dispensary, and the administrative building. This was but another example of the need for each Service possessing some organic logistic capabilities, which can truly be crucial in the early stages of a conflict.

The site of the Naval Support Detachment was nestled on the waterfront next to a small Vietnamese village. Land surrounding the base rose steeply to a high ridge, thus complicating the job of perimeter defense. On my first visit the Officer in Charge expressed his concern over the vulnerability to attack from over the ridge, despite a wire protective fence on the hillside.

However, a serious attack did not come until after the Republic of Korea troops, responsible for area security of the peninsula, were moved out. Then, on 8 November 1967, a VC team hit the Qui Nhon base with a satchel charge attack. Three charges were exploded inside the perimeter. One water tank and an empty fuel tank were ruptured. Two men were injured.

An attack on the night of 22 and 23 December was more serious. It started in the early morning hours with a diversionary explosion at the nearby junk base. What was estimated as an eight to twelve man Viet Cong sapper platoon made its way unobserved down the hill in back of the base, apparently using a gully for cover, and cut through the fence. The Chief Petty Officers' quarters were damaged by a 50–pound satchel charge. The mess hall was hit by grenades, small arms, and automatic weapons fire. Two men were killed. Small arms fire was again received on 25 December.

Following some recommendations in a message from me, Captain King, Commander Naval Support Activity, Saigon, asked the Commanding General, U.S. First Field Forces, for more area protection. The latter launched a task force on search and destroy missions. The sweep of the peninsula was in progress before the end of the month, and things remained quiet thereafter. Protective steps taken by the Naval Support Detachment included improved guard tower locations and better perimeter lighting.

Meanwhile, in addition to supporting Market Time, the Naval Support

Detachment was made responsible for assisting the establishment of a harbor defense site on the hill at the entrance to Qui Nhon, and then providing for its logistic support.

## CAM RANH BAY

Further to the south was Cam Ranh Bay, the one well protected deep–water bay along the coast.  It had been at Cam Ranh Bay where units of the Russian Fleet had assembled and prepared for the trip north to their defeat at the Tsushima Strait in the Russo–Japanese War in 1905.  Well situated for support of forces in the II Corps Tactical Zone, Cam Ranh Bay was developed into a vast logistic complex for the Army with a major Air Force airfield.  The Navy was allowed a small area on the point on the northern side of the entrance.  Equipped with two piers and some work shops the naval support base became a major repair and support facility for Market Time craft.

There were those who wanted to establish a permanent fleet base in

NH–74203

*Future site of the Naval Support Detachment, Cam Ranh Bay, 1965.*

Vietnam, for the future as well as the present.   An ambitious plan proposed by certain members of the CINCPACFLT staff to develop Cam
Ranh Bay into such a base was not deemed to be a warranted investment in
view of our other bases in the Far East; in any case, its full development was
never approved.   Quite rightly the Navy's policy was a fleet which would be
as independent of fixed bases as practicable.   A scattering of such bases,
strategically located, is desirable, but care must be taken not to dissipate
too high a percentage of available resources on fixed facilities at the expense
of mobile forces.

My staff and I were always aware of the possibility that a change in the
warfare situation might reach a point where it would be desirable to deploy
units to Vietnam for the support of major fleet units.   I envisaged sending
repair ships, tenders, floating drydocks and other support to Cam Ranh Bay
in case the war placed a demand for Seventh Fleet battle damage repairs
nearer the scene of action, but fortunately the need never arose.

Construction of berthing, messing and other support facilities in a small
valley at a pleasant but isolated beach on the ocean side of Cam Ranh Bay
took a long time, again competing as it did with the far larger Army and
Air Force complex for contractor priorities.   However, by December 1966,
some progress was being made in constructing the base.   Commander
Task Force 115 and Commander Coastal Squadron One were then relocated
from Saigon to the Cam Ranh Bay base.

Patrol aircraft engaged in Market Time operations were initially based at
Sangley Point in Manila Bay.   To save the time of flying across the South
China Sea, a decision was made to operate planes out of centrally located
Cam Ranh Bay, returning to Sangley for "depot level" maintenance.   In
May 1967, temporary billeting was provided for personnel of the Naval Air
Facility until their own accommodations could be constructed at the air
base.

That same month Seabees installed a 100–kilowatt generator and power
lines at the support base.   In July the Seabees constructed explosive ordnance
disposal and recreation facilities, and a pier extension.   They also repaired
roads, after long delays in getting the job done by the Army contractor.

The Navy acquired paved stowage pads for ammunition at the Army
Ammunition Depot.   Spin–stabilized rockets and 5–inch ammunition were
stowed there by the Naval Support Detachments for issue to the rocket
support ships (IFS and LSMR).   Other ammunition for Market Time
craft and emergency fleet supply was stored and issued.

A new type craft deployed to Cam Ranh Bay—an inshore patrol gunboat powered by gas turbine and diesel engines—provided additional logistic challenges.  The first of these, *Gallup* (PG–85), reached Cam Ranh on 30 April 1967.  A sister craft, *Asheville* (PG–84), followed in May.  The Seabees had constructed a warehouse for PG supplies in March but maintenance posed difficult problems for months.  Not only were the craft new, but the planning in Washington had been based on highly optimistic estimates of the maintenance and repair capabilities at sea.  Far more base support proved necessary than originally envisaged.

Initial planning relied on the use of a 400–ton Army floating drydock for support of Market Time craft in Cam Ranh Bay, but as this did not meet all the needs, a small Navy floating dock was later deployed.

In view of the importance of the location, the detachment was designated the Naval Support Facility, Cam Ranh Bay, on 1 September 1967, with a commanding officer under the CNO–CINCPACFLT–COMSERVPAC–COMNAVSUPPACT Saigon chain of command.  The facility's assigned mission was to provide, arrange for, maintain, and operate facilities, and provide services and material to support U.S. Naval Forces, Vietnam, and Fleet units of the operating forces of the U.S. Navy.  The allowance of 12 officers and 230 enlisted men was to provide support to approximately 1,200 personnel of Commander Task Force 115 and units under his command, to a large Naval Communications Station constructed there, to the Naval Air Facility, and to the Harbor Defense Forces.

The Naval Communications Station, a $13.2 million complex, was located at the naval support base with the receiver site located 2.5 miles north of the station and the transmitter site 5.5 miles further north.  The primary subscriber of this modern station was CTF 115 for coordinating and controlling coastal surveillance throughout Vietnam.  The station also formed a part of the Fleet net.

Established in a development status on 1 April 1967, the U.S. Naval Air Facility, Cam Ranh Bay, was co–located on the U.S. Air Force Base.  It became fully operational on 1 August.  By this time six SP–2H aircraft were based there for Market Time surveillance.  Later the patrol aircraft would total twelve P–3s.

## VUNG TAU

Still further south was Vung Tau, at the end of the peninsula jutting south into the bay just east of the Rung Sat Special Zone, a key location with regard to traffic going up the river to Saigon and convenient to the Mekong. A harbor control post was built for the harbor defense unit on the high land at the end of the peninsula. It was just south of Vung Tau that merchant ships anchored awaiting passage up the rivers.

The anchorage to the west of Vung Tau was used by our naval ships. Repair ship *Tutuila* was normally located in this area, as were *Askari* and ships of the Mobile Riverine Force from time to time. Closer to the shore was the usual location of the Service Force's Harbor Clearance Teams, two heavy lift craft, and one or two light lift craft. A small pier located there, convenient to the Naval Support Activity warehouse, was the point from which cargo was transshipped to the Mobile Riverine Force and Dong Tam. A hut built at the Vung Tau airstrip supported the Sea Wolf helicopter unit.

*Tutuila* proved to be an extremely valuable mobile support unit. The Army had asked for this internal combustion repair ship to provide support for Army craft. When it was about to deploy, the request was withdrawn. At the time, the need for this ship for Navy support seemed to me to be

1132312

*Repair ship* Tutuila *(ARG–4).*

marginal. What turned the scale was the realization that *Krishna* would, from time to time, need a relief. My request from CINCPACFLT resulted in the transfer of *Tutuila* from COMPHIBLANT to COMSERVPAC for deployment to Vietnam.

This proved to be a far sounder decision than had been anticipated. During her passage through Pearl, I found her to be in excellent condition, and with a well–trained and dedicated crew. Through the years, since World War II, there had been many additions to her shops to the point where she was very nearly the equivalent of a large repair ship (AR).

As already noted, *Tutuila*'s normal location was in the roadstead to the north of Vung Tau, near the mouth of the Long Tau River which carried traffic to Saigon. There her extensive repair capacity was always employed to the fullest. In addition to repairing craft of Market Time and Game Warden, she did much emergency work for visiting ships of the Fleet.

In April 1967 *Tutuila* was turned over to the operational control of Commander Naval Support Activity, Saigon. In May, repair parts for LSTs were added, and from then on she provided valuable repair support for the river mouth LSTs. She also was a key factor in readying ships and craft of the Mobile Riverine Assault Force for their important duties. In June 1967, *Tutuila* extended depot level maintenance support to Coastal Division Thirteen.

Not all of her duties were routine. There was, for instance, the time when she was asked to provide gunfire support with her 5–inch guns to forces operating north of the anchorage in the Rung Sat Special Zone. This she did effectively.

When *Krishna* was permitted a well needed period away for upkeep, rest and recreation, *Tutuila* took her place at An Thoi. On the second trip of *Tutuila* away from Vung Tau, this time to provide services at Kaohsiung, Taiwan, while getting some well earned recreation, USS *Markab* (AR–23) took her place at Vung Tau. The crew of *Markab* responded with great enthusiasm. Repair ships and tenders normally stayed for prolonged periods in ports like Subic and Kaohsiung working hard and receiving little glory. Not being in the combat zone they did not receive the medals of the combatants. Succeeding ARs also enjoyed the chance to relieve *Tutuila* and performed magnificently.

Earlier recommendations for the deployment of fleet repair ships in–country had been turned down by CINCPACFLT. I had then recommended a procedure whereby the ARs would remain under the control of

COMSEVENTHFLT and CTF 73, thus remaining ready to redeploy if needed elsewhere. Approval was granted.

This was another example of the depth and flexibility of the Pacific Fleet logistic system. Those in–country were not left solely to their own but had the whole of the Service Force to back them up, and the assistance of other Fleet units when needed.

On 5 November, *Markab*, at her anchorage off Vung Tau, not to be outdone by *Tutuila*'s earlier fire support mission, fired eighty–six rounds of 5–inch harassment fire against the Rung Sat Special Zone. This had all the signs of a self-generated mission. On the other hand, permission had been obtained from the proper authority and the desire for action could be appreciated.

*Tutuila* earned the Navy Unit Commendation for her outstanding per-formance at Vung Tau and An Thoi.

## CAT LO

The shore base for support of Market Time craft and assisting in the support of units sweeping and patrolling the Long Tau River was at Cat Lo, a short distance north of Vung Tau on the inboard side of the peninsula. The village of Cat Lo through which one would pass on the trip by jeep from Vung Tau was famed for the excellence of its Nuoc Mam, a fish oil greatly prized by the Vietnamese. The fragrance of this delicacy was such as to make the trip almost unbearable to my occidental nose.

At Cat Lo the facilities were co–located in crowded fashion at a Viet-namese Navy base. Competing again with larger Army and Air Force projects for contractor construction, it took almost a year to get facility construction underway so that the detachment would have the shops, berth-ing, and messing buildings they needed. Filling in land by dredging originally scheduled for the spring of 1966 was not accomplished until the end of 1968.

As has been noted before, the air cushion vehicles, PACVs, were initially based at Cat Lo where they operated from a paved ramp and were maintained by contractor personnel.

Potable water was a difficult problem at Cat Lo. When a shallow well failed, it was necessary to haul water from Vung Tau. COMSERVPAC requested three water purification plants. After several aborts, a well was dug which provided 12,000 gallons a day.

NH–74200

*Naval Support Detachment, co–located at the Vietnamese base at Cat Lo.*

By January 1967, 627 personnel were being supported at Cat Lo.

A detachment from Amphibious Construction Battalion One set up an Ammi pontoon assembly operation at Cat Lo in July 1967. The Ammi type of pontoon was a new development conceived by Dr. Amirikan, an advisor to the Naval Facilities Engineering Command. A major improvement over the World War II pontoon, it was tailored to the varying requirements for rapid construction of piers, bridges, small craft facilities, etc. Ninety by twenty–eight feet and equipped for the use of adjustable bottom spuds, these pontoons could be moored in water varying from three to forty feet in depth. They were so constructed as to permit wide flexibility of assembly and usage.

## AN THOI

The southernmost base for Market Time support was at An Thoi on the east end of Phu Quoc Island in the Gulf of Siam. This support was initially provided by *Krishna* anchored off the village where *Krishna*

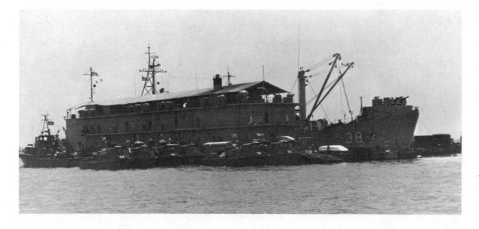

USN-1130648

*Barracks craft and* Krishna *anchored at An Thoi tending Market Time craft.*

was later joined by APL–55. The island provided shelter during the southwest monsoon, with the anchorage being shifted during the winter months so as to use the lee of the smaller islands off the eastern end of the island.

Except for the village, the adjacent Vietnamese Navy base, and our airstrip, the area was covered by a dense jungle. Of the U.S. forces only the advisors were ashore, the others being based afloat. Nine Coast Guard cutters (WPB), seventeen Swifts (PCF), and two LCMs were maintained there, and 656 personnel supported. Later, one Thai gunboat was added to the list of those supported.

Under the command of Lieutenant Commander William R. Harris, *Krishna*, which was awarded the Navy Unit Commendation, stayed continuously on station almost a year the first time, before a trip to Bangkok on four days' rest and recreation. During this time and other infrequent trips away, *Tutuila* provided interim support. In September 1967, the specially configured APL–21 relieved APL–55, the latter being towed to Sasebo for conversion for Game Warden support.

## LONG TAU RIVER

The most urgent task on the inland waterways was that of controlling the Long Tau River, the route by which crucial civilian and military supplies were delivered to Saigon. Establishment of a base to support the patrol craft and minesweepers was an essential element in the carrying out of

this task.   Such a base was established at Nha Be in addition to the secondary support provided at Cat Lo.

## NHA BE

Geographically Nha Be was the ideal location to support operations protecting shipping routes from the sea to Saigon.   Seven miles south of
Saigon, on the west bank of the Long Tau River and on the outskirts of the
town of Nha Be, the detachment's site jutted out into the juncture of the
Long Tau with the other deep–water channel to the sea, the Soirap River.
The mangrove–covered, VC-infested Rung Sat Special Zone (RSSZ) could
be seen to the south.   Across the river was considered "Viet Cong country,"
a phrase that I always objected to.   It usually meant an area over which
government control was not complete, not necessarily one over which the
VC actually exercised control.

Until the military port facilities were built to the north and east of Saigon,
ammunition ships and many others off–loaded at anchor there.   Most of
the incoming fuel was off–loaded at a large fuel tank farm just north of the
city of Nha Be.

The permanent base site was located on twenty acres of swamp real

NH–74204

*Nha Be, 1965.*

estate initially completely unusable. A major reclamation effort was needed before it could be occupied. Due to the lack of suitable real estate, a common problem in the Delta region, the Nha Be Detachment and its tenants were first co–located on a small Vietnamese River Assault Group base. Reclamation of the land started in May 1966, but it was not until December that dredging had provided enough fill to start construction of semi–permanent facilities.

In the initial stages of Nha Be's development, base support was provided by two officers and eighty–four enlisted men to support 121 Game Warden and mine countermeasure boat personnel and their craft. At this time the base loading was ten river patrol boats (PBR), four minesweeper boats (MSB), and four landing craft personnel large (LCPL). The tasking was for a full range of logistic support, including berthing, messing, small boat repair, internal security, and supply support.

At the time of my first visits to the base, the living accommodations were tents crowded together in the small Vietnamese military compound. Dunnage from ships being off–loaded in the river had been used to provide raised floors and walkways as protection against normal flooding, and to build a crude screened–in mess hall and galley.

The craft were berthed at a temporary pier made with the help of Army boat–type pontoons. Most of the piers used at NAVSUPPACT bases, even when temporary, used the watertight and sturdy pontoons used by the Navy in causeway construction. Later the new and improved Ammi pontoons were used for such piers. I was in the area in 1967 when a high wind sank the pontoon pier, including a tool room shack. A harbor clearance team and a light lift craft (LLC) came up from Vung Tau to recover it.

In June 1966, a large covered lighter (YFNB–16) was deployed to the site to provide an interim platform for berthing and repair. A crane and Advanced Base Functional Component (ABFC) equipment, destined for use ashore, were installed to provide a machine shop, repair and supply facilities on board. Because of the value of mobile support, it was later decided to keep the equipment on board and to order an additional set of ABFC equipment for "depot level" maintenance ashore of engines and hull repairs, and "intermediate level" capabilities for ordnance and elec-tronic repairs.

The top deck of YFNB–16 was provided an awning and a screened–in berthing area. Surprisingly, the Officer in Charge of the detachment told me of difficulty moving people on board. They were proud of the sacrifices they were making and didn't want to move to such luxurious quarters, at least while others still had to live in the compound.

The base loading increased to 20 PBRs and 12 MSBs, and the personnel supported now totaled 300. The plan was for 57 craft and 1,000 personnel. By the fall of 1968, eighty–four craft were being supported at Nha Be, including nine riverine assault craft assigned to help the defense of Saigon.

In August 1966 Nha Be had commenced supporting CTF 116 Sea Wolf helicopter fire teams operating in support of Game Warden craft in the RSSZ.

Many problems were encountered in developing the base. The dredge fill kept being eroded by river currents, yet it was a long time before pilings would be installed by the contractor. Effort after effort was made to drill deep wells. Potable water could not be located, and it had to be trucked in and stored on the base.

The facilities to be installed included eleven officer and enlisted quarters, a mess hall, maintenance and repair shops, four 1,000–barrel fuel tanks, an administrative building, communications space, covered stowage and warehouse, and a small boat pier. Occupancy was in stages as facilities were gradually constructed.

As the build–up of U.S. forces in Vietnam continued, Saigon became heavily crowded with many headquarters personnel of all Services. General Westmoreland instituted a plan whereby a large percentage would move outside the city. To provide the Navy's share, Commander U.S. Naval Forces, Vietnam, decided that the headquarters of the Naval Support Activity would move, along with its warehouses, to Nha Be. I opposed the move. As a very minimum I felt that Commander Naval Support Activity and key members should remain close to COMNAVFORV's headquarters. Experiences in Pearl Harbor and in Danang convinced me that a logistic support command can function with full effectiveness only if it is in daily contact with the operational commander of the forces being supported. Travel by the crowded two–lane road to Nha Be was difficult. Sometimes the route was insecure due to guerrilla activity. To make matters worse, the airport at Tan Son Nhut was on the other side of Saigon, and to get there by automobile or truck one had to make one's way slowly through all the dense traffic of the city.

Finally, it was determined, late in 1967, that the warehouses and offices would be moved to Newport, being constructed near the airport. Nevertheless, the move of the NAVSUPPACT headquarters was finally made to Nha Be late in 1968, a move I still consider to have been a mistake.

In March 1967, three BEQs (Bachelor Enlisted Quarters) were ready for occupancy, and it was finally possible to do away with the tent cantonment. Surprisingly, on my visit the next month, morale, although still good, seemed nowhere near as high as when the men had been living under the far more primitive conditions. This reaction was typical of other detachments as well. The more severe the sacrifices, the prouder the men seemed to be of their performance.

Nha Be scored a first in April 1967 when an Army crane hoisted an MSB minesweeper out of the water for hull repairs. Heretofore, only engine repairs had been accomplished for the MSBs, hull work having been accomplished previously only by the overloaded Vietnamese Navy shipyard in Saigon.

The helo pad and runway were completed the same month. This pad became a busy place. By July, in addition to supporting Sea Wolf fire teams, the base was supporting Army helo fire teams, "Firefly" helicopters,

NH–74345

*Naval Support Detachment, Nha Be, 1968.*

and other missions.  These used the helo pad for refueling and ammunition replenishment, and as an emergency medical evacuation station.

Installation of the sheet pile bulkhead did not start until 15 May 1967. Erosion of uncompleted sections would continue for a year or more.

On 3 August, Nha Be sustained a 20–minute attack from several positions from across the Soirap River east of the base and from the northeast bank of the Long Tau.  About forty rounds from 81 mm. mortars landed on the base.  As a result of an emergency sortie only one MSB was hit, and this was undergoing out–of–water repairs.  There were many shrapnel holes in the buildings but the actual damage was light.  Twenty–four men were wounded.

On 5 August the base was hit again, this time by mortars and recoilless rifle fire.  Only two rounds hit the base.  Damage was slight.

The fire fighting teams at Nha Be had their busy times.  On 3 May 1967, a Vietnamese junk at the Esso pier at Nha Be, with a cargo of sixty 55–gallon oil drums and forty drums of other inflammables, caught fire. The Nha Be Detachment fire boat fought the fire until the foam supply was exhausted, then towed the junk to a deserted rice paddy.  The area was cleared just before the junk exploded.

In June the detachment responded to a serious fire in the fuel tanker, SS *Esso Marikado*, at the Nha Be tank farm with 10,000 gallons of jet fuel on board.  First on the scene, Navy river patrol boats and a support detachment LCM towed the burning vessel away from the pier to prevent the fire from spreading to the fuel stowage.  Four members of the detachment's fire party were blown into the water by an explosion.  All were recovered with only minor injuries.

## BASES IN THE DELTA

In the Delta, riverine operations were on the increase as more craft were deployed to Vietnam.  Originally, the operations were confined almost entirely to the main rivers.  As control of these increased in 1967, the River Patrol Force started ranging into secondary waterways.  In 1967 operations were extended to routes west of Saigon used by the enemy for movement of men and supplies from Cambodia.  Major offensive operations would finally commence in the area south of the Bassac River in October 1968.  Ranging throughout this vast southern area of the Delta, this was a major joint operation in which units from Navy Task Forces 115 (Market

Time), 116 (Game Warden), and 117 (Mobile Riverine Force) all partici-
pated.  Heavy dependence was placed on the mobile support units of the
Naval Support Activity, Saigon.

As had been noted previously, such mobile support units had been in the
initial support phases.  The value of their mobility and flexibility continued
to be demonstrated as the Service Force ship and craft were redeployed to
respond to the shifting tactical situation.

It should be noted that the vast majority of the ships and craft used to
provide mobile support in the Vietnam War were those left over from
World War II.  Some were still in active service.  Others were in reserve,
and were reactivated or converted for the jobs to be done.

For base facilities to be established ashore the key ingredient was that
of previously mentioned Advanced Base Functional Components.  Despite
obsolescence, they provided the building blocks for the planning and construction of bases ashore.  As in World War II, they were tailored to provide
the personnel, material, and equipment to fit the specific job to be done in
each case.  In Vietnam the concept had to be further modified because of
the fixing of constructive standards by MACV to which all the Services had
to comply once the standards were set.

## MY THO

The most eastern base on the Mekong River proper was that at My Tho.
On the north bank of the river and connected to Saigon by the key road in
the area, My Tho was the most important city for miles around.  This made
it a frequent target for Viet Cong harassment.

Initially the Naval Support Detachment and the boats it supported were
co–located on a Vietnamese River Assault Group (RAG) base on the city's
waterfront.  Pier space was very limited.  Repairs occupied a small tent,
and supplies a small shack.  As was the case elsewhere at the start, the
ammunition magazine was a CONEX[1] surrounded by sandbags.  U.S.
personnel were crowded into the two–story Victory Hotel and the poorly
ventilated outlying buildings inside its high way.  As the River Patrol Force
continued to increase, a second berthing building was leased farther from
the waterfront.  For a while a weekly armed truck convoy delivered supplies from Saigon.

---

[1] Standard Army Shipping Container.

*Naval Support base at My Tho under construction, 1966.*

The site chosen for the U.S. base was a small park just west of the RAG base where construction of the support facilities started in November 1966. The base was completely operational in March 1967, having been the only facility for the support of Game Warden forces that was completely contractor–constructed.

The Viet Cong made two attempts to disrupt the operations at My Tho in February 1967. On 10 February, in violation of the Tet truce, a VC terrorist tossed a hand grenade into the construction site at the base waterfront. The only casualty was a U.S. sentry who suffered a minor hand wound. Damage was restricted to numerous small holes in two recently erected aluminum buildings and a fence within the base area.

On 14 February a box 18 by 24 inches floating upstream with the tide was fired on by a security watch. The box exploded in a ball of white flame described as approximately 12 feet in diameter. No damage to PBRs in the vicinity or to base site material was sustained. A large pile driver on site at the pier was apparently the intended target.

In April 1967, a 1,000–barrel fuel oil farm was constructed and a mine net laid upstream of the base. That month, fuel in an Esso barge erupted in flames 100 feet high, endangering the fuel depot and market place. The My Tho Detachment played a key role in helping put out the fire which lasted thirty minutes. Four Vietnamese civilians died and four civilian warehouses were destroyed.

Seabees completed nearby facilities for helicopters, completing the job by 1 July 1967.

The city of My Tho was hit by mortar attacks on a number of occasions. On 5 November 1967, the second personnel billet was damaged, along with two vehicles at the Naval Support Detachment. There were no casualties. My Tho was to be hit many more times, including attacks during the Tet offensive of 1968, but operational support continued with high efficiency.


## DONG TAM

At Dong Tam, 4.5 miles west of My Tho, a major base for Army and Navy forces of the Mekong Delta Assault Force was built on reconstructed land on the east side of an inlet just off the Mekong. A basin was dredged out, with the discharge providing the necessary fill to support buildings ashore. The 9th Infantry Division moved to Dong Tam in December 1966.

A Seabee detachment, sent down from I Corps, built the Navy facilities ashore, and on 27 January 1967 the Naval Support Activity Detachment, Dong Tam, debarked from USS *Brule* (AKL–28) to occupy the Navy portion of the base. Materials which had been assembled for Dong Tam were transported from Saigon by USS *Mark* (AKL–12), USS *Brule*, and YFR–889. Establishment of means to provide support to the River Assault Forces commenced. Tents, strongback structures, pontoons, and other Advanced Base Functional Component facilities were constructed. By the end of the month, three of six Ammi pontoons to form the Dong Tam pier had been mated in place. By the end of February, the site was ready for personnel, and a pier of six Ammi pontoons had been constructed and anchored temporarily awaiting arrival of a pile driver. Their job done, the Seabees returned to I Corps.

The Naval personnel ashore at Dong Tam took particular pride in their area. The buildings for berthing, messing, administration, and recreation in the Navy section were laid out in precise and orderly fashion—in contrast with the more jumbled appearance of much of the rest of the base. Streets and yards were carefully manicured despite the fact that this was filled land.

On several occasions the Navy site was hit by mortar fire. I visited there two days after the first such attack, which had been from across the basin and inlet. Well aimed mortar rounds had walked accurately through the area. The fact that only eighteen were wounded, and none seriously, seemed remarkable. All hands had reached sandbag enclosures with remarkable speed.

By March 1967 eight landing craft (LCM–3) were on station, along with a 12,000–gallon fuel barge relocated from Long Xuyen.

In April, YFNB–24, which had been configured for repairs, berthing and messing by the Ship Repair Facility, Yokosuka, arrived at Dong Tam, along with APL–26 for berthing of Army and Navy personnel and a floating derrick (YD–220). The crews of YFNB and APL conducted themselves in a smart military fashion. I suspected their strict adherence to naval customs was partly to impress the Army troops on board. As I waded through mud and up the brow on my first visit to these craft, in late April, I was greeted with boat gongs, six side boys, and a boatswain's mate piping—just as if I had been boarding a first line combatant ship in some peaceful port.

One of the early problems at Dong Tam was that the basin, having been dredged with but one entrance, did not flush. Therefore, to use the "heads" on the YFNB and APL it was necessary to construct a pipeline to the Mekong.

By May 1967, 500 to 750 Navy personnel were being berthed ashore. In June APL–26 was reconfigured at Dong Tam for support of Navy Mobile Riverine Force personnel and Army troops. Changes to the APL had been made by detachment personnel to provide office space and communications equipment for the Army headquarters unit. Soldiers and Army officers on board told me they never had it so good.

From time to time, APL–26 was placed under the operational control of CTF 117, becoming a maneuvering unit of the Mobile Riverine Force.

## VINH LONG

Further west, Vinh Long had become operational on 8 July 1966, the base being co–located at a Vietnamese RAG base. The facility consisted of a seawall, boat ramp and apron with small repair and supply shacks, a boat engine lifting rig, and a crane.

Detachment personnel, and the 144 personnel of the River Patrol Force being supported, lived in a comfortable four–story building south of the city. Another building was converted into a billet later as the forces supported increased.

Vinh Long was the only base that did not remain intact and fully operational during the Tet offensive of 1968, when the Navy Tactical Operations Center, communications equipment, supply storeroom, and its boat spares were destroyed by fire. The two billets were abandoned, but being undamaged were later reoccupied. On this occasion, one young officer of the detachment, missing for two days, was finally located fighting with United States Army Rangers.

Mobile support came to the rescue as YFNB–9 was deployed to Vinh Long to upgrade the repair capability and provide interim communications support and supply space. This craft had been planned earlier for such a move so that ten PBRs, additional to the ten already there, could be supported.

On 7 May at Vinh Long an unsuccessful attempt was made to mine the river patrol boat pier. The pier sentry observed the water spout about thirty yards off the pier.

It was finally possible to abandon the inadequate facilities ashore and go entirely afloat on 22 October 1968 as a result of deploying specially configured APL–46 to the site.

## SA DEC

Even more austere was the base at Sa Dec, which became operational on 13 July 1966. Lack of real estate again required co–location on a Vietnamese base, on an island across from the city. Repair space at the head of the pontoon pier was particularly cramped. A boat ramp was built in January 1967.

Despite the inadequacy of the facilities, the Sa Dec Detachment did as fine a job keeping the PBRs operating as bases with better facilities. This was the result of especially close teamwork on the part of personnel of the boats and those of the Naval Support Detachment. Attached to the boats was an officer who volunteered to head the maintenance effort, a mutually agreeable arrangement. His leadership and expertise were key factors in the outstanding performance in the early days.

Personnel initially lived in tents alongside a soccer field in the city. Having lunch there one day, I found they had unexcelled pride in their cuisine. This tended to be the case at almost every Navy base no matter how remote. As in ships, the traditional Navy emphasis on food preparation and a varied menu paid off in morale.

## YRBM–16

On arrival in–country on 28 March 1967, the Repair, Berthing and Messing Barge, YRBM–16, was sent to Tan Chau, a city close to the Cambodian border.

Converted from a covered lighter (YFNB) by the Ship Repair Facility, Yokosuka, YRBM–16 was efficient and comfortable. Its wardroom and living spaces were worthy of any ship of the Navy. A share of the credit goes to the maintenance staff at COMSERVPAC's headquarters, which had put much effort into guiding the design.

The security precautions of this craft were notable. Watches at the brow and bow and stern wore sound powered phones at all times, and seemed to be especially alert. The Officer in Charge, an ex–fire controlman, had the mortar battery well trained, requiring them to make frequent visits to an Army firing range. The crew was proud of its ability to go in General Quarters in a matter of seconds. Control of the battery was well organized. A grid system had been established by which fire could be directed accurately to any point within range. The craft was later to see action off Ben Tre.

Tan Chau was disestablished in July 1967 when YRBM–16 moved to Binh Thuy.   When no longer needed at Binh Thuy, YRBM–16 with twenty PBRs moved to an anchorage off Ben Tre on a branch of the Mekong, south of My Tho, which had long been an enemy stronghold.

On 7 November 1967, the armament of YRBM–16 was brought into play in a fire fight with the Viet Cong.   Forty–six rounds of 81 mm. mortars killed three VC and wounded four.   There were no U.S. casualties.

On 18 November, however, the VC scored when an explosion blew an 18 by 17 foot hole in the starboard side aft.   As far as could be determined, the charge had been placed there by a swimmer and "command detonated" by wires from the shore.

The explosion blasted through a diesel wing tank of YRBM–16 to an adjacent living space and into an engine room.   Fire, fed by the fuel, gutted the engineering and shop spaces.   USS *Hunterdon County* (LST–838), a river–mouth LST, responding to the call for assistance, helped fight the fire and took personnel aboard.   PBRs also assisted.   Fire fighting equipment was flown to the scene by aircraft of the Naval Support Activity, Saigon.

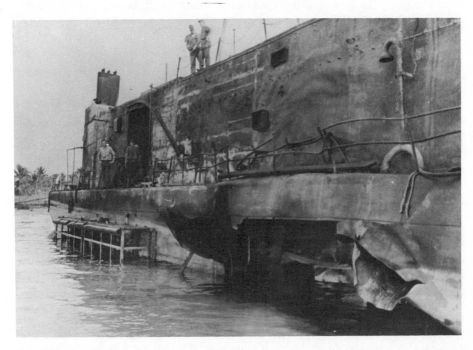

NH–74177

*Repair, messing and berthing barge YRBM–16 after Viet Cong underwater swimmer attack at Ben Tre.*

A harbor clearance team and light lift craft (LLC) were sent from Dong Tam to salvage the craft and install a temporary patch. YRBM–16 was then towed to Dong Tam for more work on the hull before being sent to Sasebo for permanent repairs. Five men were missing and eight injured. One later died.

APL–55 was then deployed to Ben Tre to resume support. APL–21 was deployed from Subic Bay to An Thoi to relieve APL–55.

## LONG XUYEN

The Naval Support Detachment at Long Xuyen on the Bassac was established on 13 July 1966 to support twenty PBRs, being co–located with the Vietnamese at their RAG base. In January 1967 the boat ramp was extended and a 120,000–gallon fuel oil barge deployed to the site. The detachment was deactivated on 28 March 1967, when the boats were relocated to areas of higher VC concentration.

One hundred and ninety–four personnel of the River Patrol Force were supported at Long Xuyen.

## BINH THUY

Next to Nha Be the largest river support base was the one near the city of Can Tho on the Bassac River.

Early operations made use of the Can Tho Vietnamese RAG base, where repair facilities included a marine railway running up into a shed. I recall being particularly impressed with the repair work done on propellers. Shallow water and floating debris took their toll of these propellers, bending, chipping, and breaking off blades. One native old timer there was able to restore the blades to excellent operating condition. How he did it without a dynamic balancing machine I shall never know.

At first, the U.S. Naval Support Detachment and the personnel it supported were housed in a villa in the city. Later the temporary base was moved west, past the Binh Thuy airstrip, and the detachment became known as the Naval Support Detachment, Binh Thuy, on 1 August 1966. The interim facility consisted of two one–story buildings of local construction with rooms for the officers and men. When I first visited the site, water was up to the door sills, and Vietnamese women were hard at work planting rocks in the short muddy stretch of road.

NH–74199

*New base at Binh Thuy.*

YRBM–9, outfitted for repair and supply at Nha Be, moved to Binh Thuy where it was moored alongside the billet in October 1966. That same month Commander River Patrol Force (CTF 116) and his staff moved to the base from Saigon.

Contractor construction of the semi–permanent facilities just east of the temporary base started in November 1966. In sharp contrast with the earlier facilities, the resultant base had efficient repair and supply buildings, communication facilities suitable for the Task Force Commander, office spaces, and comfortable barracks.

Nearby Binh Thuy airfield was a favorite target for enemy attacks, and on such occasions, the support detachment lent help, such as when, in May 1967, fifty detachment personnel helped put out a serious fire started by a VC attack.

When Tan Chau was disestablished, YRBM–16 moved to the new site at Binh Thuy until the facilities ashore could take over the load. That same month, July 1967, the shift to the new base being completed, YFNB–9 was towed to Nha Be to be outfitted as a repair barge (YR).

At this time the Navy Sea Hawk helicopters were at the Binh Thuy airfield. Later a site was constructed for them adjacent to the naval support base.

## SUPPORT EFFECTIVENESS

The preceding brief treatment of bases, ashore and afloat, has been given to impart some feeling for the austere and difficult conditions encountered. The point is that, as results of hard work around–the–clock, dedication, imagination, and innovation, a remarkable job was done in keeping the inshore and river craft in operation an extraordinarily high percentage of the time. The performance of those concerned in accomplishing unanticipated jobs attests to the flexibility and adaptability of the naval officer and bluejacket.

# CHAPTER XIII

# Construction

The undeveloped nature of much of Vietnam, the lack of ports and port facilities, the inadequacy of roads, the large number of streams to be crossed, the destruction of bridges by the enemy, the requirement for out-lying bases throughout the guerrilla–infested country, and the need for airfields and logistic areas—all placed a particularly high premium on construction. With escalating demands for facilities far in excess of construction capabilities, an extraordinary effort was required. To meet the extensive needs for construction, many of which were of great urgency, it was necessary to employ a wide variety of means. As a result, construction was accomplished by self–help; by local concerns, such as mentioned in the case of Headquarters Support Activity; by military engineers; by contractors; and, in the case of some emergency projects, by personnel of facilities maintenance organizations.

Previous chapters have included some mention of tasks carried out by the Navy Mobile Construction Battalions. The primary intent of this chapter is to tell briefly the overall story to do with these Seabees. But, first of all, brief coverage will be given to the construction effort as a whole and to the role of the major contractor for construction. Management of the latter effort was a Navy responsibility, although, unlike the Seabees, the responsibility did not in this case flow through the CINCPACFLT–COMSERVPAC chain of command.

The absence of national mobilization and a call–up of Reserves, especially limiting in the case of the Army, resulted in placing heavy reliance on a single contractor to achieve a rapid build–up of construction capabilities. The capabilities so developed under that contractor were so vast and diversi-fied as to amount essentially to a major construction industry.

## DEFENSE CONSTRUCTION AGENT

The Navy's Bureau of Yards and Docks (later to be named the Naval Facilities Engineering Command) had been designated the Department of

Defense Construction Agent in Southeast Asia for contractor construction and design in the case of all Department of Defense projects, and others as designated. In view of the expansion which was to follow, it is of interest to note the reason set forth in the implementing memorandum signed by a Deputy Assistant Secretary of Defense on 8 March 1963. This was that Southeast Asia was one of the "areas in the Far East where the current and projected workload for design and construction does not warrant the continuance of several construction agencies."

Located in Saigon was the Officer in Charge of Construction (OICC), Southeast Asia. The office was later split into two OICCs in 1965, one in Vietnam and one in Thailand. Each reported to the Chief of the Bureau of Yards and Docks through the Bureau's Pacific Division in Hawaii. This was an effective arrangement for applying the management capabilities of the bureau and the expertise of the Navy's competent Civil Engineer Corps to the tasks at hand, although it resulted at times in some added complications with regard to staff and command relationships wherein construction was concerned. It was a source of amazement to me that Rear Admiral James R. Davis (CEC) and his successor, Rear Admiral William M. Heaman (CEC), seemed to be able to keep things so well sorted out in their varied roles as the Officer in Charge of the Pacific Division, Yards and Docks, as CINCPACFLT's Civil Engineer, as COMSERVPAC's Civil Engineer, and as Commander Construction Battalions, Pacific, under COMSERVPAC. I must admit that which hat was being worn was not always clear to me, particularly when Service Force staff actions were desired concerning construction to be performed by the contractor, and when there was competition for the limited personnel available to fulfill the wide variety of responsibilities.

As Commander Service Force, my primary concern as regards contractor construction was trying to get adequate facilities built to permit fulfillment of logistic responsibilities in the I Corps Tactical Zone, and at Navy support bases elsewhere. Understandably, it was hard for these to compete favorably for priorities in the face of the many large and important projects for which the contractual effort was especially well qualified. Large airfields had to be built before land–based aircraft could be used in quantity. In early 1965, ability to use such aircraft was extremely limited, there being but three airfields, with but one runway apiece and with little in the form of base facilities. By 1968, eight major air bases had been constructed with a total of fifteen runways. Two hundred smaller airfields were also to be built, and almost as many heliports.   Major airfields were also built in nearby Thailand.   In addition, there were many Army demands for construction of major complexes, including the ones at Cam Ranh Bay and Qui Nhon, the major logistic base near Saigon, and the headquarters for Commander U.S. Military Advisory Command's large staff on the outskirts of the city.

The unified commander, CINCPAC, was responsible for the setting of priorities throughout the Pacific.   He, in turn, quite properly delegated these responsibilities for construction in Vietnam to the subordinate unified commander, COMUSMACV.   Determining priorities at the COMUS-MACV level must have been extremely difficult, particularly in such a dynamic situation.   There were demands for urgent construction far beyond the capabilities available, and the situation was further complicated by the widely scattered locations throughout the Republic.   Furthermore, the setting and changing of priorities involved more than military need, being based to a large extent on the capabilities at the time for a given type of construction and the demands for that type.   Until a Director of Construction was established under COMUSMACV in the winter of 1966, many of the decisions of the OICC amounted in effect to decisions on priority.

In the early days the problems to do with urgently needed Navy facilities in I Corps seemed particularly frustrating.   Of these problems, those to do with port development were most acute.   Whereas one of the lessons of SERVPAC's Advanced Base Section in World War II was that port development should initially take priority over the development of airfields, the reverse was true in the early days in Vietnam, when, under MACV's initial port development plan, a priority was assigned not only under airfields but under main supply routes and railroads as well.   Yet the latter would be of little use if the supplies were not able to get ashore.   Complicated by low priority and by the lack of dredges and pile drivers, there were many serious delays insofar as port development projects were concerned.   Firm commitments as to "beneficial occupancy dates" were hard to obtain from the OICC.   Often what I had understood to be milestone dates continued to slide vaguely into the future.

Rear Admiral Davis stated: "The primary planning is being done at Danang by a special planning group staffed in part from my office at Pearl Harbor working under the direct guidance and supervision of the Naval Component Commander."   The capabilities of this small group were severely limited with regard to the expanding tasks to be accomplished. Although briefed from time to time by Rear Admiral Davis as to the plans for development of Danang and Chu Lai, I had been slow to recognize how much approval and priorities depended on the prior presentation of detailed base development plans. In retrospect, it would have been desirable to have provided NAVSUPPACT from the very start with a strong construction planning staff. Such an in–house capability would have helped in base development planning but, more importantly, strengthened the ability to compete for construction priority in the critical early days.

As noted in Chapter VIII, I made a rush trip to Danang in December 1965, with selected members of my staff. There we pieced together various projects to define the overall plan for port development more completely. On briefing General Walt, he showed a full awareness of the seriousness of the situation. I believe his influence had much to do with General West-moreland's actions about a month later in assigning top priority to port development for a productive six–week period.

During the December visit it became clear that there was an urgent need for frequent personal liaison with Saigon by Commander Naval Support Activity, Danang, particularly with those involved in making decisions on construction. This was the main reason for requesting the assignment of a Navy "administrative" airplane to the activity. Before a C–117 was assigned in February 1966, it often would take three or four days to attend a meeting in Saigon and get back. In addition, the aircraft's use within I Corps, on call, proved of tremendous value for personnel and special cargoes, a value which increased as more detachments were established at outlying sites. This was one of but many confirmations of the value of "organic" aircraft, not to compete with the common airlift services supplied by the Air Force, but to complement them.

The establishment of a base development section on COMNAVFORV's staff in Saigon in April 1966, was another step which improved the situa-tion significantly. On the scene in Saigon, Rear Admiral N. G. Ward, Chief of the Naval Advisory Group, and later Commander Naval Forces, Vietnam, did his best to get bases constructed for the support of Market Time and Game Warden. Despite his many efforts, building the relatively small bases suffered delay after delay, and as noted before, much of the work planned had to be done eventually by Seabees.

The difficulties were primarily a part of the basic problem of inadequate total construction capabilities initially to meet the explosively expanding needs of all the Services in Vietnam, and the difficulties of small projects competing with larger ones. Those involved in managing the effort deserve the greatest of praise.  Everything considered, the overall accomplishments were nothing short of remarkable.

Nevertheless, the clear lesson was that the use of a contractor in such a situation is not in itself enough.  Each of the Services needed military engineer units under their own control, particularly at the start, during times of local emergencies, and in outlying combat areas.

## BUILD–UP OF CONTRACTUAL EFFORT

When the build–up started in 1965, Raymond, Morrison–Knudsen (RMK) was under contract to the Bureau of Yards and Docks for work in Vietnam. Steps were taken to mobilize the contractor's efforts in as short a time as possible.  Planning for this mobilization was complicated by the strategy of keeping the effort limited, intending to do enough but not much more. The strategy of "graduated military actions" gave little basis for meaningful projections, although clearly the required capacity for work would be enormous.

With no firm plan available, a basic assumption made by the Navy managers was that a balance construction capability was needed to permit work going on concurrently in as many projects as possible.  In January 1965, RMK was told to gear up to a workload of $5 million per month.  In May, the estimate was a future monthly placement rate of $12 million.  In August, the objective was $15 million by January 1966.  Two more contractors were added, as the combination became Raymond, Morrison–Knudsen, Brown and Root, J. A. Jones (RMK–BRJ).  By January the goal was to achieve construction at the rate of $40 million per month by October 1966, and to sustain this level of effort for one year.  This workload estimate proved to be about 25 percent higher than what was subsequently authorized in Washington and a phaseback was required.

By June 1966, contractor projects were underway at forty–seven different sites.  Two months later when the gradual cutback was started, the total contractor personnel had reached a peak of 52,730.

As has been mentioned already, one of the most difficult problems in South Vietnam was that of dredging.  Until another contract was assigned for dredging at Tan My in 1967, all the United States dredging effort was managed by RMK–BRJ.  In those days of dredging deficiencies in 1965 and 1966, I often wondered if it would not have been worthwhile for the

Navy to have some organic dredging capability of its own, as it did in World War II.

The acquiring of materials for the construction effort could not await precise definition of projects. Thus, the contractor procured materials in bulk on the basis of general estimates.

Starting in May 1965, a supply base had been built by the contractor at Poro Point on the Philippine island of Luzon for the transshipment of materials. MSTS was unable to provide the LSTs required and shipments had to be made mainly by regular cargo ships. As a result the contractor acquired two LSTs, one in April 1966, the other in June. Sixteen aircraft were chartered by the contractor.

One of the side effects of the early build–up of construction capabilities, strongly felt in Danang in particular, was that a heavy flow of construction materials was set in motion both by the contractor, and by the military engineers (Navy, Marines, and Army). These materials contributed to the high volumes of cargoes arriving in Danang, volumes at times well in advance of immediate needs. The large quantities of such cargoes, and the fact that many consisted of items hard to handle, added greatly to the initial over–taxing of Danang's limited terminal capacities.

Despite the difficulties, it is hard to visualize how the build–up and per-formance of contractor construction could have been more rapid to meet the dynamically changing and expanding requirements and the need to compress "crash" programs.

## CONTROLS

The problems were further complicated by the use of procedures similar to those in time of peace for approval of most of the construction. Construc-tion was programmed, authorized, and appropriated under the time consuming, laborious MILCON (Military Construction) procedures, pro-cedures difficult even in more normal times. Detailed justification, all the way to Washington, was often required on a project–by–project basis.

On 28 November 1965, during a visit to Vietnam, Secretary McNamara was advised that $1 billion worth of construction would be needed to meet urgent requirements. On his return to Washington, he initiated steps to control the construction program within his own office. As I understood it at the time, the reason was to ensure that adequate assistance was given to meet the imposing needs of the Vietnam War in timely fashion. Undeniably these steps were of great help at the start and some measure of overall control was required over such a costly program, but I felt there were also adverse effects resulting from the detailed nature of the role played by the Office of the Secretary of Defense in construction management, control of reprogramming, certification of requirements, and allocation of contingency funds. Much paper work was involved, as more and more detailed reports were required of the status of projects and funding.

The Secretary also reached the conclusion that a construction "Tzar" was needed. On 6 January 1966, the Deputy Secretary of Defense approved an "engineer construction boss" in Saigon to be "responsive" to COMUS-MACV, even though both Admiral Sharp and General Westmoreland felt that the problems were more basic than organizational, and favored the functions of coordination and control being performed by COMUSMACV's staff. Nevertheless, the Construction Directorate MACV was established on 11 February with a staff of 50 percent Army, 25 percent Navy and 25 percent Air Force. Mission and functions assigned by COMUSMACV were based on an Office of the Secretary of Defense memorandum, with the Director being given extensive authority over both contractor and military construction. His authority extended to the setting of standards and even to passing on requirements. It also encompassed control of military engineer units not assigned to major combat forces.

In addition to this construction "Tzar" on the scene, the Secretary of Defense established a general officer under the Assistant Secretary of Defense (Installations and Logistics), as Staff Director of Southeast Asia Construction.

The result was that special lines of authority were set up for construction, superimposed on other lines of responsibility and authority for command and support. What really made the setup work was that the in–country Director of Construction did in effect function as though his primary responsibility was to COMUSMACV.

### SEABEES

It was primarily the Seabees on whom we depended for urgent construction in the north. The occasional help of the Seabees was invaluable to the early development of Navy base facilities in the southern part of the Republic of Vietnam as well.

The Naval Mobile Construction Battalion organization had its roots in the experiences of World War II in building advanced bases and in the support of the Marines. As a result of the needs of construction in the British Isles, Iceland, and Lend–Lease naval bases, Naval Reserves had been recruited in 1941 to form "Headquarters Construction Companies." Following the attack on Pearl Harbor, the experiences at Wake, Cavite, and Guam made it clear that specially trained and disciplined naval construction forces were needed. On the request of Rear Admiral Ben Moreell (CEC) on 28 December 1941, construction companies were organized to work on advanced bases. The manning of these was accelerated by drawing heavily upon civilian construction engineers for the officer corps and by offering immediate petty officer status to qualified construction workers.

A nucleus of a construction battalion organization had been kept in existence after World War II through the determined sponsorship of the Bureau of Yards and Docks and the strong support of the Marine Corps. Although the units were not manned at the levels of World War II battalions, the result was a balance of capabilities for "horizontal" and "vertical" construction that was well fitted to the needs of 1965 and 1966. Later, as the war moved further from the initial base areas, the needs shifted more to those of horizontal construction, and the manning and equipment were changed accordingly.

In the early days of 1965, it was often said that the young Seabees were a far cry from their older and more experienced predecessors of World War II. Whether true or not at the start, it took very little time before these dedicated officers and men had proved themselves to be true professionals and seasoned veterans. Working in advanced areas as well as at the major bases, their accomplishments were a key to both combat and logistic operations throughout I Corps as they engaged in port development; built airfields, helopads and airstrips; constructed and improved roads; put up cantonments and warehouses; developed fortifications; dug wells; prepared missile sites; set up refrigeration stowage, water purification plants, dairy plants, ice plants, and utilities; built galleys, recreation facilities, open and covered stowage, fuel tanks and distribution systems, water stowage, ramps, causeways, piers, and bridges; and did countless other jobs. The assignments were numerous and varied. For instance, one of many notable jobs in the Danang area in 1965 was the cutting off of the top of heavily–jungled Monkey Mountain in order to provide a commanding site for a Hawk anti–air missile battalion. Later, in 1967, a ridge of this same mountain was leveled and concrete laid in site preparation for a transmission antenna system for the Naval Support Activity communication facilities.

As has been mentioned before, the airstrip at Dong Ha in March 1967 underwent major repair by the Seabees. Matting was removed, the sub-grade restabilized and the matting re–laid with a minimum of interruption to the use of the field. An airfield was built at An Hoa. Heloports were constructed at Chu Lai, Danang, Danang East, Phu Bai, and Dong Ha.

Remote quarries for crushed rock were operated despite a number of enemy attacks. A bridge 2,400 feet long, the Liberty bridge, was constructed twenty miles south of Danang. Two spans of this bridge, the longest ever built by Seabees, were dropped by the Viet Cong on 6 September 1967. It was put back in operation in thirty–two hours.

Highly responsive to the needs of the Marines and the Navy alike, the Seabees reacted in a minimum of time to build what was needed. There was always the matter of priorities, but as adjudicated within the I CTZ by General Walt, there was an absolute minimum of red tape insofar as construction battalion work was concerned. The battalions fully established

NH–74342

*The Liberty Bridge spanning the Thu Bon River, under construction.*

the indispensable nature of organic military construction forces in the combat theater. Valuable as the contribution of the civilian construction firm was for many of the larger jobs, the most urgent and crucial assignments were usually those of the Mobile Naval Construction Battalions.

One of the biggest problems confronting the Seabees in the early days pertained to repairing the construction equipment and machinery. The sand, dust and grit, and the operating environment, had far more adverse effects than had been anticipated. As a result, extraordinary action had to be taken to get an adequate supply of parts and much effort was required in maintenance actions. An Okinawa Seabee detachment, established on 19 August 1965, at the Marine Corps Air Station, Futema, Okinawa, was given the assignment of coordinating the shipment of new parts, equipment, and machinery from the continental U.S. to the in—country battalions.

By the summer of 1965, three of the five Pacific Fleet Mobile Construction Battalions were deployed to Vietnam. These were formed into the 30th Naval Construction Regiment under Captain Harold F. Liberty (CEC), USNR, and after September 1966 under Captain Albert R. Marschall. More battalions were needed for further build—up and to establish a reasonable rotation schedule. To provide more strength, NMCB–8 was transferred permanently to SERVPAC from the Atlantic on 5 August 1965, followed by NMCB–4 on 7 November. The former deployed to Danang on 29 December to become the fourth battalion in—country.

In December 1965, the Chief of Naval Operations decided that all the Atlantic battalions would join in the rotation to Vietnam. Rear Admiral H. A. Renken, COMSERVLANT, and his construction battalions commander visited Pearl Harbor to help work out the details. While Commander Construction Battalions, Atlantic, retained responsibility for administration, certain other command functions, including inspections, were assigned to Commander Construction Battalions, Pacific, under COMSERVPAC, for the duration of each deployment.

What with duty in Guam and Vietnam, it was eleven and a half months before NMCB–3 could get home on its initial cycle. Since the goal for Seabee deployments was set as eight months overseas and six months at the homeport, new battalions had to be created for rotation purposes alone. NMCB–40 was commissioned on 1 February 1966, and NMCB–58 on 15 September at Davisville, Rhode Island. The Construction Battalion Camp, Gulfport, Mississippi, was reactivated and NMCBs 62 and 133 were commissioned there on 1 July and 15 September 1966.

On 18 May 1966, to provide a means for command attention over the larger force on the West Coast of the United States, the 31st Naval Construction Regiment (NCR) had been established at Port Hueneme, California. COMCBPAC's Equipment Branch was transferred to the 31st NCR from Pearl Harbor. The question was raised as to whether or not the entire Construction Battalion Center should report to Commander Service Force. This was not desirable from my point of view in the light of the many tenant activities at the Center, including research and development, and Bureau of Naval Personnel schools. The final decision was that the Commanding Officer of the Center, while remaining under the command of Facilities Engineering Command, would report to COMSERVPAC for "additional duty."

As was the case with the Naval Support Activity, Danang, special attention was required to ensure adequate liaison with the various headquarters in Saigon. This was particularly true in the case of construction in view of the extent of centralized decision making in this area by the COMUS-MACV staff and the Director of Construction. To compete with those on the scene demanded a flow of informal information at the flag and general officer level and below, in addition to the formal transmissions. Rear Admiral Heaman (CEC), who had transferred from his job of Officer in Charge of Construction, Vietnam, to relieve Rear Admiral Davis upon the latter's retirement, strongly advocated the establishment of a third construction brigade with headquarters in Saigon. His advocacy of the concept to me and Admiral Johnson was paralleled by similar recommendations at the Washington level.

From the point of view of principles of organization, management and command, such a step made little sense. It meant placing a flag officer in command of a construction brigade over a single regiment that also was commanded by a flag officer. Although giving expression to such views at the time, I decided not to raise formal objection because of the liaison requirement. Not only was the situation with regard to construction extremely critical at the time, but also the extent of authority of the newly established Director of Construction over the employment of military engineers was such as to make the matter of liaison at the right level a matter of special concern.

In June 1966, the Chief of Naval Operations authorized the commissioning of this brigade under the command of Rear Admiral R. R. Wooding (CEC) who was relieved on 9 December 1966 by Rear Admiral P. E. Seufer

(CEC). Later, as a result of further build–up, a new organization was placed into effect, when on 1 August 1967 the Third Naval Construction Brigade headquarters was moved from Saigon to Danang to be co–located with the 30th Naval Construction Regiment. Captain Marschall, who served as temporary commander of the Third Naval Construction Brigade, supervised the move until he was relieved on 31 August by Rear Admiral J. V. Bartlett (CEC). A representative remained in Saigon. At the same time, the 32nd Naval Construction Regiment was established, with headquarters at Phu Bai, to be responsible for all Seabee construction north of the Hai Van Pass.

Three more Navy Mobile Construction Battalions (NMCB) had been deployed to Vietnam in the spring of 1966. Still more arrived in Vietnam in August 1966, April 1967, May 1967, and November 1967. One additional was to arrive in 1968, for a total of twelve deployed battalions.

Meanwhile, to sustain these deployments the total number of NMCBs in the Navy increased to twenty–one, from the eight battalions at the start of the war. In addition, the personnel in each battalion had been increased from an initial strength of 21 officers and 568 men to 24 officers and 738 men per battalion. Despite the expansion, high standards of effectiveness of all the battalions were achieved through intensive training of battalions when back in the homeport areas.

Manning the additional battalions meant a drain on the number of so–called "Group VIII" personnel throughout the Navy. Drawing upon World War II experiences, the aid of labor unions and contractors was sought to encourage enlistments, and a direct Group VIII Construction Petty Officer Procurement Program was established. The program achieved remarkable results, providing all the petty officers that were needed, and more. Reserves were finally mobilized for the last two battalions authorized at the time of the *Pueblo* crisis.

Operations of the Seabees extended to many scattered locations. Details from a parent battalion, usually numbering less than thirty men each, provided construction support not only to the Navy and Marines, but also to U.S. Special Forces and other Army, Air Force, and allied units operating in the more remote areas of the I Corps zone. Seabee details did a wide variety of jobs in other zones as well. These included the building of the 250–man U.S. Navy portion of the Mobile Riverine Force base at Dong Tam in the Mekong Delta; construction in support of major Army units at Cu Chi, Pleiku, and Long Binh; construction support of AID at Quang

Ngai, and Nha Trang; and airfield upgrading and cantonment construction at An Khe.

The most crucial work continued to be that in the north. For instance, in February 1967, a 104–man detachment of Naval Mobile Construction Battalion Five was assigned the job of designing and building observation towers along the thirty miles of the Demilitarized Zone. In March these Seabees constructed two 50–foot towers north of Gio Linh and set up four 20–foot towers at other scattered locations.

The Seabees in this area had their share of combat. Actions were especially sharp at Con Thien, two miles south of the DMZ, where NMCB–4 had the job of constructing a camp. On 29 April 1967, the North Vietnamese hit the camp with approximately 110 rounds of mortar and artillery fire, followed by a probing of the half-completed perimeter. The construction type activities were harassed by enemy mortar and artillery fire for six of the next eight months. Early on the eighth of May, Con Thien was attacked by an estimated two reinforced North Vietnamese Army battalions. The Seabees helped defend the camp after 600 to 1,000 mortar rounds had driven Marines and Special Forces troops back from the perimeter. This was the last of the enemy assaults on the camp, but the Seabees continually encountered enemy mortar and artillery fire while completing the camp's various underground bunkers, and the supply and berthing areas. Eleven of the twenty–five–man Seabee team were wounded during the period of 29 April to 13 May as the job was completed. Hundreds of the enemy were killed during their attacks on this important outpost.

Operating as they did, the Seabees saw much combat action in many other outlying locations as well, ranging from VC mining incidents to direct engagement with enemy forces. At Ba To and Thuong Duc, Seabee details from NMCB–9 weathered VC attacks while building fortified camps for the Army's Special Forces. At Tam Ky, one Seabee was killed and others wounded when the MACV advisors' compound came under VC mortar attack in October 1966. These are typical of experiences at many other locations as well.


## SEABEE TEAMS

The versatile capabilities of the Seabees made them particularly valuable in civic action projects, in which every unit did its bit. They built schools, bridges, roads, hospitals, and resettlement villages. "Well digging" teams have been mentioned. While increasingly the focus of Seabee effort was on support of combat forces in advanced areas, the work of Seabee teams in assisting and teaching Vietnamese villagers continued to make helpful contributions as a part of the Agency for International Development (AID) effort. In the winter of 1967, the teams in Vietnam expanded from four to six upon the request of the U.S. Ambassador. A further doubling of these teams was requested in 1968.

# CHAPTER XIV

# Salvage

One of the most interesting and rewarding responsibilities of Commander Service Force was that of salvage. It was interesting because of the dangerous nature of so many of the operations, the fact that each had its own unique set of problems, and the fact that success often hinged on the promptness of action and the soundness of the decisions which governed those actions. It was rewarding because of the importance of recovery of valuable ships and craft to serve again, and the saving of often high–cost cargoes which were sometimes crucial to the war effort.

The requirements for salvage rose sharply during the Vietnam Conflict. Enemy action was but one of the reasons. For instance, the need for continuous logistic support often meant operating ships and craft close to a lee shore pounded by high seas, such as occurred along I Corps during the northeast monsoon. It sometimes meant the landing of supplies through high surf or the entering of treacherous inlets. In the many waterways within the Republic, there were natural hazards, often accompanied by hostile action. Furthermore, the approaches to Vietnam were dotted by the many dangerous reefs in the South China Sea. Still another contributing factor was the old age of cargo ships reactivated from the National Defense Reserve Fleet, and the increased probability of breakdowns at sea, particularly when battling heavy seas during transits of the stormy North Pacific. The resultant demands for salvage operations encompassed rescue and assistance, including a number of rescue tows; fire fighting and emergency repairs; afloat salvage of ships damaged at sea; offshore salvage; refloating stranded or sunken ships in exposed locations along the coast, or on reefs or islands; harbor salvage; harbor and river clearance of damaged or sunken ships and craft, and of damaged bridges and piers; aircraft salvage; cargo salvage; and the demolition of wrecks. At times the operations were conducted under combat conditions.

The responsibility of Commander Service Force for command of salvage operations was a carry over from World War II. Starting with the recovery of ships at Pearl Harbor, the art in the U.S. Navy had advanced greatly in the war that followed. In the Pacific, a Fleet Salvage Officer had been established under Commander Service Force. The powerful salvage ships (ARS), developed at that time, remained as Service Force assets, along with the fleet tugs (ATF) which were fitted for offshore salvage as well as towing duties.

During the years following World War II, assignment of overall management responsibilities for salvage to the Bureau of Ships (later Naval Ship Systems Command) played a great part in keeping the art alive within the Navy and ensuring retention of the associated capabilities. The Ship Systems Command's responsibilities were exercised through a Supervisor of Salvage who was charged with providing salvage material; providing expert advice and technical assistance when necessary; entering into and administering contracts with private enterprise for salvage services to public and private vessels and aircraft; processing and settling of claims for salvage services rendered by the Navy; assuming salvage responsibilities upon agreement of the Service Force Commander concerned or when directed by the Chief of Naval Operations; exercising technical control of methods and procedures for salvage work; and training salvage experts.

USN–1062970

*Powerful salvage ships, such as* Deliver *(ARS–23), built in World War II, were invaluable in the Vietnam War.*

Public Law 513 authorizes the Secretary of the Navy to provide necessary salvage facilities for both public and private vessels upon such terms and conditions as he may, in his discretion, determine to be in the best interests of the United States.  It further authorizes the Secretary of the Navy to settle any claim for salvage services rendered by the Navy to other than U.S. Naval vessels.  Within the capabilities available, the policy of the Navy was to assist in the salvage of other than Navy ships or aircraft when such assistance was requested and where adequate privately owned salvage facilities did not exist or where not reasonably available.  Such action was contingent on a request from the owner or master.  The owners would then pay for the services of the salvage ships and other charges.

Close cooperation between Commander Service Force and the Supervisor of Salvage was an important feature in the more difficult operations.  Information and assistance of the supervisor and the rest of the Bureau of Ships would be requested, such as to determine information on stability, the strength of the ship's structure, calculations of the buoyancy which would be required, loading stresses, ship's plans, etc., when the information was not readily available to the Service Force.  The supervisor would be contacted also when additional material or equipment was desired.  An additional responsibility was the consummation of agreements with private owners.

Upon arrival of salvage forces on the scene the cognizant Service Force Commander was charged with the assumption of command of the distressed ship or unit, and became responsible for the conduct of the salvage operation.  In addition to the Fleet Salvage Officer on COMSERVPAC's staff and a senior salvage officer assigned to the staff of Commander Service Group Three, specially trained salvage officers were assigned to ARSs and ATFs.  These officers, many of whom were "engineering duty only" officers, combined diving qualifications with specialized training in salvage techniques, in ship stability, and in hull repairs.  The salvage officers on the scene took charge on the wreck, while overall command of the entire operation and operational control of the ships involved was assigned to a line officer qualified for command at sea.  Normally, the latter was a service group or squadron commander, or for smaller operations, the captain of a salvage ship or fleet tug.

Specialized equipment and materials under the custody and control of the Supervisor of Salvage were stored at supply activities strategically located around the world, and released to the Service Force Commander on request.

Promptness of action is of special importance in the case of ships and craft exposed to the seas. Avoiding the wrong actions and taking the right steps early in the game frequently spells the difference between success and failure. For this reason I made it clear on many occasions that the group and squadron commanders, salvage officers, and commanding officers were to get moving immediately upon knowledge of a ship or craft in distress, without waiting to be so ordered. As a result, it was not unusual for them to be already on the way to the scene by the time the word reached me.

SERVPAC's salvage forces made many notable contributions to the war effort. These forces were almost continuously occupied during the Vietnam Conflict. New heights of professionalism were achieved, and additional capabilities were developed, particularly in the clearance of rivers and harbors, and in underwater salvage. All in all, the salvors were an ingenious, brave and hardy lot, and possessed the stamina required for diving and underwater work. Picking up a tow in mountainous seas, diving in treacherous waters, and working inside a grounded ship being pounded by breakers was hardly work for the timid. Almost without exception, the commanding officers of the tugs and salvage ships were outstanding skippers and fine ship handlers. About a half were "mustangs" who had come up through the ranks; the rest were young officers well fitted for the challenges of command. The ships were, as a rule, particularly sharp and shipshape. Augmenting their salvage work, there was a seemingly endless series of requirements for tows in the Far East, across the Pacific, or off the West Coast of the United States.

## FRANK KNOX

As noted in a previous chapter, one of the most urgent problems confronting me when I took over responsibilities as Commander Service Force was that to do with efforts to save destroyer *Frank Knox*, which had run high on Pratas Reef in the South China Sea only a little over a day before. This was to be but the start; there was one salvage operation after another during my thirty–one months as Commander Service Force. Sometimes several were going on at the same time. Few were routine; each had its own set of challenges.

By the time I relieved Admiral Irvin, it was clear that the chances of *Frank Knox*'s being saved were at best marginal. In addition to the efforts of those on the scene, her salvage would occupy much of the time of my staff and myself for a period of seven weeks.  Despite many requests by COMSERVPAC's Fleet Salvage Officer, Commander E. B. Mitchell, to go to the scene, I held him at the headquarters.  I could understand his wanting to be where the action was, but keeping him in Pearl Harbor proved to be a wise move.  Constantly conferring with me, and in frequent contact with the Supervisor of Salvage of the Bureau of Ships, Captain W. F. Searle, Jr., and with other organizations which could help, the headquarters was an ideal location to initiate and follow–up on the obtaining of whatever could help the difficult operation—an operation greatly complicated by seas and a 5– to 6–knot lateral current, and one in which the nature and contour of the hard coral made the setting of beach gear difficult.

Only a few hours after the grounding on the morning of 18 July 1965, a team of Nationalist Chinese Navy underwater demolition divers from nearby Pratas Island found the ship to be aground from frame 20 to frame 130, with one blade of each propeller bent and the others chipped.  In the early morning hours, within less than an hour and a half of the time of grounding, Commander Service Group Three had ordered salvage forces to the scene.  USS *Grapple* (ARS–7), USS *Munsee* (ATF–107), USS *Cocopa* (ATF–101) and Service Group Three's salvage officer, Lieutenant Commander J. H. Boyd, Jr., arrived by the next morning.  USS *Mahopac* (ATA–196) got there later that day.  Conditions were evaluated and plans made for a pull at high tide on 20 July with one set of beach gear attached [1] to the destroyer and two sets to *Grapple*.  A barge brought to the scene started off–loading ammunition to lighten the ship; fuel was pumped into another barge; and water was pumped over the side.

When the pull succeeded in moving the ship twelve feet, prospects looked more promising.  However, Tropical Storm Guilda moved into the area, not only preventing a pull the next day, but also placing the ship in a most precarious condition as a result of high winds and 10– to 12–foot swells from the south breaking over the destroyer's fantail.  Pumps attempted to combat leakage but the engine spaces were flooded to the waterline by midnight.  During the storm, *Grapple* had continued her efforts until dragging placed her dangerously close to the reef in the high seas, when it became necessary to slip the beach gear and cut the tow wire.

The destroyer, working in laborious fashion in response to the pounding of the seas, had moved laterally and was now even harder aground.  The

---

[1] Rig of special anchors placed to seaward to furnish a pulling force.

NH–74179

*Refloating destroyer Frank Knox after grounding on Pratas Reef.*

fact that one set of beach gear attached to her stern stayed in place undoubtedly saved her from a complete loss.

Before I was relieved, Admiral Irvin had phoned Rear Admiral J. W. Williams, Jr., Commander Service Group Three, directing him to seek the approval of Commander Seventh Fleet to proceed to the scene. Admiral Williams arrived at Pratas Reef on 21 July. Carrier *Midway* provided helicopter services to transport men and equipment to the wreck until USS *Iwo Jima* (LPH–2) arrived 22 July. USS *Conserver* (ARS–39), USS *Sioux* (ATF–75), USS *Greenlet* (ASR–10), and additional salvage personnel were dispatched to Pratas Reef. Other ships of the Fleet helped.

After much work on the ship and other necessary preparations, a major pull on 26 July moved the ship thirty feet, as Typhoon Harriet, passing nearby, raised the wind and seas and endangered the entire operation. Another typhoon threatened a couple of days later, but fortunately changed course.

There is not space to cover the complete story of the supreme efforts being made on the wreck and by the salvage ships. It was indeed touch and go the entire time. Sheer strakes of *Frank Knox* were buckled. The keel was broken in several areas. Much of the bottom was open to the seas. Boilers and machinery came loose from their foundations. At one stage those on the scene and on my staff recommended cutting the ship in two. I opted to keep on fighting, even though the probability of recovering the ship then seemed no greater than 10 percent.

Many ingenious ideas were tried, a number of which were originated by COMSERVPAC or the BUSHIPS Supervisor of Salvage. Strengthening the longitudinals, selective coral blasting, judicious use of beach gear, and dewatering by the use of a new technique of cast–in–place foam were, in particular, essential to success. Nor could the job have been done without the delivery of pumps, materials, and personnel to the ships by Seventh Fleet helicopters when weather was too rough for other means.

Finally, on 24 August, with five salvage ships and *Knox* herself pulling to beach gear, the destroyer was refloated. This may have been the most difficult single successful ship salvage job in history. The story of her recovery and subsequent restoration to full service by the Ship Repair Facility, Yokosuka, is one of ingenuity, hard work, perseverance and bravery. Lessons learned would prove of great value in subsequent salvage operations.

A number of steps were taken to incorporate these lessons in training and to acquire better equipment. For instance, training in the laying of beach gear had previously been confined to exercises in Middle Loch, Pearl Harbor. This was important basic training, but in itself it hardly prepared crews for operations in the open seas. To give more advanced training we had a hulk sunk on the exposed shore of Lanai, one of the Hawaiian Islands. Operations on this hulk paid great dividends in preparation for the many salvage operations to come.

One of the difficulties of the *Frank Knox* operations, the unreliability of the portable gas–driven pumps and other equipment left over from World War II, led the Supervisor of Salvage to purchase modern lightweight diesel–driven equipment which, when acquired, proved far more effective and reliable. Submersible pumps were rehabilitated. New lightweight submersible pumps were acquired. Velocity power tools were redesigned. New salvage work boats of greater size and power were delivered to salvage ships. Foam, such as that used in *Frank Knox*, was added to the inventory. Better underwater object locators, and portable communication transceivers were acquired. As a result of a thorough study by an ATA skipper, it was found possible to equip these smaller ocean–going tugs with one set of beach gear. The capabilities of the fleet tugs were increased by equipping them with a second set.

## COMBAT SALVAGE

The first operation after *Frank Knox* was a combat salvage operation on the coast of Vietnam in the Gulf of Siam which did not involve the regular salvage forces. It was accomplished by nearby *Krishna* and USCG Cutter *Point Young*. Two Viet Cong junks delivering cargoes to the enemy had been sunk, one in twenty feet of water and the other in thirty feet. Both were patched, raised and towed to An Thoi on 19 September 1965. The contraband cargo recovered included grenades, rifles and ammunition.

The next combat salvage job involved a United States ship when USS *Terrell County* (LST–1157) broached in the surf on the hostile shore of Tuy Hoa on 22 November. Rear Admiral Frederick E. Janney, the new Commander Service Group Three, flew to the scene. USS *Molala* (ATF–106) laid one set of beach gear, passed a tow wire to *Terrell County* with much difficulty in the high surf, and pulled her off on 25 November with *Mahopac* assisting in a tandem pull. The ship was patched, pumped dry, and towed to a repair base.

On 13 December, USS *Hitchiti* (ATF–103) salvaged LCU–1494 which had been damaged on a beach near Danang. Three days later the same ship raised a USMC LVT from twenty feet of water near Phu Thu, recovering bodies of the Marines who had gone down with the amphibious vehicle. That same day USS *Safeguard* (ARS–25) was assigned the task of recovering special equipment of an RA–5C aircraft which had crashed off the coast of Vietnam. Three days later, the capsizing and sinking of a 60–ton Army crane at Qui Nhon and the grounding of a freighter of Panamanian register were investigated. Salvage was found to be infeasible.

## RESCUE TOWS

Meanwhile the salvage forces were busy in other salvage operations in widely scattered areas of the Pacific. On 3 October, SS *Britain Victory* lost power in the South China Sea; *Conserver* and the small tug, LT–431, provided emergency assistance.

The next salvage operation was one of the few that did not end in success. On this occasion the Greek ship SS *Ekaterini G.*—a five-hold Liberty ship operated by Global Chartering and Brokerage Company, New York—was taken in tow by USS *Tawakoni* (ATF–114) after losing a propeller 600 miles south of Adak. In high winds and heavy seas the stricken ship was towed toward Adak, the nearest sheltered port. Unfortunately, *Ekaterini*'s anchor chain, being used as part of the tow rig, parted in a storm off the coast of Adak as the fleet tug and its tow awaited a break in the weather to permit entering port. It was impossible to recover the ship during the fury of the storm and she grounded on Great Sitkin Island. All of the crew members were saved by a Navy helicopter but the ship was a total loss.

This was followed by a success in the same area when SS *Tai–Nam*, a Nationalist Chinese freighter, lost propulsion power on 21 December as a result of propeller shaft difficulties and flooding of her shaft alley about 600 miles from Adak. SERVPAC's Alaskan–station fleet tug, then USS *Mataco* (ATF–86), took *Tai–Nam* in tow in extremely heavy weather. The ship was later delivered to a rendezvous with *Sudbury Two*, a civilian tug dispatched from the West Coast of the United States.

## THE THREAT OF BLOCKED CHANNELS

During the earlier war against the French, the Viet Minh forces had made extensive use of mines against ships and craft on inland waters. Similar actions had been taken to disrupt operations within the Republic of Vietnam. The seriousness of the threat and the need for specialized salvage capabilities was brought home to the United States when a former "jeep–carrier" engaged in ferrying aircraft to Vietnam, USNS *Card*, was sunk at Saigon on 2 May 1964, and later refloated by Service Force salvors.

Just as speed was of transcending importance during salvage operations in locations exposed to high seas, speed was often of crucial importance in inland waters as well. In addition to the importance of restoring ships and craft to service, the sinking might be in such a location as to block a vital channel or an important off–loading site. There was particular concern over the critical need for the delivery of military and civilian supplies up the river to Saigon.

To clear wrecks from critical locations in an absolute minimum of time, specialized salvage capabilities were needed.

## HARBOR CLEARANCE UNIT ONE

After a series of recommendations, the Secretary of Defense authorized the establishment of a "harbor clearance unit" capable of clearing the Saigon River, or any other vital waterway or port in Vietnam, should it become blocked by enemy action. Harbor Clearance Unit One was activated on 1 February 1966 at Subic Bay with a skeleton crew of 5 officers and 65 enlisted men. It soon built up to 20 officers and 159 enlisted men, all hand-picked for the job. The Supervisor of Salvage, Captain W. F. Searle, Jr., and SERVPAC's Fleet Salvage Officer, Commander E. B. Mitchell, deserve major credit for success in establishing the unit in an extraordinarily short period of time.

The core of the unit consisted of four ancient British heavy lift craft (HLC) which had seen service in the Suez Canal. For large lifts, the craft normally operated in pairs, one on each side of the ship to be lifted. Saddling the ships on large steel cables, the HLC would take on water ballast and, after tightening the cables, pump the ballast out. Operated in this fashion, each was capable of lifting 750 tons.

The four heavy lift craft were leased from the British and towed to Subic. A considerable amount of rehabilitation had to be done before the HLC were ready to operate efficiently in Vietnam waters. Equipment was old. With tiny bunks, cramped space, no power ventilation, and primitive galley and heads, living conditions were inadequate. Rehabilitation was essential.

As a result of extraordinary attention by my staff and high priority at the Ship Repair Facility, Subic, the job was done in a remarkably short period of time.

By March, the heavy lift craft were ready for emergency deployment. Salvage machinery and equipment had been overhauled, well–stowed and palletized for airlift. Arrangements had been made for transporting equipment and personnel by aircraft on twelve hours notice.

A design was completed to provide smaller craft for light lifts through the modification of landing craft. The result was the conversion of three LCU by Fleet Activities, Sasebo, into light lift craft (LLC), each capable of bow lifts of 25 tons. In addition, a covered lighter (YFNB) was converted into a salvage tender with shops, fire fighting equipment, demolition materials, salvage machinery and equipment, offices, and living accommodations.

Meanwhile, intensive effort was focused upon the task of obtaining qualified personnel in the shortest time possible. Commander Mitchell spent much time in locating the best salvors available anywhere in the Navy. The

NH–74176

*Light lift craft converted from LCU for service in Vietnam.*

result was indeed an elite group. A nucleus of this group was in Subic even before the HLCs were ready.

I proposed a basic plan for control of Harbor Clearance Unit One, whereby it was placed directly under COMSERVPAC's operational control, except for teams deployed to Vietnam or teams on a salvage operation elsewhere. When teams of the unit were in Vietnam, they were placed under the operational control of Commander Naval Forces, Vietnam; and when on a salvage operation elsewhere in the Far East, they were placed under the operational control of CTF 73 (COMSERVGRU Three), under Commander Seventh Fleet. COMSEVENTHFLT and COMNAVFORV concurred, and CINCPACFLT approved the concept.

Personnel were outfitted and trained to work under combat conditions. And, as soon as the HLCs were ready, training in the specialized techniques of lift operations commenced using submerged hulks in the Subic area.

The normal policy was to keep two HLCs in the Subic Bay area for maintenance and training and to rotate them from time to time to Vietnam, where two were stationed, normally at Vung Tau.

In 1967, additional personnel and craft were provided to meet the increasing needs of river warfare in Vietnam, and in particular to permit assigning detachments to the Mobile Riverine Forces during major operations. With the goal of achieving improved capabilities in underwater salvage at deep depths, COMSERVPAC obtained permission for six divers of HCU–1 to participate in trials of an advanced diving system, ADS IV. While on a

K–79477

Crilley *(YHLC–1), with* Crandell *(YHLC–2) in the background—two modern heavy lift craft acquired from Germany.*

"saturation dive" conducting a bottom survey of the future site of SeaLab III, Chief Boatswain's Mate Richard Villasenor set a U.S. Navy open sea diving record of 440 feet. The air transportable system was leased and deployed at Subic Bay where training was conducted in readiness for possible requirements in the future. Using *Safeguard* as a platform for the ADS IV system, the wreckage of an A–3 aircraft was recovered from 136 feet of water in Subic Bay in September 1967.

By now the Harbor Clearance Unit's strength had increased to 29 officers and 231 enlisted men, with six teams, the four Admiralty lift craft, five light craft, two diving boats, and a net tender specially configured for salvage work with the riverine operations. To improve the capability even further, two modern heavy lift craft with a lift capacity of 2,500 tons each were purchased from a German firm. These, the world famous *Energie* and *Andauer*, which had been work horses of the Suez operation, became, on 15 October, YHLCs 1 and 2, named *Crilley* and *Crandall* after two former divers who had been awarded Congressional Medals of Honor.

## ACCELERATING TEMPO OF SALVAGE OPERATIONS

The year 1966 was to be a busy one. It started with the recovery of a large MSTS transport ship, USNS *Sultan* which had, on 14 January, grounded on Rukon Shoal at the entrance to Naha, Okinawa. Rear Admiral Janney and his salvage officer flew immediately to the scene. Using indigenous resources, Army tugs, improvised beach gear, and shore–based construction machinery, *Sultan* was refloated two days later and proceeded under her own power to Sasebo for repairs.

PCF–4, sunk by a mine in the Gulf of Siam, was raised by salvage personnel of *Krishna* on 17 February 1966, in an operation subjected to periodic VC sniper fire. Later that month, SS *Sea Raven*, a Panamanian registry T–1 tanker owned by Esso International, grounded at Chu Lai. The ship's engine room and pump room were flooded to a depth of twelve feet. Dewatering and pulling with beach gear by USS *Reclaimer* (ARS–42) and USS *Bolster* (ARS–38) resulted in successful refloating on 5 March.

On 11 March, USS *Summit County* (LST–1146) ran aground at Chu Lai, puncturing her hull and flooding the engine room. *Hitchiti* divers installed a patch, made temporary repairs, and, when weather permitted, towed the LST out of the river. *Bolster* made the tow to Sasebo. Then on 18 March, USNS *Cassotot*, a T–2 tanker, went aground off the entrance of

Pearl Harbor. The ship was refloated with the help of harbor tugs the same day.

The first operation by personnel of Harbor Clearance Unit One was in mid–April when an underwater bridge sectioning was completed for the Naval Support Activity, Danang. In late April, Harbor Clearance Team One (four officers and thirty enlisted men) deployed to Vung Tau with one light lift craft. Another Viet Cong trawler was forced ashore on the southern tip of Vietnam on 13 May. Under gunfire from the enemy, Harbor Clearance Team One and LLC–1 salvaged the contraband cargo.

## EXCELLENCY

A major offshore salvage job presented itself when SS *Excellency*, a 15,000–ton cargo ship owned by the U.S. Department of Commerce, grounded on Triton Island in the Paracels on 24 April. *Bolster, Reclaimer,* USS *Coucal* (ASR–8), USS *Ute* (ATF–76) and Service Group Three's salvage officer were dispatched to the scene. The ship was found to be hard aground forward with twenty fathoms of water under the stern. After unloading several hundred tons of critical Air Force ammunition into an LST, with *Bolster, Reclaimer* and *Ute* heaving on six sets of beach gear, and with *Coucal* pulling on her engines, *Excellency* was refloated 30 April.

Meanwhile SS *Washington Maid* and SS *Ohio* had collided 200 miles southwest of Inchon on 26 April. USS *Surfbird* (ADG–383) followed the former to Inchon and rendered damage control assistance.

## RIVER CLEARANCE

The first use of heavy lift craft was when a team was sent up the Mekong to My Tho on 20 May to commence work on removal of an 850–ton French ship sunk there in World War II. Two heavy lift craft and a second team were sent from Subic, arriving on 4 June. The operation was successfully completed on 14 June. The star on this and many other major harbor clearance operations was Lieutenant Billie L. Delanoy. While the operation was still in progress, six divers from the team were diverted for a time to Saigon to search for limpet mines on ships moored in the Saigon River.

In the mid–Pacific, USS *Radford* (DD–446) had gone aground on 25 May off Pearl Harbor. With the help of *Hitchiti*, USS *Deliver* (ARS–23) and four harbor tugs, she was refloated the same day. Two days later

1116799

*Two of the four old heavy lift craft, leased from the British, raise the hull of French ship* Paul Bert *at My Tho.*

*Safeguard* and a YFN with an embarked crane recovered parts from a Marine fighter which had crashed in Kaneohe Bay.  SS *Gertrude Therese* grounded on 6 June at Adele Island off Darby on the northern coast of Australia.  U.S. Navy cargo on board, consisting of high frequency radio transmitters destined for the Northwest Cape Facility, was valued at ten million dollars.  The SERVGRUTHREE salvage officer flew to the scene.  Four and a half hours after arrival of *Reclaimer*, she and commercial tug *Zuna* refloated the ship.

Back in Vietnam, SS *Baton Rouge Victory*, under charter to MSTS and proceeding with a full load of U.S. Government cargo en route from Vung Tau to Saigon, was severely damaged by a Viet Cong mine in the Long Tau River.  Seven days later, using two heavy lift craft, Harbor Clearance Unit One refloated the damaged ship from a precarious position in the Long Tau River and beached her in the estuary near Vung Tau.  Bodies of seven missing crewmen were recovered and valuable cargo off–loaded.  The large damaged area was patched; *Baton Rouge Victory* was refloated and

NH–74183

*Lieutenant DeLanoy is awarded the Bronze Star for the key role he played in salvage operations.*

towed to Singapore for repairs. Later in August, a barge sank with a load of ammunition on board, blocking the entrance to Cat Lo. It was raised by Harbor Clearance Team Two with the help of a light lift craft (LLC–2).

On 12 September, *Desal II*, a 10,000–ton barge en route from the United States to Japan and under tow by a civilian tug, became adrift and grounded on Wake Island. Using compressed air, *Safeguard* refloated the barge and towed it to Pearl Harbor.

On 1 October, a Vietnamese monitor sank near Vinh Long in sixty feet of water as the result of a hull leak. Harbor Clearance Unit One and a heavy lift craft (HLC–2) raised the craft. This was the first of three operations to be conducted by Harbor Clearance Unit One that month. On 12 October, when a tear in the shell plating of SS *Clarksburg Victory* resulted in flooding the engine room, Harbor Clearance Unit personnel patched the hull and dewatered the space. Then on 20 October, LLC–3 was used by Teams One and Five to remove an old sunken Dutch dredge which was partially blocking the Danang River.

## PRAIRIE GROVE

A particularly difficult rescue tow was required when SS *Prairie Grove*, a jumboized T–2 tanker carrying a U.S. Government cargo of jet fuel to Japan, under MSTS charter, lost a propeller about sixty miles south of Adak on 19 October 1966. USS *Cree* (ATF–84) took the ship in tow in heavy weather. Encountering 20–foot seas, *Cree's* tow wire parted on the fourth night. By next morning *Cree* had the ship back in tow using the emergency nylon towing hawser. Despite the heavy going, *Cree* recovered 1,700 feet of tow wire splicing and "end for ending" it. On the sixth day the tow was back on the main tow wire. Later the tow was transferred to a Japanese tug.

November was another busy month, starting on 2 November when a minesweeper (MSB–54) was sunk by enemy fire in the Long Tau River. The Harbor Clearance Unit raised the wreck with LLC–2 and delivered it to Saigon. Submarine USS *Tiru* (SS–416) grounded on 3 November in the Coral Sea. COMSERVGRUTHREE was airlifted to the scene. With the help of civilian tug *Carlock* and HMAS *Vendetta*, pulling in tandem, *Tiru* was refloated. On 7 November, SS *Old Westbury* suffered a boiler casualty 850 miles northeast of Guam and was towed to Guam first by USS *Sunnadin* (ATA–197) and, when fuel was low, by USS *Wandank* (ATA–204). Also in November, HCU–1 personnel salvaged an Army barge (BC–644), which had capsized near Vung Tau.

In December, there were a series of instances off the coast of Vietnam in which resupply barges were lost by their towing ships in heavy northeast monsoonal seas and grounded on the storm–tossed shore. After being cast adrift in a storm, YFRN–412 went on the beach 2,000 yards north of the Perfume River on the coast of Vietnam. In the face of the heavy surf, USS *Arikara* (ATF–98) landed a salvage party and patched and pumped the pounding barge. Beach gear was laid and the barge hauled to seaward when she struck a sand bar. Further hauling resulted in refloating. Salvage jobs such as this in heavy surf off a lee shore required a particularly high degree of seamanship, courage, and salvage skill. A MSTS barge grounded off Vung Ro on 4 December, and motor vessel *Tiburon* broached and capsized at Cua Viet on 30 December. Salvage ships were dispatched to the scenes, but in each case the owners decided the salvage not to be worth the cost. SS *Sea Train Texas* was mined while at anchor at Nha Be on 21 December. Harbor Clearance Unit One completed emergency repairs the next day.

## MAHNOMEN COUNTY

The first operation of 1967 was not rewarded with success despite valiant efforts for a full month. On New Year's Eve 1966, an LST anchored off Chu Lai, USS *Mahnomen County* (LST–912), had suffered a broken anchor chain in a sudden shift in the weather, and broached parallel to the beach off Rosemary Point. Harbor Clearance Unit One personnel were dispatched to the scene along with *Grapple*, *Sioux*, and Commander Service Group Three's salvage officer, at the time Commander John Orem, Jr. The LST was found hard aground in an extremely rocky section with high seas breaking over the ship. Northeast monsoon weather was full blown with winds up to 45 knots and surf 12 to 18 feet high.

The salvage forces labored continuously under extremely hazardous conditions, employing all possible salvage techniques. Quantities of foam, first used in the *Frank Knox* operation, were flown to the scene, and blasting of rocks on the seaward side was attempted. One member of the team, C. G. Gordon, AO1, lost his life as a result of disregard of his own safety in helping a man in distress in the engine room. Finally in mid–January, with all bottom tanks open to the seas, and *Mahnomen County* breaking up, the effort had to be abandoned. On 31 January 1967, the ship was stricken from the *Naval Vessel Register*, and later stripped and demolished.

## JAMAICA BAY

Meanwhile, a large dredge well along in years, *Jamaica Bay*, had been severely damaged and sunk in the Mekong during a pre–dawn attack by VC swimmers on 9 January. The dredge blocked the approach to the LST ramp to be employed in support of the Dong Tam base, then under construction. Dredging operations in the base development would have been severely handicapped unless the *Jamaica Bay* hulk could be removed by early March, when the replacement dredge *New Jersey* was due to arrive.

After sinking, *Jamaica Bay* rested on her starboard spud at a 30 degree port list in 35 feet of water, which rose at high tide to the dredge's 03 level.[2] The force of the explosion had blown large holes on both quarters and created general weakness in the hull. About forty years old, the dredge had no watertight subdivisions; open from the keel to the 01 level, she was

---

[2] The third level above the main deck.

NH-74178

*Refloating* Jamaica Bay.

compared to a bathtub full of water. In view of the importance of the job
and expected difficulties, I sent the Fleet Salvage Officer, Commander
E. B. Mitchell, to the scene, much to his pleasure.

The extremely difficult job of floating the wreck started on 10 January.
Following an around–the–clock effort, seven days a week, by 167 dedicated
officers and men of Harbor Clearance Unit One, *Jamaica Bay* was finally
towed from the scene on 12 March. The technical aspects of the job were
extremely complex in that refloating by conventional patching and pumping
was not feasible.

Lifting operations on *Jamaica Bay* commenced on 5 February, marked
the first time the U.S. Navy had used four lift craft in a simultaneous
lift operation. There was only one other known instance in the world of
such a lift. Operations were hampered when HLC–2 sank during the night
after being holed by a jagged projection from the wreck. The craft was
refloated and restored to operation in only one week.

Never have diving conditions been more difficult. Silt in the water was
so dense that zero visibility prevailed at depths of more than about one foot
below the surface, and all underwater work had to be accomplished by feel.
Swift currents made it difficult for the divers to remain in position, and

jagged edges of plating protruding out from the damaged area increased the hazards. A further complication was harassing sniper fire, mostly at night. After four rounds of mortar fire landed within 100 yards of the operation, U.S. Army Ninth Infantry Division spotters were positioned on board the salvage craft to direct 105 mm. howitzer fire from the Dong Tam base area.

The lift was accomplished in six steps up a specially dredged gradient 800 feet long. Patching and pump placement operations commenced on 21 February. Pumping operations commenced on 3 March. Cradled between two heavy lift craft, *Jamaica Bay* was refloated on 8 March.

In an unfortunate sequel, *Jamaica Bay*, while being towed by a civilian tug in the open stretch between the Mekong and Vung Tau, was hit by a sudden storm, and began breaking up. When they were ordered to leave the dredge, men of the Harbor Clearance Unit were inside the wreck attempting to stem the flow through cracked seams with their own clothing.

## DIVERSIFIED OPERATIONS

Other important salvage operations were required in January. On the ninth, destroyer *Waddell* damaged both propellers on touching bottom at Midway Island. The ship was towed to Pearl Harbor by USS *Takelma* (ATF–113). On 13 January, *Mataco* extinguished a fire on fishing boat *Mondego* off San Diego. Also, on 13 January, SS *Guam Bear* and SS *Esso Victory* collided off Apra Harbor. With a 30–foot hole extending from gunwhale to keel and engine room flooded, *Guam Bear* was towed into the harbor and beached alongside the breakwater. Personnel from USS *Grasp* (ARS–24) and the Ship Repair Facility laid beach gear promptly, thus preventing her from sliding into deep water. Valuable cargo was removed. Out in Vietnam on that same fateful 13th (14 January west of the date-line), MSB–14, rammed and sunk by a French ship, *Mui Finn*, was refloated by LCC–2.

Then SS *Teh Hu*, 1,900 miles northwest of Pearl Harbor, suffered an engine room explosion. *Greenlet* and *Florikan* rendered assistance and towed the ship toward Japan for a rendezvous with a commercial tug.

On 16 February an EC–135 airplane crashed off Honolulu. To help the Air Force to determine the cause, pieces and parts of the plane were recovered by *Reclaimer* and *Hitchiti*. On 3 March it was a Marine F–8U in Kaneohe Bay. *Deliver* recovered the components. On 21 March, it was an Air Force F–102 which crashed off Pearl Harbor. Again the job was done by *Deliver*. Also in March, *Reclaimer* had a rescue tow when SS *Norbega* lost propulsion 510 miles east of Midway. Next, it was SS *Oceanic Tide* which had lost power 700 miles northwest of Pearl Harbor. *Deliver* was successful in saving the ship and, with portable generators, the refrigerated U.S. Government cargo. The ship was towed to Honolulu. In still another operation that month, *Sioux* picked up SS *Evanthie* south of Tokyo Bay and towed her toward Yokohama until relieved by a Japanese tug.

In April, *Conserver* used one set of beach gear to refloat LCU–1500 from Molokai. USS *Current* (ARS–22) recovered LCM–8 which had broached at Qui Nhon. On the twelfth, MV *Amastra*, a general purpose tanker of 18,000 tons and British registry, was mined at Nha Trang. An 8–foot hole was blown in the port quarter in the area of the engine room, the ship settling until the stern was awash. *Current*, *Greenlet*, and Commander J. B. Orem were ordered to the scene. A temporary patch was put in place and the engine room was dewatered. Sufficient diesel oil was transferred to another tanker to raise the damage area and install a permanent patch so that the ship could be towed away for repairs.

In a subsequent operation that month, Harbor Clearance Team Three (HCT–3) and *Greenlet* recovered bodies, personal effects, and weapons from an AC–141 aircraft which crashed off Cam Ranh Bay on 14 April. HCT–3 repeated the job when an Army helicopter crashed in the same area a week later, and then recovered remnants of a Navy US–2C aircraft which crashed at An Thoi on 12 May.

### MINOT VICTORY

The next major salvage job was that resulting from the grounding of MSTS chartered SS *Minot Victory* on North Reef in the Paracels on 16 May. The ship was found to be about 1,700 tons aground forward on coral and limestone. An ARS, three ATFs, an ATA, and the Service Group Three salvage officer were ordered to the scene. Tanks were deballasted and fuel removed. *Tawakoni* (ATF–114) and *Mataco* (ATF–86), the first on the scene laid beach gear, but pulled without success. Vietnam–destined cargo was off–loaded to a converted LST which had been towed to the scene from Danang. Four sets of beach gear were then laid and connected to the wreck. *Current*, with two sets of beach gear, pulled with *Mahopac* in tandem; *Mataco* with one set of beach gear, *Tawakoni* with another set, and

*Hitchiti* in tandem also pulled. The first attempt on 21 May failed, but a second try two days later succeeded.

On 10 June, HCT–5 refloated an Army barge section sunk off Vung Tau. Then, on 25 June, the team, with the help of LLC–2 and USS *Oak Hill* (LSD–7) refloated a Swift boat (PCF–97) sunk off the coast.

It was on 29 June that LST *Coconino County* was mined at the ramp inside the mouth of the Cua Viet River. Busy *Hitchiti* delivered her to Danang for repairs. On the same day, fleet tug *Molala* was herself the embarrassed victim when she suffered a main propulsion casualty heading back from Yokosuka toward Pearl Harbor from a highly successful tour with the Seventh Fleet. A SERVPAC Store Ship, USS *Aludra* (AF–55), performed the rescue on 3 July and transferred the ship to USS *Lipan* (ATF–106) two days later to complete the tow to Hawaii.

In Subic Bay it was discovered that the hulk of the old cruiser, *Rochester* which had been towed out from the pier and sunk as the Japanese approached early in World War II, lay at the site planned for a fuel transfer buoy to accommodate large tankers. Harbor Clearance Unit One demolished the wreck with explosives.

It was in August 1967 that Harbor Clearance Unit One received the Navy Unit Commendation. Craft and personnel of the unit in Vietnam worked on a variety of salvage operations that month. These included assistance to the Riverine Assault Force for the recovery of equipment, search for an Army utility landing craft ramp off An Thoi, Army mechanized landing craft salvage operations at Tan An, and truck recovery at My Tho.

It was on 23 August that *Hitchiti* joined USS *Asheville* (PG–84) at Danang to escort her to Yokosuka for repair of a casualty to her main propulsion transmission system. Three days later when just south of Taiwan, *Hitchiti* took *Asheville* in tow and commenced evading Typhoon Marge. The two ships later retired to Subic Bay.

## STONER

SS *R.C. Stoner*, a Standard Oil tanker, ran aground at Wake Island on 5 September 1967, with 130,000 barrels of aviation fuel on board. Immediately after grounding, *Stoner* commenced leaking fuel into the sea, onto the beach, and into the small boat harbor causing a serious fire hazard. All but key personnel left the ship. U.S. Coast Guard Cutter *Mallow* was diverted to Wake and *Conserver* sailed from Pearl Harbor to render assistance.

*Mataco* en route from the Western Pacific was also diverted to the scene and I sent Commander Orem, who had relieved Commander Mitchell as Fleet Salvage Officer. Pumps were air shipped from Pearl Harbor.

A detailed survey conducted on 7 September revealed that the after steering room, the engine room, a cofferdam and six tanks were holed and flooding. The ship had assumed a 10 degree list broadside to the reef. USS *Noxubee* (AOG–56) was diverted to the scene on 7 September to assist in off–loading fuel. *Grapple* sailed from Pearl harbor and USS *Wandank* (ATA–204) from Guam. Harbor Clearance Team Two flew in from Subic. However, the effects of rough surf took their toll before recovery forces could get control of the situation, and *Stoner* commenced breaking up on 8 September. Six days later, the owners declared the ship a total loss, and the salvage personnel removed masts from the wreck because of their interference with the island's aircraft instrument landing system.

Typhoon Sarah hit Wake Island the next day with winds up to 145 knots, creating extensive damage. The salvage forces rendered invaluable assistance, providing the initial power for radio and telephone systems with their power packs, and repairing critical damage.

NH–74180

*SS R.C. Stoner.*

After the storm the salvors flattened the wreck. This proved to be more than routine, for, in addition to high winds and high seas, sharks added to the hazards. For reasons never explained, large numbers would gather at the wreck each time an explosive charge was detonated. Possibly the answer lay in the occasional use of the stunning effects of explosives in the South Pacific for fishing.

Operations in the Western Pacific continued at a high rate that fall. On 18 September, *Grasp* assisted in refloating the 378–foot Chinese Navy Dry-dock Number One in Tsoying Harbor, Taiwan. On 2 October submarine USS *Diodon* (SS–349) suffered a fire and propulsion casualty south of Japan. *Hitchiti* went to the scene and towed *Diodon* to Yokosuka. The next day USNS *Geiger* went aground at Danang. Fuel and troops were off–loaded. Dredge *Davidson* removed sand along the port bow, and USS *Abnaki* (ATF–96) refloated *Geiger* with the help of two sets of beach gear.

In anticipation of the increased demands on the monsoon and the critical situation in northern I Corps in the fall of 1967, CINCPACFLT approved my recommendation to deploy an additional salvage ship to the Western Pacific until spring. The deployment of USS *Bolster* (ARS–38) permitted the continuous stationing of such a ship at Danang starting 24 October. In addition to the many salvage tasks, *Bolster* helped in the repair of off-shore fuel lines damaged by the seas.

On 6 November, Coastal Patrol Craft, PCF–76, broached and sank 200 yards off the Cua Viet River. Her crew was rescued by a Naval Support Activity amphibious craft, a pusher boat, and a helicopter. On 4 November one Army reefer barge and two fuel barges washed ashore at Duc Pho and were refloated by the Naval Support Activity. LCU–1494 broached at Duc Pho. She was retracted and towed to Danang by *Bolster*.

On 16 December YC–51, aground near Danang, was refloated and towed to Danang. Also in December, USS *Chowanoc* (ATF–100) sailed from Adak to assist disabled SS *Steel Flyer*. Although damaged while passing a line in heavy seas, she towed the ship toward Seattle until met by a civilian tug. During *Chowanoc*'s absence, *Hitchiti* went north from Pearl Harbor to assume the duties of a northern Pacific search and rescue ship.

## GUARDFISH

There would be one more difficult salvage job before the year came to an end. On Christmas Eve, nuclear submarine *Guardfish* (SSN–612) went aground on a trough of hard coral east of the entrance buoy to Pearl Harbor, in storm weather. *Current*, Captain T. Grabowski (then COMSERV-RONFIVE), and the Fleet Salvage Officer were on their way within half an hour. *Current* was soon joined by *Grapple* and four harbor tugs (YTB–761, YTB–657, YTM–757, and YTM–195). On 25 December, USS *Arikara* (ATF–98) joined the salvage group. There being no suitable fittings for the purpose, the after escape truck upper hatch of *Guardfish* was removed and a tow wire was reeved through it. With *Grapple* and *Current* pulling to two sets of beach gear, a start was made on Christmas Day. The day after, with *Arikara* also pulling, *Guardfish* pivoted on coral heads and was pulled slowly clear.

The high tempo of salvage operations continued in 1968, but the story will end here. Needless to say, the salvors far more than paid their way with their unsurpassed performance, their professionalism, and valor.

CHAPTER XV

# Surveillance and Special Operations

Shortly after reaching my quarters in Makalapa on the evening of 22 January 1968, the Service Force duty officer advised me of a message just received by the Commander in Chief, U.S. Pacific Fleet, indicating USS *Pueblo* (AGER–2) was being approached by North Korean men of war. I had a double check made to ensure that Admiral Hyland, then CINCPAC-FLT, or his deputy, Vice Admiral Baumberger, had the word and asked to be kept up–to–date. Additional messages advised of an order to "Heave to or I will fire" and one to "Follow my wake, I have pilot aboard." Other information was received of MIG aircraft overhead, a boarding attempt, being fired upon, and the serious condition of a man who had lost his leg.

*Pueblo* was a Service Force intelligence collection ship on her first operation. Later the full story would unfold of how the ship was led inside the 12–mile limit claimed as territorial waters by North Korea, boarded, and captured; of enemy acquisition of intelligence equipment and documents; of the lack of a military response on the part of the United States; and of compromising actions at the national level to gain return of the crew.

Individual ships had from time to time been given intelligence gathering duties as secondary functions, but it was only recently that intelligence collection ships had appeared as a specific type. To some extent we were following the lead of the Soviets who had long been gathering electronic and other intelligence by specially equipped trawlers, designated AGIs. These often operated in the vicinity of our carriers on Yankee Station and off Guam, Hawaii, the coast of the United States, and other strategic locations.

The first intelligence collection ships assigned to the Service Force were *Oxford* and *Jamestown*, two Liberty ships, converted into "Auxiliary General Technical Research Ships" (AGTRs). USS *Oxford* (AGTR–1) arrived in the Western Pacific on 3 June 1965, and USS *Jamestown* (AGTR–3) on 2 January 1966. They were employed in the South China Sea area most of the time. It was a sister ship, *Liberty*, that was attacked and severely damaged by Israeli aircraft in the eastern Mediterranean in June 1967.

*Pueblo* was the second of a smaller type designated "General Environmental Research Vessels" (AGERs). Equipped for signal and electronic intelligence, and for the collection of hydrographic information, the AGERs were conversions from auxiliary light cargo ships (AKLs) which had originally been constructed for the Army in World War II under an "FS" designation. Previous mention has been made of the important resupply functions carried out for the Naval Support Activity, Saigon, by two AKLs, *Mark* and *Brule*.

## BANNER

The first of the class was USS *Banner* (AGER–1). As AKL–25, *Banner*'s duties had been those of transporting supplies throughout the Trust Territories. In July 1965, she was transferred from Commander Naval Forces, Marianas, to Commander Service Force, U.S. Pacific Fleet, and ordered back for alterations.

Conversion by the Puget Sound Naval Shipyard, Bremerton, Washington, under the leadership of the extremely capable Rear Admiral Floyd B. Shultz, had been done expertly and in a surprisingly short period of time.

NH–74181

Banner, *the first of the "environmental research ships."*

*Banner* (now AGER–1) deployed to Yokosuka, joining Service Squadron Three under Commander Service Group Three. Placed under the operational control of Commander Naval Forces, Japan, who in turn was directly under the Commander in Chief, U.S. Pacific Fleet, she commenced her first surveillance patrol on 30 October 1965.

The organization of the AGERs and the AGTRs was abnormal. Each had a security group detachment with responsibilities to the Naval Security Group in Washington and the National Security Agency, who determined the equipment to be installed and the tasks to be performed. Under the tight cloak of secrecy, the security group operated in a semi–autonomous fashion. Until it was changed as a result of recommendations from Pearl Harbor, the head of the detachment in *Banner* was higher in rank than the commanding officer, a potentially awkward situation even though the former was not eligible for command at sea. Fortunately, the Commanding Officer, Lieutenant Robert Bishop, was one who assumed full authority without interfering unduly with the intelligence responsibilities of the security group. Under him and his successor, Commander Charles R. Clark, USS *Banner* performed exceptionally well in carrying out many missions in the Far East.

It was as a result of the achievements of *Banner* that a decision was made to convert two more ships to the AGER configuration. FS–344 from Mare Island and FS–217 from Norfolk were towed to Bremerton for the conversion. One was to become the ill–fated USS *Pueblo* (AKL–44), later AGER–2. The other, *Palm Beach*, was to be sent to the Atlantic Fleet.

## PUEBLO

As is customary in the case of ships about to be commissioned, the Prospective Commanding Officer, Commander L. M. Bucher, reported to the Commandant, Thirteenth Naval District until the end of the fitting out period. During the conversion period, Captain A. S. Chapman, my Force Maintenance Officer, and others of his staff followed the conversion closely and visited the ship a number of times to check her progress although, unlike normal ships, spaces and equipment associated with the intelligence mission were so highly classified that members of my staff could not view them or the associated plans. Where other areas of the ship were involved, they attempted to uncover potential difficulties, advise the commanding officer, and assist in getting support for corrective measures.

In sharp contrast with *Banner*'s experience, difficulties and delays were encountered, apparently stemming from many design changes and improper installation of intelligence equipment. Following their visits Captain Chapman and his people gave me favorable reports concerning Commander Bucher and the job he was doing during this period. It was clear that he was highly aggressive in raising issues and trying to get everything possible done for his ship. I considered this to be to his credit, despite hints that a more diplomatic approach might sometimes have produced better results.

One matter of concern that arose during conversion was the lack of a ready means for scuttling the ship. Captain Chapman reported to me that during a trip to Puget Sound he had "discussed with the officers of both ships means of scuttling the ship rapidly. *Pueblo* and *Palm Beach* are single compartment ships and would sink rapidly if the engine space was flooded. I recommended that the engineer keep a sledge hammer in the engine room so sea valves could be knocked away from the skin of the ship." In Captain Chapman's view, scuttling by this means could be "accomplished with dispatch in an emergency."

After being placed in commission, *Pueblo* conducted shakedown training under the Training Command in San Diego. Before World War II such training had been the commanding officer's direct responsibility. Then, because of the large number of inexperienced officers during the massive expansion of that war, Training Commands had been established in each ocean. In the case of *Pueblo*, security considerations excluded the Training Command's overseeing of training in intelligence operations. Subject to certain remarks, the shakedown training report concluded that *Pueblo* was "ready for unrestricted operations."

Next, a predeployment readiness inspection was conducted in the San Diego area by Commander Service Group One. The latter indicated that the deficiencies uncovered were easily correctable and that the ship was ready for unrestricted operations. One discrepancy of concern in the report, "to be corrected as soon as possible thereafter," required action to "promulgate emergency destruction bill, post in all spaces, provide weighted bags where needed."

A *Pueblo* letter of 9 June 1967 included a request for an explosive destruction device to destroy sensitive and classified equipment quickly. In addition to a favorable recommendation, the COMSERVPAC endorsement instructed the commanding officer "to initiate a jettison and destruction bill for sensitive materials and to conduct periodic exercises to ensure proficiency." Prior to receipt of the endorsements up the chain of command, which took abnormally long, the Office of the Chief of Naval Operations had directed the installation of a destruction device. This order was reversed, however, and reference made to other means to achieve destruction, as a result of advice by the Naval Ship Systems Command concerning the effectiveness of certain specific equipment.

As was customary, officers from various sections of my staff boarded the ship when she arrived in Pearl Harbor in November 1967, to see what needed to be done to help her attain the best possible state of readiness for operations in the forward area. A matter of particular concern was the recurring difficulties the ship had been having with her steering engine. Troubles were analyzed and an effort was made to get problems rectified by the Pearl Harbor Naval Shipyard, but their efforts to determine the basic cause and effect corrective measures were unsuccessful in the two days available. My staff then made the arrangements whereby the repairs were accomplished later in Yokosuka.

Officers and men of the ship came up to the headquarters for briefings. Normally these would have covered the full gambit of operations and support in WESTPAC. In this case, the basic briefing on operations was done by CINCPACFLT's staff in view of the highly classified and specialized nature of the mission.

Commander Bucher paid a long call on me, during which the problems and conditions of the ship and the training of her crew were discussed. Although not fully informed of the details of the operations of the intelligence ships, I discussed the harassment *Banner* had experienced on certain missions and the measures taken, including the presence of a protecting destroyer on one occasion. With this in mind, I stressed the importance of learning all he could from *Banner*'s captain. He told me of gaining some knowledge of the operations in a previous assignment, of having already had discussions with Lieutenant Bishop, and of the receipt of later information by mail.

In discussing deficiencies uncovered in the predeployment inspection, I was concerned to learn that the bill for destruction and disposal of classified material had not yet been completed. He advised me it would soon be ready. When in Yokosuka, he finally reported completion, including the receipt of weighted bags.

Aside from the delay in the destruction bill, my overall reaction to the conference with Commander Bucher was very favorable. He impressed me with his knowledge of his ship, with his statements of the actions he was taking to ready the ship for operations in the Western Pacific, and with the impression of dedication and resoluteness he conveyed.

Unable to inspect his ship that afternoon, I sent Captain Dan Drain, my Chief of Staff, who was given special clearance to inspect the security spaces. Captain Drain reported that "Bucher, and all the other officers on board, were intensely proud of the ship and expressed pleasure to me of all the support they were receiving." The reports of others of the staff were equally favorable. I paid a short visit next morning before the ship's departure, although the captain was not then on board. My aide, Lieutenant Commander Frederick J. Howell, accompanied me but was restrained from following me into the security spaces. *Pueblo* was in shipshape condition and all I saw gave an impression of high morale on the part of the crew and pride in their jobs.

As in the case of other SERVPAC ships homeported in the Western Pacific, once *Pueblo* crossed the date line she became a part of Service Squadron Three under Rear Admiral N. G. Ward, who had taken over this job after his tour in Vietnam. However, in this case his command responsibilities were somewhat diluted, in comparison with those to do with other types of ships in his squadron, as a result of the extraordinary rules having to do with the intelligence activities and the special tasks directed by CINCPACFLT and Commander Naval Forces, Japan.

After leaving Pearl Harbor, the Chief of Naval Operations directed the installation of two 50–caliber machine guns, which were mounted when the ship was in Yokosuka. My message of 18 December directed the ship "to conduct test firings and gun crew training to insure weapons can be employed effectively."

Other ships deployed to the Western Pacific, including *Oxford* and *Jamestown*, were normally under the operational control of Commander Seventh Fleet. The situation was different in regard to *Banner* and *Pueblo*. Although the former had on occasion operated as part of the Seventh Fleet, during the vast majority of the time she was under the operational control of Commander Naval Forces, Japan, Rear Admiral Frank L. Johnson, who was designated Commander Task Force 96. In addition to having operational control of *Pueblo*, the latter had responsibilities to do with preparing and instructing the ship for her coming operations.

The capture and subsequent events have been recorded in the Court of Inquiry and a report by a Congressional subcommittee. In this book I shall not attempt to analyze or pass judgment on the actions taken off Korea and those during imprisonment. It is clear, however, that the image of United States resolve suffered, especially in the Orient. The long term effects are hard to assess, but the events brought to mind the underestimation of our resolve by Germans in decisions pertaining to the U–boat attacks leading up to World War I and a similar underestimation of American reactions on the part of the Japanese in their decision to attack Pearl Harbor. The events also brought to mind an earlier stage in our history when, on 29 December 1798, the Secretary of the Navy issued a circular to commanders of vessels, stating:

> It is the positive command of the President, that on no pretense whatever, you permit the public Vessel of War under your Command, to be detained, or searched, nor any of the Officers and men belonging to her, to be taken from her, by the Ships or Vessels of any Foreign Nation, so long as you are in a capacity to repel such outrage on the honor of the American Flag; —If force should be exerted to compel your Submission, you are to resist that force to the utmost of your power. . . .[1]

In the actions which followed seizure of *Pueblo*, the Service Force had its usual roles to play. Underway replenishment ships were deployed north in anticipation of possible action, carrying specially tailored loads of ammunition. An earlier decision by the Secretary of Defense was soon reversed in order to reconstitute stocks of ammunition in northeast Asia, stocks which had been depleted to meet Southeast Asia needs.

### "BLOCKING SHIPS"

In turn, the Soviet collection ships created additional tasks for Service Force units. The Pacific Fleet kept track of these ships particularly when they were near our forces or our bases. At such times as they engaged in operations in Hawaiian waters or close to the West Coast of the United States, it invariably was a fleet tug (ATF) or a salvage ship (ARS) that was assigned to assure that the Soviet ship stayed outside of the three mile limit and did nothing unlawful. These were fairly uneventful operations, but the situation in the Western Pacific was quite another matter.

Most of the time, such a Soviet ship was stationed near our Task Force

---

[1] U.S. Office of Naval Records and Library, *Naval Documents Related to the Quasi-War between the United States and France: Naval Operations from November 1798 to March 1799* (Washington: GPO, 1935), p. 135.

77 in the Tonkin Gulf. Except when there were special requirements, such an extraordinary salvage demands, a fleet tug or salvage ship would be assigned as "blocking ship." It was the duty of the "blocking ship" to counter the collection effort when practicable, and to prevent interference with carrier flight operations. To do the latter required extensive knowledge of the Rules of the Road, great skill in seamanship and ship handling, and a willingness to take risks.

A proper interpretation of the Rules of the Road would have meant that the Soviet ship would have kept clear of carriers engaged in launching and recovering aircraft, and displaying the appropriate international signal. Instead, the Soviet SIGINT ships would often attempt to create situations where the carrier might be influenced to make radical maneuvers. It was the job of the "blocking ship" to prevent such interference. The result was what resembled a "dog fight" by the ships concerned, as the "blocking ship" would attempt to interpose itself so as to become the "privileged" ship under International Law. In such battles of determination, the ships at times would close to within a few feet from collision before the Soviets would break off.

K–86133

*Fleet ocean tug (ATF).*

The greatest challenges usually occurred when a new "blocking ship" arrived on the scene. Then, like a small boy at a new school, the SIGINT ship would test the resolve and abilities of the newly arrived captain. Once the latter had proved that he had what it took, the challenges subsided. Almost without exception our captains were completely successful against their skilled opponents. These Service Force captains gained great respect from others at Yankee Station, and on a number of occasions, received high praise for their determination and skill.

## SURVEY OPERATIONS

Among those conducting important missions in Vietnam waters were the Service Force's survey ships. Charts of the Vietnam coast, based as they were on old French charts, were incomplete and the outpourings of rivers and actions of the seas had created significant changes in contours and depths in the coastal areas. Vice Admiral Paul P. Blackburn, Jr., Commander Seventh Fleet in 1965, highlighted this as a serious problem, observing that

> in order to provide logistic support from the sea, it is obviously necessary to have good, and current info on harbor facilities, beach gradients, tidal data, meteorological data, etc. In the case of the east coast of Vietnam, this was sparse, non-existent, or badly outdated.

With the roots of the Hydrographic Office going back to 1830, and in the tradition of Matthew F. Maury, the Navy had long been proud of its survey work and the excellence of the charts it produced. With the far-flung operations, the needs of amphibious operations and advanced bases had undergone explosive growth in World War II—with almost 42 million copies of charts having been printed for 1944. Although the needs in Vietnam were relatively modest, they were urgent.

Planning and scheduling hydrographic surveys to meet urgent operational requirements was no longer a simple Navy problem; for reasons I have yet to understand other organizations were now in on the act. By the time of the Vietnam build-up, the Defense Intelligence Agency (DIA) had been established and then assigned the responsibility to develop plans, programs, policies, and procedures for intelligence, mapping, charting, and geodetic programs. DIA's authority extended to the management of hydrographic survey resources, and its functions included the requirement to supervise, determine priorities, and validate requirements. It was responsi-

ble for the assigning and reassigning of survey projects to the Military
Departments.

In any case, by the time I reported, the demands for survey operations
were on the increase. USS *Rehoboth* (AGS–50) returned from the northern Pacific only to be deployed to the Western Pacific a month later for intensive operations in Vietnam waters, assisted by USS *Sunnadin* (ATA–197)
until February 1966.

The deployment of USS *Maury* (AGS–16) and USS *Serrano* (AGS–24)
in November 1965 was met with a flurry of requests. Meeting the requirements posed many challenges. Of eight priority areas, an advance party
found only three secure enough from enemy attack for the fixing of beacons,
and only a limited amount of advanced geodetic work could be done between
operations. Despite strong requests, helicopters were not assigned and had
to be obtained mission by mission.

Surveys were conducted at Cam Ranh Bay, Nha Trang, Phan Rang,
and their approaches, plus an unscheduled operation at the mouth of the
Bassac River. A sound boat was taken under fire on 9 December. Seven
small areas at Vung Tau and Nha Trang were added in January, and a
second Bassac operation required sound boats to operate around the clock.

The ships then moved north to conduct surveys at Chu Lai and the mouth
of the Perfume River. The beach camp at Chu Lai was under fire on
several occasions and a sound boat offshore was hit.

Starting home after a normal tour, *Maury* was recalled to accomplish
another still urgent survey. Only one numbered field chart had been
completed by a survey ship since World War II. On this tour, nine numbered and one unnumbered charts were produced by *Maury*.

Then, with demands still growing, USS *Tanner* (AGS–15), USS *Shel-
drake* (AGS–19), and USS *Towhee* (AGS–28) were transferred to
SERVPAC from the Atlantic in July 1966, and deployed to WESTPAC as
*Maury* and *Serrano* carried out assignments in the middle and eastern
Pacific. Operations in the Far East included surveys off Danang, off Subic
Bay, in the Mekong and Soirap Rivers, off Vung Tau, and in the Rung Sat
Special Zone.

In January 1967, *Maury* and *Serrano* returned to take over the Vietnam
surveys. This time surveys in the Delta were conducted in enemy infested
areas and patrol boat escorts for *Maury*'s sound boats were provided by
Task Force 115. One sound boat received heavy and sustained fire near
the Co Chien River and was holed below the waterline. In February and

March, *Serrano* operated in I Corps where small arms fire was received. There was hardly a letup as operations by both ships continued in the Delta and at selected areas along the coast. Meanwhile, *Maury* produced twelve four–color hydrographic office field charts promptly on the spot, once again proving the value of these ships to naval units operating in strange waters.

## MOBILE COMMUNICATIONS SUPPORT

The post World War II era had brought with it a requirement for tight command and control of deterrent forces and possible nuclear operations. In addition, there was an increasing tendency to centralize even detailed decisions at high levels in Washington, with resultant extraordinary demands for prompt and voluminous information from the scene. Unprecedented demands were placed on radio communications to satisfy the desires for this information and the transmission of orders in detail. Further complications arose from the poor electromagnetic propagation conditions in the South China Sea and the overloaded state of communications facilities in the area.

These demands and conditions created a requirement for mobile communication support of the Seventh Fleet in this area. USS *Annapolis* (AGMR–1) was transferred from the Atlantic to SERVPAC on 13 August 1965 for continuous duty in the Western Pacific. About a year later, USS *Arlington* (AGMR–2) was similarly transferred. Both provided increasingly valuable support to the ships and commands off Vietnam, relaying messages and performing other communications support. As a dividend, these ships repaired teletype and cryptographic repair services as time permitted. No ships spent a higher percentage of their time at sea.

## OTHER OPERATIONS

The variety of operations for Service Force ships seemed to have no end. For example, *Rehoboth, Neptune* (ARC–2) and *Peregrine* (AG–176) were conducting oceanographic surveys, and *Granville S. Hall* (YAG–40) and *George Eastman* (YAG–39) carried out seven ecological, biological, meteorological, and epidemiological surveys.

Still another type of operation had to do with the two icebreakers, which performed many important duties in the northern and southern polar

NH-74450

Annapolis, *first of the communications relay ships.*

regions. Rightly or wrongly, the Navy later got out of this business. These icebreakers were transferred within the next two years to the Coast Guard, along with similar ships from the Atlantic Fleet.

## POSTAL SERVICES

This is probably as good a place as any to mention the all important role of the Service Force in the delivery of mail. With responsibilities for routing and coordinating the mail for the Navy, Marine Corps, and Military Sea Transportation Service—including chartered ships—daily actions were required at the headquarters. Only by keeping up to date on ship movements and changes in plans could mail be rerouted in time. By far the most difficult problems were those to do with MSTS–chartered ships which had frequent diversions unaccompanied by prompt notification. In July 1965, 1,333,786 pounds of mail were processed. The volume doubled in the next year with a peak of 3,628,371. In November and December 1967, 11,133,000 pounds were processed.

Carrying out this responsibility was a complex process involving SERV-PAC's Fleet Post Office in San Francisco, a later detachment in Seattle, Mobile Navy Post Offices, the Navy Post Office at Subic Bay and at fourteen locations in Vietnam, and my staff.

# CHAPTER XVI

# Western Pacific Bases

In earlier chapters, the importance of a maximum of independence of fixed bases on the part of mobile forces of the Navy—ships, task forces, fleets—has been stressed. The high degree of logistic independence of individual ships and their ability to operate in remote areas stem from their design, the nature of the equipment and supplies they carry, and the qualifications of their personnel. And, augmenting the logistic capabilities of the individual ships are units of the Mobile Support Force, the successor to the "fleet train" of old. Fleet independence of shore bases reached a peak in operations of the U.S. Navy in the Pacific in World War II, when ships were kept west of Pearl Harbor almost indefinitely. Only in the case of extensive damage was it felt desirable to return them to the navy yards.

During more normal periods, it is not practical or economical to provide such extensive mobile capabilities as were developed in World War II. Thus, the bases and shore activities established in the Western Pacific after World War II proved to be of inestimable value in the Vietnam Conflict. These bases were of particularly great value in eliminating the need for long transit times, such as would have otherwise been required to return units of the Fleet, ships, craft, and aircraft to Hawaii or continental United States. These were secondary benefits as well. Major economies resulted from the lower pay scales of workers in the Far East. Depots of supply and storages of ammunition at these bases greatly improved the effectiveness and economy of logistic support. Opportunities were given for rest and recreation on the part of the crews of fleet units.

Most of the facilities for support of aircraft were under Commander Naval Air Forces, U.S. Pacific Fleet. Most for support of the Marines were under the Commanding General Fleet Marine Force, U.S. Pacific Fleet. As related previously, essentially all of the remainder were activities of the Service Force. The accomplishments of these activities and the dedication of those who manned them deserve far more treatment than the space in this book affords.

All the naval facilities throughout the Western Pacific were to feel the impact of the high tempo of fleet operations, of the workload accompanying increases in the number of ships deployed to the Seventh Fleet, of the tasks involved in reactivations and conversions of ships and craft to meet new and expanding needs, of the requirements for back–up support of U.S. and a number of allied forces in Vietnam, and of expanded military assistance programs—especially for the Vietnamese. Impact would even be felt by the Headquarters Support Activity, Taiwan. In addition to its duties in providing common support to all U.S. forces on that island, added tasks and expansions in workload would accompany the greatly increased number of ship visits for recreation and upkeep.

At the start of the Vietnam build–up, the bulk of the shore based support of the Seventh Fleet was in Japan at facilities which had previously served the Japanese Fleet, augmented by contractual effort on the part of a highly developed industry. Most important was the major complex at Yokosuka which included a large shipyard and many other activities suitable to a large naval base. U.S. facilities there included Fleet Activity, Yokosuka, with its many services and activities, the Ship Repair Facility, the Naval Supply Depot, Naval Ordnance Facility, the equivalent of a naval station, and a naval hospital. Fleet Activity, Sasebo, included repair and supply departments. Several requests were made to make the former a Naval Repair Facility but I felt that its size did not warrant it. Furthermore, much contractual support was received from Japanese shipbuilding and repair facilities there in Sasebo. Also at Sasebo was the Naval Ordnance Facility, which provided extensive support to the Marines as well as the Navy.

Okinawa, labeled the "Gibraltar of the Pacific" by the Army, had neither a good fleet harbor nor was it a focal point for commerce. It was well located for air operations and provided real estate for the Marines and their training, but Naha's harbor was small and Buckner Bay dangerously exposed to seas from the southeast—as was learned in World War II and many times since by visiting ships of the Fleet. Fleet Activity, Ryukyus, was limited in its capabilities to not much more than services.

The one Western Pacific naval base on U.S. territory was at Guam, where Service Force activities included the Ship Repair Facility, Naval Supply Depot, Naval Magazine, and Naval Station. Guam was centrally located with regard to operations throughout the Western Pacific. An arc of a circle of a 1,300–mile radius from Guam would swing through Japan, Okinawa, Taiwan, and Luzon. Yet real estate and natural resources there were limited, and under normal conditions, Japan was far more preferable as a main base location for the Seventh Fleet. This proved especially true in the Korean War when Sasebo, Japan, only ninety miles from Pusan, became such an important base. Much of the support in Sasebo was afloat. Remnants of Mobile Support Unit Three were still in use there at the start of the Vietnam War, and proved their value in Danang in 1965.

The naval shore activities on Guam were at a low ebb in early 1965 as a result of severe personnel cuts. An earlier typhoon had destroyed or extensively damaged many of the buildings, and those were gradually being replaced. Much would have to be done before Guam could carry its share of the load.

With commitments to the protection of Taiwan and to the Southeast Asia Treaty Organization, operations of fleet units had often ranged south and some time was spent in Subic Bay. Although an important airfield had been carved out of a mountain at Cubi Point, most of the Subic Bay facilities were of World War II advanced base type construction. The facilities, their equipment, and their manning levels fell far short of the needs that would develop. The SERVPAC facilities encompassed the Naval Base, Naval Station, Ship Repair Facility, Supply Depot, and Naval Magazine. The base also included the Naval Air Station, Cubi Point, and a hospital, together with other facilities for support of the Navy and Marines. The shift of the center of gravity of Seventh Fleet operations to the South China Sea and the relative nearness to Vietnam were to tax all of these facilities to the utmost.

## REPAIR

Commander Service Force exercised direct command over the Ship Repair Facilities, and controlled the assignment of overhauls, activations, and conversions. Tasked by COMSERVPAC with coordination of afloat and base facilities work allocations in the Western Pacific and charged with operational control of the mobile support forces assigned to the Seventh Fleet, Commander Service Group Three employed repair ships and tenders, mobile technical units, and other assets in a way which would best meet the changing and expanding requirements for repair and maintenance.

In August 1965, COMSERVPAC, with the concurrence of CINCPAC-FLT, established a general priority listing for work at the repair facilities. This was for guidance to which strict compliance was not required of COMSERVGRUTHREE when he felt adjustments in priority were required.  Some measure of the scope of work can be gained from a listing of these priorities, namely:

| Priority | Work or Project |
| --- | --- |
| 1 | Polaris Missile casualty restoration |
| 2 | Seventh Fleet casualty restoration (At SRF Subic: 2.1.  Fast Patrol Boat casualties, 2.2.  Preparation of craft for NAVSUPPACT, Danang, 2.3.  Preparation of craft for Market Time, 2.4.  Special shore electronics, 2.5.  Emergency harbor tug repairs.) |
| 3 | Polaris Missile urgent repairs |
| 4 | Seventh Fleet urgent repairs (At SRF Subic: 4.1.  Fast Patrol Boat continuing support, 4.2.  NAVSUPPACT, Danang, continuing support, 4.3.  Market Time continuing support, 4.4.  Landing craft rehabilitation.) |
| 5 | Seventh Fleet scheduled overhauls and urgent shore electronics work |
| 6 | Emergency repairs to area service craft and boats, ships of other government agencies, friendly foreign naval ships, and privately owned ships |
| 7 | Scheduled repairs and overhauls of area service craft and boats |
| 8 | Military Assistance Program ship repairs and overhauls |
| 9 | Seventh Fleet desirable repairs, including type commander funded work on homeported ships |
| 10 | Routine work for other government agencies |

Extraordinary additions to the workload, particularly at Subic, stemmed from occasional cases of battle damage, such as to destroyers *O'Brien*, *Ozbourn, Turner Joy*, and *Edson*, and the damaging fires experienced by carriers *Oriskany* and *Forrestal*.  Groundings and storm damage added their share, of which repair of *Frank Knox* by Yokosuka was the most notable achievement.  Almost a total loss, with keel and other structural members broken, hull extensively destroyed, machinery broken loose from foundations, and spaces filled with solidified foam, she was somehow restored to first class condition.

Many steps were required to increase the capabilities of the repair facilities, particularly at Subic.  Of particular importance was the augmentation by units of the mobile support force.  The total number of repair ships (AR) and tenders (AD) deployed was increased from three to four.  Two were kept in Subic Bay most of the time and one was occasionally stationed off Manila.  To permit more visits to Taiwan, one of the repair ships or tenders was kept in Kaohsiung most of the time.

One of the key elements in the provision of effective repair support from facilities afloat and ashore to the many customers was the great effort and imaginative guidance provided by SERVPAC's Fleet Maintenance Office under the leadership first of Rear Admiral E. A. Grantham and after 7 September 1965, Captain N. Frankenberger who was soon promoted to Rear Admiral.

The Ship Repair Facility, Subic, was neither outfitted nor manned for the increasing workload and emergency peaks. Before the build–up, a larger percentage of the work then had to do with maintenance of local service craft, with military assistance programs, and with work for other government agencies. To meet the needs of the fleet and forces in Vietnam it was necessary to divert work elsewhere and build up Subic's capabilities as rapidly as possible. The seriousness of the situation struck me forcibly during my first visit as COMSERVPAC, in August 1965. Noting the 56–hour work week plus 50 percent overtime and rapidly increasing demands, I became concerned that the facility was on the verge of being completely overwhelmed and was nearing the breaking point. I was soon to learn that the reputation with some units of the Fleet, who sought far more than could possibly be provided, was not the best. But this changed within the year. Later I was to hear nothing but praise, which grew to the point where the captains of ship after ship and unit commanders would tell me even of their preference for SRF Subic over any shipyard in the United States.

This took a lot of doing. The physical plant consisted of World War II Quonsets, other substandard facilities, and obsolete tools and equipment. It would take a long time to replace or augment the plant through the slow moving and involved Military Construction Program, and new tools and equipment were not readily available.

A two–fold program was established, encompassing personnel and facilities. The staff of highly qualified officers was increased, step by step. Determination was made of how many workers and supervisors would be required, how rapidly they could be assimilated and trained, and what facilities would be needed.

Manned mainly by civilian Filipinos, there was essentially no base of trained personnel in the Philippines to draw upon, particularly in the most critical structural, pipefitting, and electronic skills. During the fall of 1965, a helper to the journeyman training program was set up with the goal of adding 400 to the work force by April 1966. Further increases would follow and were authorized as soon as the facility established that it could

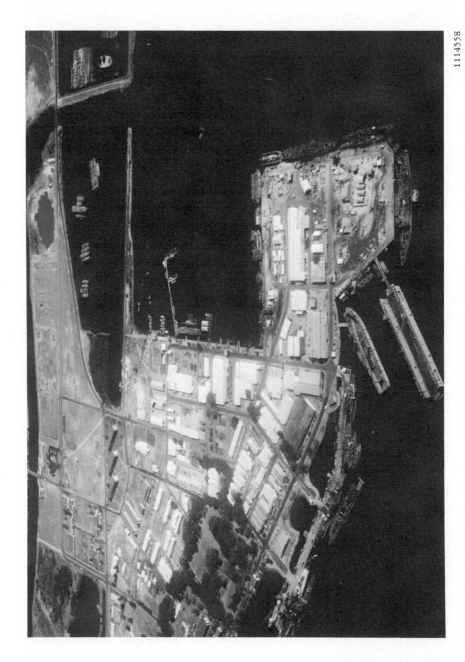

1114558

*Ship Repair Facility, Subic Bay.*

use the additional manpower. The force went from 2,396 in 1965 to 4,405 in 1967. Further increases were to take place the next year.

The shutdown of the New York Shipyard provided a quick source of needed machine tools and equipment. Additional floating drydocks were activated. Improvements in management practices were placed in effect. By the time of my inspection in 1967, the facility's operations had become amazingly effective and efficient.

To make way for fleet repairs, other work, such as that to do with Military Assistance Programs, was shifted to Guam in 1965. Despite these diversions, the total workload at Subic increased by 66 percent by the next summer with fleet work doubling. The dollar value of Seventh Fleet work went from $1,763,000 in 1964 to $7,500,000 in 1966, and further increases were in the offing.

The build-up in the Ship Repair Facility, Guam, was also a major effort. In this case, most of the manpower was provided from a Philippine labor contract with some augmentation of skills and management personnel from the U.S. In the spring of 1965 only a little over 700 were on the rolls of the work force at the Repair Facility. By June 1966, 1,700 were employed with an additional 300 being recruited.

A steady stream of overhauls of Military Assistance Program ships were scheduled for Guam. Increasing numbers of ships en route across the Pacific would stop there for repairs. Four DERs were homeported in Guam in July 1965 and thirteen LSTs followed. But the most significant impact for the next year or two came from the accelerated requirements for service craft needed in Vietnam.

In Japan, as a result of the highly trained and dedicated work force, the excellent facilities, and the commercial backup, the problems were met with much greater ease.


## SUPPLY


The Supply Depots in the Western Pacific encountered their share of problems. As more ships and aircraft were deployed, and as more hours were steamed and flown, the requirements for repair parts and general stores underwent a rapid upward trend. In a four month period starting in July 1965, the workload at the Naval Supply Depot, Yokosuka, went up 63 percent. At Subic the increase was 107 percent. Meanwhile, the net

effectiveness (i.e., the ability to supply what is on the allowance list)
declined to 65 percent at the latter location.

Depletion of stocks in the Western Pacific was followed by depletions
in depots in the continental United States. Together with a growing backlog of cargo for shipment from the West Coast, this meant increased order
and shipping times and a further aggravation of the situation. The struggle
upward was a difficult one. Major follow–up and expediting programs
were initiated. Special stocks of Fleet Program Material were placed at one
or more depots. Industrial support material was positioned. Load lists for
specific maintenance programs were developed and items shipped to appropriate depots. Fleet Issue Loads for ninety days were stocked at Subic and
Yokosuka. Casualty reports were analyzed to identify items to be added.
Additional Navy Stock Funds were obtained for projected requirements.
A new supply management program was instituted.

For the tremendous success of supply activities throughout the Service
Force, primary credit belongs to the truly outstanding officers of the Fleet
and Force Supply Division of my staff, initially under Rear Admiral Bieri
and after mid–1967 Rear Admiral Elton W. Sutherling.

As in the case of other types of shore activities, Subic Bay was by far
the hardest hit. Old storage buildings were inadequate, inefficient, and
poorly located among the buildings of the Ship Repair Facility. Manning
was extremely deficient in contrast with the demands of the growing fleet,
those of the expanding forces in Vietnam, and the increasing needs of the
many local activities being supported.

It was many months before the construction program provided the sort
of facilities really required, but augmenting the depot with supply officers
of the highest qualifications and management improvements soon began to
pay off. Despite a more than a tripling of sales, net effectiveness at Subic
was averaging 83.5 percent by fiscal year 1967 and by December 1968 was
up to 93.8 percent. During all of this time, net effectiveness of the Naval
Supply Depots, Yokosuka and Guam, was near or above the 90 percent
level. By any measure the performance of all these facilities was outstanding. Statistics cannot tell the story; for the high responsiveness to the
operating forces and to others stemmed from dedicated men working long
hours, often seven days a week.

## OTHER ACTIVITIES

The scope of this book does not permit thorough treatment of the many shore activities of the Service Force. Throughout, the highest standards were maintained and all could take pride in rendering the best possible "Service to the Fleet."

# CHAPTER XVII

# Ammunition

In Chapter V, five sets of problems were highlighted as requiring immediate and special attention when I first reported as Commander Service Force, U.S. Pacific Fleet. The second of these had to do with ammunition. It seemed as if hardly a day went by during the thirty–one months' tour in which command attention was not required in one form or another. For this reason, the subject of ammunition logistics receives special attention in this chapter.

As has been mentioned before, no other operational logistic area was more challenging or more demanding in the Vietnam War than that of ammunition logistics. None differed so radically from peace to war.

In peacetime, expenditure rates are low and confined to the relatively stable and predictable requirements of training and tests. Distribution is simple and straightforward. Time is not a critical factor.

In wartime, ammunition assumes an overwhelming importance, being the one essential and final ingredient in the application of power by all combatant forces. As was the case in World War II, the Korean War, and, in fact, all wars, ammunition required special and continuous attention at all levels of command. Its logistics are fundamentally different from the problems of supply of other products and other items. Separate management is required involving judgments which combine the results of operational experience, technical knowledge, and an understanding of operational logistics. Techniques must be developed for the unique requirements of ammunition reporting and distribution in time of combat.

During the Vietnam War, the problems of Navy ammunition logistics were complicated by a number of special factors. Perhaps the most fundamental one was that the quantities of war reserve stocks, at least in the case of the Navy, were well below comfortable levels. Understandably, peacetime ammunition production was often deferred to apply limited funds for investments in ships, aircraft, sensors, and weapon systems. Judgment in this regard was at times biased by honest doubts that expenditures in war would in fact be as high as forecast. In actual fact the forecasts later proved to be low in many cases, as extraordinary demands arose and as there was unforeseen escalation of the scope and tempo of the conflict. Production decisions were influenced by memories of the vast stocks of ammunition left over from World War II, sometimes without an understanding of the inevitability of much of this as a result of the sudden capitulation following the shock of two atomic bombs amidst a period of massive build–up for the expected invasion of Japan itself. Although of much lesser magnitude, the amounts left over from the Korean War were also remembered; yet these obsolescent weapons proved invaluable in 1965 and 1966.

Concern over the possibilities of excesses, even when world–wide stocks were well below objectives and the stress on limiting current dollar expenditures to an absolute minimum meant an insufficient allowance for escalation, surges, and emergencies. In the case of some types of munitions, this continued to be the case until after my return to Washington in the spring of 1968. The unprecedented expenditures accompanying the Tet and spring offensives of that year helped make the point, as did the *Pueblo* incident, but even at the end of that year world–wide Navy stocks were still below the minimum objectives.

Rather than savings, the results of short term frugal policies were often higher monetary expenditures and uneconomical practices in the long run. With little or no margin of safety, production lines were subjected to frequent changes, often on a highly urgent basis when economic rates had to take second place. There was hardly a time when there were not requirements for expensive shipments of ammunition of one kind or another by air, not only of newly developed weapons but of the standard ones as well. Higher stock levels would have prevented much of this.

At times, there was a tendency to base production decisions on past expenditures rather than future forecasts. Yet up until the time of the de–escalation in November 1968, this war of "graduated military actions" was almost continuously on the increase and seasonal factors and enemy actions could distort the picture greatly. Combat expenditures of ammunition give a measure of the increase resulting from the escalation. In the case of naval air ammunition, peak monthly combat expenditures in short tons were June 1965, 4,000; September 1965, 8,000; May 1966, 12,000; May 1967, 23,500; May 1968, 31,300. Combat expenditures of 5"/38 gun ammunition form another indicator: July 1965, 2,500 rounds; November 1965, 15,000; August 1966, 22,000; November 1966, 30,000; May 1967, 32,000; January 1967, 41,000; March 1968, 41,000.

USN–1130916

*An A–7 aircraft being catapulted for a strike against North Vietnam.  Modern aircraft, such as this Corsair, carried extraordinarily heavy bomb loads.*

Furthermore, past experience was heavily biased by the fact that for many months the combatant expenditures in some categories of ammunition were limited by the restricted stocks.  The bias was particularly significant in the cases where shortages forced the use of substitute weapons.  Those using past experience as a measure of the future drew faulty conclusions as a result. For example, there was a long time when shortages of 500–pound bombs resulted in inflated use of the less effective 250–pound variety.  As more Mark 82 low drag bombs became available, expenditures of 500–pound bombs went up ten–fold from March 1966 to March 1967.

Past experience could also be misleading as result of the fact that usage varied with targeting, not only as to the mix of weapons used, but also as to quantity.  For example, in strikes against heavily defended targets near Hanoi and Haiphong a high percentage of aircraft would be used for supporting missions, such as fighter protection, antimissile and antiflak duties. In certain strikes against targets in South Vietnam, it was customary for most aircraft to deliver a full load of bombs.  The type of aircraft on the line was another variant and as time went on, aircraft with greater bomb carrying capacities, such as the A–7, were deployed with the carriers.

The expenditures of ships on gunfire support missions exceeded expectations. One reason was the fact that where there was jungle cover it was difficult to assess results, and a few more rounds would invariably be called in. Also the number of gunfire support ships off South Vietnam increased as the war went on, and the tempo of operations varied depending on the operations of forces ashore, friend and enemy. The initiation of Sea Dragon operations against WBLC, an abbreviation for waterborne logistic craft (pronounced "WIBLIC"), lines of communications, and other targets ashore added still more requirements.

There were seasonal variations as well, many of which could be traced directly or indirectly to the weather. Unfortunately the season of low expenditures came in the fall of each year, and coincided with the period when the Department of Defense and the Bureau of the Budget were making the final hard adjustments to the budget in preparation for presentation to the Congress. In the fall of 1967, for example, we found out belatedly that someone in Washington, in the light of recent expenditure experience, had cut "requirements" of both gun and bomb munitions to a figure below that forecast by CINCPACFLT. This intensified the difficulties when actual requirements increased markedly month after month in the following winter and spring. With the inevitable time lags in recognizing requirements, getting decisions, increasing production, and effecting deliveries to the combatant forces, the situation was critical for months.

Added to the above difficulties was the evidence that many did not appreciate the full significance of the unique differences of fleet ammunition logistics from that of ground forces and ground–based aircraft. In these latter cases the normal "pipeline" was point to point from the production line or depot in the U.S. to a depot overseas, such as at an airfield from which strikes would be launched. Conversely, the fleet's logistics were inherently more complex, additional allowances stemming from the mobility of its units and the realities of underway replenishment.

The cargoes of the ammunition ships (AE) were adjusted from time to time by COMSERVPAC and Commander Service Group Three, in response to changes in usage rates of the various types and "mods" of weapons, with continuing allowance for the fact that antiair and ASW weapons must be available in case the enemy, or his allies, decided to take action against ships at sea. As a result, it was necessary for ammunition ships to return to port due to shortages of the most critical item, even though varying quantities of other types of ammunition would still remain on board. During one period that we analyzed, 26 percent of the tonnage, on the average, so remained. On top of all this was the need for ammunition at a base such as Subic where point to point MSTS ships could make deliveries and where the ammunition ships could take on their loads.

Factors such as the above combined to make the operational logistic actions in the case of ammunition extremely difficult. The fact that there were always critical items placed a premium on flexible controls, on prompt action, and on anticipation.

## RESPONSIBILITIES

COMSERVPAC had a number of specific ammunition responsibilities assigned by the Commander in Chief, U.S. Pacific Fleet. Foremost among them were:

> a. Develop procedures and plans for stock maintenance, distribution, and control of expendable ordnance.
> b. Achieve and maintain readiness and adequacy of stocks of expendable ordnance.
> c. Carry out inventory and distribution of expendable ordnance.

These responsibilities encompassed aviation ordnance for the Marines as well as the Navy. Marine ground ammunition, not being common to the Navy, was the responsibility of the Commanding General Fleet, Marine Force. Even in the latter category the Service Force had a role to play in the provision of stowage at Service Force Activities. In August 1965 a 15–day supply of such ammunition was established at the Naval Magazine, Subic, to be drawn on in case of emergency. The stocks of Marine ground ammunition at the Naval Ordnance Facility, Sasebo, were increased in January 1966 with the approval of CINCPACFLT. This activity then assumed a major logistic role in regard to management of such ammunition, becoming the main supply and inventory control point for Marine ground ammunition in the Western Pacific.

Under Commander Service Force, Commander Service Group Three was charged with supervising and directing the distribution of ammunition in the Western Pacific, including air munitions for the Marines.

In addition to Navy and Marine requirements, SERVPAC activities provided limited ammunition support to the Air Force. During the more critical times, some of the Air Force ordnance was transshipped through the Naval Magazine, Subic, or transferred from Navy stocks in stowage there. The major involvement with the Air Force was at Guam, as the result of the use of that island as a base for B–52 strikes of increasing intensity. The Navy Supply Depot performed the off–loading of bombs at the ammunition wharf in Apra Harbor and deliveries were made to Andersen Air Force Base by the Naval Magazine

## FORECASTING

As has been mentioned previously, I instituted an ammunition requirements study in August 1965 which took into account the dynamics of fleet operational logistics, and made projections based on production schedules and on high and average weekly expenditures already experienced. The forecasts indicated a situation far more serious than I had expected, and others in the Pacific shared my concern. When presenting the picture to representatives from Washington, the impression was gained that they felt the concern was over–expressed. Yet a year later total fleet assets were within the predicted envelopes and well on the pessimistic side. From time to time, we had hardly enough to fill all ships and AEs, and in some cases had even less than shipfills. On the other side of the coin, whereas planning in Washington seemed, at times, to fall far short of the mark, the responsiveness to our emergency requests was tremendous throughout my tour.

To keep the war going it was often necessary to go to air shipment for certain items, sometimes for prolonged periods. Stocks in northeast Asia were sent south, ammunition needed to fill magazines of ships in the mid and east Pacific was diverted to Southeast Asia, and preferred ammunition was diverted from the Atlantic Fleet as its stocks were cut to a critically low level.

The logistics of shore bombardment ammunition gives a sample of some of the sorts of extraordinary actions that were required. In October 1965, at the request of COMSERVPAC, the Bureau of Naval Weapons provided 100,000 rounds of 5″/38 projectiles in which point detonating fuzes had been substituted for antiair fuzes. In the first two days of usage off Vietnam, three destroyers experienced low order prematures in their barrels. Usage was suspended. The Bureau of Weapons determined the cause. Plastic liners were air shipped to the Naval Magazine, Subic, which made the change directed by the Bureau. Meanwhile, training expenditures were curtailed and the magazine allowances of ships not deployed were cut 50 percent. Later these allowances were cut to 25 percent in the case of 5"/38 bombardment and AA common projectiles, and to 40 percent in the case of illumination rounds. As a result of continuing shortages, COM-SERVPAC requested modification of an additional 100,000 rounds in April 1966. In December 1967, 50,000 more were requested. In the case of 5"/54, similar changes were requested but world–wide stocks were so low that only 16,500 could be converted.

These are but examples of the reason why intensive management was required at the operational logistic levels.

## MANAGEMENT

My predecessor, Rear Admiral Irvin, had recognized the seriousness of the ammunition situation early. In addition to making these views known to his superiors, he had initiated steps to acquire automatic data processing and had gained a marginal capability with some old punch card equipment. Even so, the management system in use in the summer of 1965 was basically that developed to meet peacetime needs. Many more steps had to be taken to take care of the changed and expanded needs of warfare. As of the summer of 1965, COMSERVPAC was receiving ammunition reports from fifty–four Pacific activities for fleet issue ammunition. Additional information was obtained through other channels, and often was as much as four months old. Many command levels were imposing their own ammunition reporting requirements on the ships of the Fleet.

My staff and I took steps to establish a uniform reporting system with substantial improvements in the content and format of status reports, and a conversion from manual accounting to computer processing. Many reports were eliminated, such as type commander training expenditure reports, and Ships Parts Control Center quarterly asset and expenditure reports. Report procedures were simplified. As a result, the administrative effort of reporting fleet units was reduced 50 percent and the communications lessened accordingly.

A system was established to keep track of ammunition en route across the Pacific, a particularly difficult problem. As a result, COMSERVPAC was able to follow all Navy ammunition moving for the Pacific theater, from the time of leaving a production facility to its receipt at final destination, including daily monitoring of the position of ships as they transited the Pacific Ocean. Distribution problems were rapidly detected and corrective actions promptly initiated.

For a long time, continuing difficulties and controversies arose from the fact that the Office of the Chief of Naval Operations, the Joint Staff, and the Officer of the Secretary of Defense would use raw information from many sources. When finally they started using information provided by COMSERVPAC, accurate and consistent information was available for the first time. In addition to its own needs, COMSERVPAC furnished reports to CINCPACFLT and subordinate commands, including the Commanders of the First and Seventh Fleets, and to the Type Commanders and COM-SERVGRUTHREE. Logistic status data and information for the CNO world–wide ammunition report were transmitted by COMSERVPAC to the Naval Material Command who provided CNO with the data. Starting 1 January 1967, COMSERVPAC sent a critical surface expenditures report direct to CNO. Heretofore incomplete and unconsolidated information direct from fleet ships had resulted in much misinformation. In addition, COMSERVPAC transmitted a controlled munitions report to CINCPAC, who in turn sent the information to the Office of the Secretary of Defense (OSD), while CNO provided OSD with a selected item status report. All now had accurate and consistent information. Meanwhile, reporting demands increased, the number of ammunition components under intensive reporting doubling in fiscal year 1967.

In 1967 COMSERVPAC developed a Navy reporting system for the Chief of Naval Operations that was adopted world–wide.

All this made clear the importance of information flowing up the chain of responsibility. I once recall having read an otherwise excellent book on organization in which three channels were advocated, one executory, one planning, and one informational. For simplicity, for accountability, for responsiveness, and for relevancy, all three should normally coincide. Modern communications and automatic data processing increase the temptation to by–pass chains of responsibility and command. This does not mean that information need pass through each and every command in the chain of responsibility. In fact, this would be impracticable. It does mean that information should be monitored and, when warranted, interpreted by suitable command levels before passing on. Raw information without being verified, assembled, and interpreted by those in a position of responsibility often results in incomplete and faulty information, and erroneous decisions.

Some of the early sources of information difficulties stemmed from the fact that individual components, bomb bodies, tails, various fuzes, arming wires, etc., were handled and accounted for individually. Ensuring that usable rounds were available when and where needed was a difficult problem, particularly since there was no appreciable reserve and the munitions were being used almost as soon as received. As a result, COMSERVPAC requested that certain air ordnance items be shipped only as complete rounds, with a coding system which would facilitate monitoring. At a conference at the Naval Weapons Station, Concord, California, in September 1965, the Bureau of Weapons agreed to provide the necessary instructions. The concept of Complete Round Shipment (CRAMSHIP) was promulgated by the Chief of Naval Material in February 1966 by message and implemented in March. COMSERVPAC designated the components to be shipped concurrently. The criterion followed was that each must be a usable round; it did not mean that each must have all possible configurations.

From the very start this system worked remarkably well. It was extended in May to surface ammunition and other air ordnance. Further modifications and refinements followed.

Meanwhile, steps had been underway to reduce the time in getting new production ammunition to Subic in an absolute minimum of time. A "push" system was started in August 1965 whereby certain types of ammunition would be shipped automatically to the Pacific as soon as it was produced, and a requirement was established for all ammunition to be palletized.

New ammunition components were subjected to some delays in shipments to the Fleet from production as a result of the lack of advanced technical logistic information. COMSERVPAC accelerated the inclusions of these items on Fleet inventory control reports through the publication of technical information from SERVPAC files, 90 to 120 days in advance of inclusion in Navy catalogues.

One source of delays was the availability of MSTS ships. To reduce these delays, a "Movement Control Unit" was established at Concord with responsibilities to COMSERVPAC. As a result of these and other steps, the time for Navy ammunition to reach the combatant forces from production lines was reduced by 120 to 70 days. By the summer of 1967 it was averaging 55 days.

Other difficulties arose from the fact that the management of ammunition within the Navy Material Establishment had become fragmented through reorganization. In previous wars responsibility had been concentrated in the Bureau of Ordnance. By 1965 this had been merged with the Bureau of Aeronautics into the massive Bureau of Weapons, and an activity of the Bureau of Supplies and Accounts, the Ships Parts Control Center at Mechanicsburg, Pa., had been given ammunition supply responsibilities. The situation was further complicated when "systems commands" replaced the bureaus. Now responsibilities were split between the Ordnance Systems Command and the Air Systems Command, with Ordnance doing all the ammunition loading and managing the depots and weapons stations. I personally considered this splitting of ammunition responsibilities an unfortunate move. The old division of responsibilities had been highly successful and developed the superior weapons—slim bombs, the "Eye" weapons, Sidewinder, etc.—used by Navy and Air Force alike. But whether or not the decision was correct, the resultant setup was a fragmented one.

In January 1966, I recommended that one office in the Naval Material Support Establishment be assigned responsibility for "monitoring, expediting and reporting critical ammunition from the completion of shipping until shipment from the continental U.S." The Chief of Naval Material established an organization for this purpose at the Ships Parts Control Center. It began functioning in the spring and became fully operational on 1 July.

Through all this time we had been improving our information system, including an orderly acquisition of modern automatic data processing equipment and the developments effective programs. Information from this system not only helped the distribution management but assisted in controlling expenditures of the critical ordnance. This is a story by itself. Step by step improvements were made until, in 1967, a full scale modern computer was serving some eight divisions on the staff, of which the Weapons Division was but one.

## SHORTAGES

Suddenly in April 1966, several Air Force bases in Vietnam ran out of bombs or critical bomb components. To fill in the deficiencies, Admiral Sharp, Commander of the Pacific Command, on 19 April, ordered transfers of 1,000 250–pound bombs, 1,000 500–pound bombs and 400 1,000–pound bombs from in–country Marine stocks. On 26 April we were ordered to transfer 2,500 more 1,000–pound bombs from the Navy assets. By the end of June such transfers from the Navy and Marines, including those to the Vietnamese and Loatian Armed Forces, totaled 41,793. In return, the next two months saw 16,027 ordered transferred to the Navy, mostly 250–pound bombs from Air Force stocks not yet shipped from the continental U.S. Twenty–nine transfers of varying amounts of air munitions were ordered between the Services during the next fiscal year.

There was an urgent meeting at Camp Smith, Admiral Sharp's headquarters, attended by two Assistant Secretaries of Defense, Paul R. Ignatius (Installations and Logistics) and Alain C. Enthoven (Systems Analysis). I presented our forecast of August 1965, the record since then, and predictions for the future. The predictions showed that the low point in many weapons would be reached in about three months, and that, as had been the case before, we could run out of some types if expenditures were not restrained. The knowledge of the location of Navy and Marine usable bombs was complete and up to date.

Mr. Ignatius took aggressive steps to increase production, especially 500–pound bombs. But constructive steps such as these were followed by what I viewed as unfortunate results as well, in the form of new centralized controls. The Secretary of Defense established tight controls and required special reports. For about three months we were required to submit daily reports on the location of each and every complete round of "controlled air munitions." Whether or not this frequency of reporting was necessary, our system handled it, as daily reports from ships and activities, on a usable round basis, were obtained and consolidated at the Service Force headquarters. Later the reporting of assets was relaxed to ten days and then to semi–monthly. New "temporary" ammunition organizations were established in the Office of the Secretary of Defense (OSD), on the Joint Staff of the JCS and on CINCPAC's staff. Our good management continued, but with far more difficulty. In Washington, OSD approvals were to be required for most management actions to do with air ammunitions, including each change in the production schedule, a practice which was later extended to gun ammunition. When the 250– and 500–pound bomb situation improved in the fall of 1966, I requested that "push" shipments of the Mark 81 and Mark 82 weapons stop, and that future shipments be in accordance with our requisitions. It took over a month before permission was obtained.

At the Camp Smith meeting there was evidence that some wanted to extend detailed Washington controls (Joint Staff or OSD) to combat usage and even distribution within the Pacific. Fortunately, Admiral Sharp emphasized his own responsibilities and made it clear what he would do with regard to the control of air munitions. He established monthly expenditure allocations for the Air Force, Navy and Marines, and set up a requirement for forty–five days of "operating stocks" in–theater to guard against emergencies. This was intended, and initially stated, as a minimum goal, but some started treating it as a maximum as well. The Secretary of Defense allowed a 135–day pipeline from the production line, including stocks in Southeast Asia. It was specified that this was not to be exceeded. Although there was logic in some overall controls, as initially applied they created instabilities. Every time there was a change in monthly require- ments, or allocations, the change in the authorized pipeline would be magnified (four and a half times for air and five for ship gun munitions) up or down as the case might be. As is always the case involving dynamic systems with time lags—such as in the decision process in production line changes, and in distribution—the overswings would be magnified still further. A more stable policy was finally adopted by the Navy in late 1968.

The preceding discussion should not be interpreted as an intent to be critical of individuals faced with extraordinarily difficult decisions. Rather it is hoped that the discussion will provide insights for those who may encounter similar problems in the future.

## SUBIC

One of the keys to ammunition support of the Seventh Fleet and the Marines was SERVPAC's Naval Magazine, Subic.

Early steps to increase the throughput and increase stowage have been discussed in Chapter IV.

There was no harder working group than the personnel at NAVMAG Subic, who worked a seven day week around the clock during my entire tour. In addition to ammunition movement and storage, there were many tasks normally associated only with a major naval weapons station. These included banding and putting retrofit lugs on bombs; overhauling and reno- vating powder charges; refuzing projectiles, rockets and bombs; altering fuzes; X–raying of primers.

In addition to requirements of the Seventh Fleet and Marines, a 60–day resupply level of ammunition for Market Time was established at Subic.

In order to realize the considerable savings in time and money, which would result if testing and minor repairs to air launched missiles could be effected in the Western Pacific, steps were initiated early in 1967 to provide

NH–74182

*Pier at the Naval Magazine, Subic Bay, 1965.*

NAVMAG Subic with additional facilities, such as trailers with test equipment for Sidewinder, Shrike, and Walleye missiles. The testing and repairs were later extended to Bullpup and Sparrow missiles.

Vice Admiral Thomas F. Connolly, Commander Naval Air Force, Pacific Fleet, was, as I recall, the first to suggest the idea of testing Sparrow missiles at NAVMAG Subic and thus eliminating the need for such testing on board ship. He volunteered to transfer personnel on a temporary duty for this purpose. In August 1966 action was taken to establish an interim Sparrow testing facility. It was April 1967 before it was approved and funded.

In February 1967 Commander Service Force had requested the Naval Air Systems Command to advise as to the feasibility of providing NAVMAG Subic with additional facilities, such as mobile trailers with test equipment for Sidewinder, Shrike, and Walleye, in order to avoid returning missiles to the United States for testing and minor repairs.

In cooperation with COMNAVAIRPAC, COMSERVPAC made arrangements with the Naval Air Systems Command for a portable Walleye test van to be air shipped to the Naval Magazine, Subic. The test van was placed in operation on 12 June 1967. Testing and minor repairs were later extended to Sidewinder, Shrike, Walleye, Bullpup, and Sparrow.

## MINES

A high point in logistic responsiveness was reached when the decision was made on short notice in February 1967 to mine certain inland waterways in North Vietnam. The required mines and associated equipment were assembled and tested by the Naval Magazine, Subic Bay, where they were loaded in USS *Sacramento* (AOE–1). *Sacramento* proceeded at 27 knots to deliver them to attack carriers at Yankee Station. Fifty–three hours after the order was received, the seeding of river mouths had been completed.

## NORTHEAST ASIA

Mention has previously been made of the shifting of certain of the underway replenishment ships to the Northeast Asian area at the time of the *Pueblo* crisis and the revision of their ammunition loads so as to prepare them to meet, if necessary, the needs of a different type of war. The Secretary of Defense reversed his early decision and ordered immediate reconstitution of ammunition stocks in Northeast Asia. To this end shipments were diverted and redistributions were effected in the Far East. Many of the problems would not have arisen if world-wide stock levels of ammunition had been maintained at a more adequate level.

These were but samples of the many extraordinary actions that were required monthly, weekly, and even daily to keep the Fleet and Marines supplied with ammunition where and when needed. Despite the many difficulties, actions at all levels of the logistic system met the challenge and maintained the effectiveness of the operating forces in combat in Southeast Asia.

# CHAPTER XVIII

# The Lifeline By Sea

No story of logistic support of forces overseas would be complete without at least some mention of the indispensable role played by ocean shipping.

In the Vietnam War it was necessary to deliver cargoes to the other side of the world, 6,900 nautical miles from San Francisco, when weather permitted using the great circle route, and 12,400 miles from New York via the Panama Canal. Moreover, the appetites of modern armed forces, their vehicles, and their weapons had grown greatly—even since the Korean War.

By the time of the Vietnam build–up, major advances in transport aircraft had greatly enhanced their ability to deliver urgent cargoes and high value reparables in a minimum of time. In the march of progress, aircraft have gone from small, low–powered propeller driven airplanes flying in the dense lower altitudes to jet–propelled, optimum–shaped airplanes flying at high speeds in the thinner atmosphere of high altitude. The point had been reached where the new C–141s, which assisted in delivery of supplies to Vietnam, were able to average 21 tons of cargo per aircraft.

But the basic laws of physics were unchanged; the only practicable way of transporting the bulk of the cargoes was still by displacement vessels operating on the sea. Important as high speed transportation by air was, only a very small fraction of the total tonnage could be delivered by this mode. Furthermore, ocean–going ships too had made spectacular progress, albeit over a much longer period of time. Propulsion had gone from sail to coal to petroleum fuels, and more recently gas turbines began to be used. Nuclear power could have been applied to merchantmen. In size, ships had grown in steps from tiny vessels to mammoth giants of the sea. In the latter part of the twentieth century the limits of size seemed to be only those imposed by depths of water and terminal facilities, as large shps proved capable of transporting as much as 300,000 tons or more in the case of liquid cargoes.

The laws of physics also continued to result in a major differential in cost. There used to be a rule of thumb that it cost ten times as much to transport a ton by land as by sea and one hundred times as much by air. The cost ratios commonly used in the case of air and sea in the Vietnam Conflict were much smaller. However, I suspect that the earlier rule of thumb was still roughly true, if one were to take into account all the factors, including true terminal costs and amortization of vehicle and terminal investment costs. Whatever the true ratios of cost were, they had little effect on the total tonnages at the time of Vietnam, when they were considered, as a rule, to be outweighed by military considerations.

All of the bulk fuel for the Army, Navy, Air Force, and Marines delivered to Vietnam, Thailand, and other Western Pacific bases was transported by ocean tankers. Demand for such fuel was substantial. In Vietnam alone, requirements went from less than 3 million barrels [1] in 1964 to over 8 million in 1965, to 25 million in 1966, to 38 million in 1967, and would increase still further.

In the case of ammunition, many high priority shipments were required by air, but these still accounted for only one percent of the total tonnage. The remaining 99 percent went by sealift.

In the case of dry cargo over 95 percent of the tonnage arriving in Vietnam came by sea. Because of the need for integrated movement of organized operational units and their equipment, and the initial low capacity of airports, the percentage was even higher in the early phase of the build–up.

The only area of transportation which departed from former experience was that of personnel. In the early stage of the build–up, the movement of organized units and their equipment and other considerations resulted in about half the personnel to Vietnam going by sea in 1965. As result of development of jet airfield capabilities, increasing security, and the fact that a large number of personnel movements were those caused by the end of the one year tours, the percentage that went by air increased to 80 percent in 1966 and about 90 percent in 1967.

## MILITARY SEA TRANSPORTATION SERVICE

Occasionally Service Force and amphibious ships transported special cargoes, such as in "lifts of opportunity," but these were just drops in the bucket for which the Military Sea Transportation Service (MSTS) was responsible.

MSTS originated in 1949 when the Secretary of Defense had consolidated

---

[1] One barrel is the equivalent of 42 gallons.

sea transportation into a unified service under the Department of the Navy. Although the stated reasons were economy and efficiency, there were other reasons why this was a sound move. Some of these had to do with the familiarity of the Navy with ships and operations at sea, and with the existence of repair and other supporting capabilities, ashore and afloat, which could service merchant as well as naval ships.

Reasons perhaps of even greater basic importance were those pertaining to war at sea. The seriousness of the U–boat threat in World War I had been such that the necessity of having naval crews on all vessels passing through the war zone had frequently been urged upon the Shipping Board on account of instances of cowardice and disobedience, such as the showing of lights. A joint recommendation by the War and Navy Departments, on 12 July 1917, that vessels for permanent employment as transports be commissioned in the Navy was approved by the President. On 17 December, the Secretary of War expressed the desire that the Navy man and operate all vessels carrying animals, cargoes, and munitions for the War Department, and have complete control of these vessels at sea. The Naval Overseas Transportation Service was organized on 9 January 1918.[2]

Similar problems were encountered in World War II. Samuel Eliot Morison, after "considerable study," expressed his "emphatic opinion that if and when another war occurs, the merchant marine should either be absorbed by the Navy or made an auxiliary service under military discipline."[3]

There having been no war at sea since World War II, many viewed MSTS essentially as a manager of ships such as a shipping company. Yet the threat of war against ships at sea had grown markedly, especially as a result of the build–up of the Soviet submarine fleet and antiship missiles. In this era, Navy control of shipping would perhaps be even more necessary than ever before. Meanwhile, training and readiness for such control has been greatly enhanced by organizing MSTS as one of the "operating forces" of the Navy under the Chief of Naval Operations, and by occasional exercises which included the participation of merchant ships.

This is not the place to tell the story of how the Navy carried out its sealift responsibilities through MSTS, but brief mention should be made of some

---

[2] Lewis P. Clephane, *History of the Naval Overseas Transportation Service in World War I* (Washington: Government Printing Office, 1969), pp. xviii, 1, 61–63.

[3] Samuel E. Morison, *History of United States Naval Operations in World War II*, vol. I (Boston: Little, Brown and Co., 1954), p. 300.

of the many difficult problems which had to be solved. In the Vietnam War, the tasks of MSTS were greatly complicated by the graduated strategy and the secrecy of planning. As a result, future build–ups were often not anticipated and, when they were, only limited actions could be taken in timely fashion without compromising the imposed security restrictions.

By mid–1965, cargo requirements were already greatly exceeding the capacity of available lift, which then totaled 120 ships, 89 of which were in the MSTS nucleus fleet.

Through 1965, all fuel for forces in Vietnam was supplied by contractors. Because of foreign tax implications, the majority continued to be delivered commercially in later years. Nevertheless, the Navy's Military Sea Transportation Service (MSTS) deliveries climbed from zero in 1965 to 13 percent in 1966, and to 39 percent in 1967, peaking at 43 percent the next year. In addition to the MSTS nucleus fleet and tankers chartered by MSTS, it was often necessary to charter some ships flying foreign flags—particularly after the closing of the Suez Canal in June 1967. MSTS also provided T–2 tankers for floating storage at Cam Ranh Bay and Danang because of the lack of sufficient storage ashore, and furnished smaller T–1s for shuttle service along the coast and in the waterways of Vietnam.

In the dry cargo category, there were many problems arising from the nature of specialized cargoes. For example, delivery of outsized cargoes

USN–1113980

*USNS* Core, *a MSTS ship delivering aircraft to Saigon, 1965.*

required special attention.   Requirements for transport of the vast numbers of helicopters imposed their own problems, solved by obtaining of aircraft ferries (T–AKB) and an amphibious LPH from the Atlantic.   Roll–on/roll–off ships had to be chartered for delivery of vehicles.   Container services were acquired by contract.   LSTs and other ramp–equipped units were needed for over–the–shore deliveries.

In response to requirements of the Army and COMUSMACV, MSTS negotiated the largest cost–plus–award–fee contract in its history, a contract with Alaskan Barge and Transport, Inc., for transportation, lighterage, and terminal services in the Vietnam area.

The usual practice of requisitioning ships in time of war to fulfill the expanding needs was not permitted in this "limited conflict."   Rather surprisingly, it was a strike by maritime workers which saved the day in the summer of 1965, when time was needed to activate ships left over from World War II which had been retained in the National Defense Reserve Fleet.   As a result of the strike, which lasted from 15 June to 1 September 1965, ships became available immediately which otherwise would have been on their normal runs.

Despite all that was done, deficiencies in sealift continued for some time.   As late as September 1966 the deficiency was forty–three ships, and continuing actions were needed to acquire more ships.

By July 1967 the MSTS–controlled fleet had grown to 527, of which there were 117 in the nucleus fleet, 244 under charter, and 166 under the General Agency Agreement.   The latter were the reactivated ships, owned by the Government and operated by a general agency appointed by the Maritime Administration.   These old ships suffered more than their share of breakdowns, and with inferior personnel accommodations, were the last choice of the crews manning the merchant fleet.

A complication was the shortage of trained men for the merchant service and the fact that their average age had advanced reputedly to forty-five. Further, despite extraordinary efforts by the units and contractors, there were serious delays in ship sailings which over one period of thirty–four months totaled some 2,796 ship days.

Such factors as the long distances to Vietnam, and the slow turn around before adequate port capabilities could be developed, added complicating factors to the MSTS job of furnishing sealift services.   The fact that shipping requirements were met is a tribute to all concerned.

CHAPTER XIX

# Epilogue

In many respects, a Military Service may be likened to the human body. Solely to view the body's exterior and its external actions is not sufficient. Beneath the surface are the "logistic" systems which supply the energy, repair and replace cells, and carry out other functions upon which bodily action and even life itself depend.

So it is that military operations are made possible only by a combination of combat and logistic actions. Each affects the other. Logistic actions must be so tailored as to meet the needs of military operations, whether in time of war or in time of peace. Conversely, strategic and tactical decisions, and the employment of the combat forces, must be tailored to the capabilities logistics is able to provide. Complex as the relationships between combat and logistic forces are, an appreciation of these relationships is essential to a true understanding of warfare—for both are a part of the whole.

The combination must be such as to optimize the readiness and operational effectiveness of the forces involved. To effect such an optimization, the logistic systems of each Military Service have developed both obvious and subtle differences. In the case of the Navy, effectiveness depends on the ability of individual units and small and large groupings of these units to range the seven seas, operate in sustained fashion essentially anywhere on more than two–thirds of the earth's surface, and, if need be, project and support power ashore as well as at sea. Effectiveness depends on the ability to redeploy on little or no notice, forming task groups, task forces, and fleets appropriate to the job at hand. Complicated by the wide variety of naval missions and tasks, and by the ocean environment, these effectiveness requirements place unique demands on naval logistics.

To meet these demands, in peace and war, an extremely effective and flexible naval operational logistic system has been developed over the years. In the Vietnam War the system has again proved its worth, meeting not only the more usual requirements of naval operating forces but responding rapidly, efficiently and effectively to challenging requirements that were not anticipated. It is of extreme importance that the strengths of this system, and of the overall naval logistic system which backs it up, be understood and preserved.

In presenting the story of the Service Force over a relatively short, although important span of time, and as seen by its Commander, I have hoped to increase the understanding of naval operational logistics and its relationships with the total military effort. I have hoped to provide insights from experience which may be of help to those faced with problems in future conflict situations. I have hoped to reflect credit on the tens of thousands of individuals under my command who performed so magnificently during this difficult period, and thereby also to gain better recognition for the vast number of those in uniform in all the Services, in all areas of the world, and in other periods of time, who through logistics have served the Nation in dedicated fashion in war and peace. I have hoped to convey, in some measure, the importance of operational logistic activities, the extreme challenge of the problems one often faces in logistics, and the need for prompt, decisive actions to ensure overall military effectiveness; and thus to tempt others to devote some portion of their careers to this vital area of military effort.

In the recounting of this story and in efforts to keep it down to reasonable size, it has been difficult to know where to draw the line. Regretfully, it has been necessary to leave out many important areas and sub–areas, and to neglect many activities which made fundamental contributions to the war effort. The number of groups and individuals deserving of credit has been far too great to accord them proper recognition, and this I sorely regret.

The activities of the Service Force continued to grow for several months after my departure, reaching a peak in regard to Seventh Fleet and I Corps operations in the spring of 1968. Throughout the next year the size, tempo, and scope of operations in the Delta expanded at a spectacular rate and placed heavy demands on operational logistic support. The Vietnamization program, with transfers of large numbers of craft to the Vietnamese Navy, was accompanied by continuing demands on the Service Force for support, including training assistance for those who would pick up the ball. In all these activities, those then in the Force sustained notably high levels of performance and service.

I should like to close with an overall observation.

It is of the greatest importance to the future that we learn lessons from our experiences in war. In the case of Vietnam, this is made extraordinarily difficult by the uniqueness of the conflict, and even more by the critical and emotional climate which developed in the United States with regard to it. Perhaps there has never been a greater tendency for so many to seek to place blame on individuals or specific groups for our prolonged involvement in a worthy but unpopular effort, or for the way the war was fought. The danger lies in discouraging frank and objective evaluations of overall strategies and policies, which seek not to criticize, but to provide better understanding for the future.

There are important logistic lessons to be learned from Vietnam. Hopefully this limited account will help to identify some of them.

# Types of Ships and Craft in the Service Force, U.S. Pacific Fleet

| *Abbreviation* | *Name* |
|---|---|
| ADG | Degaussing Ship |
| AE | Ammunition Ship |
| AF | Store Ship |
| AFDB | Large Auxiliary Floating Drydock |
| AFDL | Small Auxiliary Floating Drydock |
| AFDM | Medium Auxiliary Floating Drydock |
| AFS | Combat Store Ship |
| AG | Auxiliary, Miscellaneous Ship |
| AGB | Icebreaker |
| AGER | Environmental Research Ship |
| AGMR | Major Communications Relay Ship |
| AGS | Surveying Ship |
| AGTR | Technical Research Ship |
| AH | Hospital Ship |
| AKL | Light Cargo Ship |
| AKS | Stores Issue Ship |
| AN | Net Laying Ship |
| AO | Oiler |
| AOE | Fast Combat Support Ship |
| AOG | Gasoline Tanker |
| AOR | Replenishment Oiler |
| APL | Barracks Craft (non–self–propelled) |
| AR | Repair Ship |
| ARC | Cable Repairing or Laying Ship |

| | |
|---|---|
| ARD | Auxiliary Repair Drydock |
| ARG | Internal Combustion Engine Repair Ship |
| ARL | Landing Craft Repair Ship |
| ARS | Salvage Ship |
| ATA | Auxiliary Ocean Tug |
| ATF | Fleet Ocean Tug |
| HLC | Heavy Lift Craft (later designated YHLC or YMLC according to size) |
| LCM | Landing Craft Medium |
| LCM–3 | Landing Craft Medium (MARK III) |
| LCM–6 | Landing Craft Medium (MARK VI) |
| LCM–8 | Landing Craft Medium (MARK VIII) |
| LCPL | Landing Craft Personnel, Large |
| LCU | Landing Craft, Utility |
| LLC | Light Lift Craft (Later YLLC) |
| LST | Landing Ship, Tank |
| YAG | Miscellaneous Auxiliary |
| YC | Open Lighter |
| YCV | Aircraft Transportation Lighter |
| YD | Floating Crane |
| YDB | Large Floating Crane |
| YDT | Diving Tender |
| YF | Covered Lighter (self–propelled) |
| YFB | Ferryboat or Launcher |
| YFN | Covered Lighter (non–self–propelled) |
| YFNB | Large Covered Lighter |
| YFND | Drydock Companion Craft |
| YFNX | Lighter (Special Purpose) |
| YFR | Refrigerated Covered Lighter (self–propelled) |
| YFRN | Refrigerated Covered Lighter (non–self–propelled) |

| | |
|---|---|
| YFRT | Covered Lighter (Range Tender) |
| YFU | Harbor Craft, Utility |
| YG | Garbage Lighter (self–propelled) |
| YHLC | Salvage Lift Craft, Heavy (non–self–propelled) |
| YLLC | Salvage Lift Craft, Light (self–propelled) |
| YMLC | Salvage Lift Craft, Medium (non–self–propelled) |
| YNG | Gate Craft |
| YO | Fuel Oil Barge (self–propelled) |
| YOG | Gasoline Barge (self–propelled) |
| YOGN | Gasoline Barge (non–self–propelled) |
| YON | Fuel Oil Barge |
| YOS | Oil Storage Barge |
| YR | Floating Workshop |
| YRBM | Repair, Berthing and Messing Barge |
| YRDH | Floating Drydock Workshop (Hull) |
| YRDM | Floating Drydock Workshop (Machinery) |
| YRST | Diving Tender Salvage |
| YSD | Seaplane Wrecking Derrick |
| YSR | Sludge Removal Barge |
| YTB | Large Harbor Tug |
| YTL | Small Harbor Tug |
| YTM | Medium Harbor Tug |
| YV | Drone Aircraft Catapult Control Craft |
| YW | Water Barge (self–propelled) |
| YWN | Water Barge (non–self–propelled) |

# Index

Ships in this Index are USS unless otherwise specified. Personnel are USN unless otherwise specified.

## A

*Abnaki* (ATF-96), 217
Acheson, Secretary of State Dean, 10
Adak Island, 202, 210, 217
Adamson, Rear Admiral Robert E., Jr., 81
Adele Island, 208
Advanced Base Functional Components (ABFC), 73, 78, 80
    concept, 37, 170
    construction, 75, 88, 95, 173
    equipment, 24, 143, 166
Advanced Base and Shore Activity Division, 29, 38
Advanced Bases, 69, 97, 148, 187
    concept, viii, 15, 16, 37
    World War II, 73, 75, 78, 82, 227
Advanced Base Section, viii, 38, 182
Advanced diving system (ADS) IV, 205, 206
AFDL-23, 94
Agency for International Development (AID), 14, 82, 191, 193
Air Cofat, 62, 138-9, 146
Aircraft carriers, 14, 35, 42, 46-7, 51, 200
Aircraft ferry (T-AKB), 258
Air Force, U.S., 64, 213
    ammunition support, 35, 207, 244, 245, 249-51
    bases, 97, 157, 159, 249
    construction, 64, 158, 162, 191
    logistic support, 49, 60, 63, 255
Air Systems Command, Naval, 252
Alaskan Barge and Transport, Inc., 258
Alava Wharf, Subic Bay, 53
ALUDRA (AF-55), 96, 215
*SS Amastra*, 214
Amirikan, Dr., 163
Ammi pontoon, 154, 163, 166, 173
Ammunition, 36, 37, 43, 46, 52, 53-4, 79, 81, 103, 119, 143, 209, 240-53
    management, 36, 37, 44, 132, 140, 225, 240, 244-49, 255
    stowage, 35, 36, 100, 158, 231, 244, 245
    support to other services, x, 35, 36, 104, 207, 244
    underway replenishment, 23, 47, 48, 54, 56, 57, 243

Ammunition Depot, U.S. Army, Cam Ranh Bay, 158
Ammunition ships (AE), 21, 36, 44, 52-8, 165, 243-5, 253
Amphibious Assault Buoyant Fuel System, 95, 114
Amphibious Assault Ship (LPH), 258
Amphibious Construction Battalion (ACB) One, 163
Amphibious Force, U.S. Atlantic Fleet, 131
Amphibious Force, U.S. Pacific Fleet, 131, 146, 148, 149
Amphibious Group One, U.S. Pacific Fleet, 13, 40
Amphibious Logistic Support Group (CTG-76.4), 71
Amphibious ships, 42, 51, 114, 125, 147, 255
Amphibious Squadron Seven, 71
Amphibious Task Force, U.S. Seventh Fleet, 40, 42, 68, 71, 74, 106, 107
Amphibious Training Command, Pacific, 78
*Andauer* (German heavy lift craft), 206
Andersen Air Force Base, 79, 245
An Hoa, 98, 126, 188
An Khe, 192
Annam, 10, 91
Annamite Mountains, 67, 68
*Annapolis* (AGMR-1), 44, 229
An Thoi; see Naval Support Activity, Saigon, Detachments
Anti-Submarine Warfare (ASW) Group, 50
An Xuyen, 133
APL-5, 74, 107
APL-21, 164, 177
APL-25, 74
APL-26, 151, 173, 174
APL-30, 74
APL-46, 174
APL-55, 132, 164, 177
Apra Harbor, Guam, 79, 213, 245
Area Commander, 28
*Arikara* (ATF-98), 210, 218
*Arlington* (AGMR-2), 44, 229
Army, U.S. (USA), 79, 88, 90, 97, 142, 144, 148, 158, 160, 220
    construction, 155, 158, 162, 182, 191
    equipment, 131, 148, 159, 166, 202, 206

Army, U.S.—Continued
   installations, 109, 139, 155, 157, 172
   supply support, 7, 61, 62, 63, 70, 142, 255, 258
A Shau Valley, 110
*Asheville* (PG–84), 159, 215
*Askari* (ARL–30), 148, 149, 151, 160
Atlantic Fleet, U.S., 71, 189, 245
   ship transfers, 53, 57, 145, 228, 229, 230, 258
Auxiliary Squadron, 21, 22

B

Baer, Rear Admiral Donald G., 35
"Banjo Dike," 145
*Banner* (AKL–25) later (AGER–1), 220–4
Bao Dai, 10, 12, 13
Barges, 23, 35, 81, 86, 131, 209, 210, 215
   barracks, 123, 148
   fuel, 74, 173, 177, 217
   repair, 75, 94, 130, 131, 148, 178
   water, 74, 144
Bartell, James (civilian), 123
Bartlett, Rear Admiral J. V. (CEC), 191
Base Force, U.S. Pacific Fleet, 22, 23; see also
   Fleet Base Force, U.S. Fleet
Bassac River, 134, 145, 147, 169, 177, 228
Ba To, 192
SS *Baton Rouge Victory*, 208
Baumberger, Vice Admiral Walter H., 18N, 219
BC–644 (Army barge), 210
*Beans, Bullets, and Black Oil* (Carter), v, viii, 47
*Benewah* (APB–35), 151
Ben Hai River, 67
Ben Tre, 175, 176, 177
Berthing (billeting) and messing, 63, 97, 138, 178
   facilities afloat, 74, 107, 154, 166–7, 174
   facilities ashore, 59, 61, 158, 162, 166–7, 174
Bien Hoa Air Base, 63
Bieri, Rear Admiral B. H., Jr. (SC), 26, 238
*Bigelow* (DD–942), 77
Binh Thuy; see Naval Support Activity, Saigon, Detachments
Bishop, Lieutenant Robert, 221, 223
Blackburn, Vice Admiral Paul P., Jr., 71, 130, 227
Blocking operations, 45, 225–7
Blouin, Vice Admiral F. J., 132
*Bolster* (ARS–38), 206, 207, 217
Bonner, Rear Admiral Emmet P., 81
Bosco, Lieutenant Commander C. V., 79
Boyd, Lieutenant Commander J. H., Jr., 198
SS *Britain Victory*, 202
Brown, Vice Admiral Robert (MC), 100

*Brule* (AKL–28), 131, 138, 144, 145, 173, 220
Bucher, Commander L. M., 221–4
Buckner Bay, Okinawa, 232
Bureaus
   Aeronautics (BUAER), 249; see also Air Systems Command
   Medicine and Surgery (BUMED), 17
   Ordnance (BUORD); see Ordnance Systems Command
   Naval Personnel (BUPERS), 17, 190
   Ships (BUSHIPS), 39, 196; see also Ships Systems Command
   Supplies and Accounts (BUSandA), 26, 79, 249; see also Supply Systems Command
   Naval Weapons (BUWEPS), 245, 248, 249
   Yards and Docks (BUDOCKS); see Facilities Engineering Command

C

Calhoun, Vice Admiral W. L., 23
Ca Mau, 64
Cambodia, 6, 10, 133, 169
Cam Ranh Bay, 6, 40, 79, 157, 158, 214, 228; see also Naval Support Activity, Saigon, Detachments
Canaga, Captain Bruce L., Jr. (MC), 75
*Canberra* (CAG–1), 56
Can Tho; see Naval Support Activity, Saigon, Detachments
USNS *Card*, 203
Cargo Handling Battalion One, 71
Cargo Handling Battalion Two, 69, 71, 79, 90
Cargo ships, 58, 124, 131, 144, 145, 220
*Carlock* (civilian tug), 210
*Caroline County* (LST–525), 122
Carroll, Camp, 122
Carter, Rear Admiral W. R., v, viii
USNS *Cassotot*, 206
Cargo Handling Battalion One, 71
Cat Lo; see Naval Support Activity, Saigon, Detachments
Cau Hai Bay, 154, 155
Chaplain services, 43–4, 61, 151–2
Chapman, Captain A. S., 221, 222
*Chara* (AE–31), 53
Chau Doc, 134, 140
Chief of Naval Operations (CNO), 17, 70, 97, 195, 223, 224
   command relationships, 14, 17 25–6, 37, 150, 189–190
   logistic system support, 35, 67, 107, 247, 256
China, 1, 4, 5, 128
China Beach Recreation Facility, 97
Cholon, 63–4

*Chowanoc* (ATF–100), 217
Chu Lai, 42, 70–1, 100, 109, 206, 228; see also Naval Support Activity, Danang, Detachments
Civic action, 65, 101, 192
Civil Engineer Corps (CEC), 181
Clarey, Vice Admiral Bernard A., 18N, 37
Clark, Commander Charles R., 221
Clark Field, Philippines, 60
*SS Clarksburg Victory*, 209
"Clearwater," Operation, 155
Coastal Division Thirteen, 161
Coastal Squadron One, 158
Coastal Surveillance Force (CTF–115), 38, 130; see also Market Time
Coastal waters, 88, 128, 153
    enemy supply effort, 5, 88, 129
    patrol of, 42, 129, 131
    surveillance forces, 10, 75
Coast Guard, U.S., 105, 129, 133, 153, 164, 230
Coast Guard, U.S. Squadron One, 130
Coast Guard, U.S. Squadron Twelve, 130
Co Chien River, 146, 228
Cochin China, 10, 91
*Coconino County* (LST–603), 123, 215
*Cocopa* (ATF–101), 198
COD aircraft, 47
Col Co (Colonial Company) ramp, 113–15
*Colleton* (APB–36), 151
Combs, Rear Admiral Walter V., 48
Commander in Chief, Pacific (CINCPAC), 53; see also Sharp, Admiral U. S. G.
    command relationships, 18–20, 37, 61, 70
    logistic management, 182, 247, 249, 250
Commander in Chief, U.S. Air Forces, Pacific, 18
Commander in Chief, U.S. Army, Pacific (USARPA), 18, 70
Commander in Chief, U.S. Pacific Fleet (CINCPACFLT), 25, 29, 31, 37–8, 137, 161, 217, 224
    command relationships, 17–18, 20, 25, 26, 29, 32, 37, 70, 81, 137, 205, 221, 223
    logistic management, 29, 67, 132, 136, 149, 158, 233, 243, 244, 247
    responsibilities, 29, 30, 70, 180, 244
Communications, 43–4, 74, 77, 174, 178, 229
Cong Hoa, Military Hospital, 65
Connolly, Vice Admiral Thomas F., 252
*Conserver* (ARS–39), 200, 202, 214, 215
Con Son Island, 143, 146
*Constellation* (CVA–64), 15
*Constitution*, 68
Construction, 14, 36, 53, 64, 75, 77, 97, 106–107, 123, 140, 142–3, 154, 155, 156, 163, 166, 170, 172, 173, 180–93, 238; see also

Construction—Continued
    Seabees, Naval Mobile Construction Battalions.
        air facilities, 71, 106, 127, 172, 187, 188
        billeting facilities, 156, 162, 178
        fuel facilities, 95, 107, 115, 172
        port development, 67, 70, 85, 86–90, 114, 155, 182, 187
        ramps, 104, 124–5, 175, 187
        stowage facilities, 94, 100, 107, 159, 187
Construction Agent, Department of Defense, 180–4
Construction Battalion Camp, Gulfport, Mississippi, 189
Construction Battalion Center; see Naval Construction Battalion Center
Construction Battalions, Atlantic, 189
Construction Battalions, Pacific, 181, 189
Con Thien, x, 111, 192
*Coral Sea* (CVA–43), 15, 42
*Coucal* (ASR–8), 207
Cowan, Rear Admiral John (MC), 100
*Crandall* (YHLC–2, formerly German *Energie*), 206
*Cree* (ATF–84), 210
*Crilley* (YHLC–1, formerly German *Andauer*), 206
Cruiser-Destroyer Force, U.S. Pacific Fleet, 32
Cua Viet; see Naval Support Activity, Danang, Detachments
Cua Viet River, x, 111, 119–22, 124–6, 154–5, 217
Cubi Point, Philippines, 47, 53, 233
Cu Chi, 191
*Current* (ARS–22), 214, 218
Cus Ho, 104, 106

**D**

Danang (Tourane), 68, 91–2, 122, 123, 228; see also Naval Support Activity, Danang
Danang Air Base, 63
Danang Bay, 67, 68, 90
Danang East, x, 71, 75, 93–4, 96, 188
Danang River, 209
Danang Support Group, 130
*Davidson* (Army dredge), 124, 125, 217
Davis, Rear Admiral James R. (CEC), 181, 182, 190
Defense, U.S. Department of (DOD), 14, 30, 181, 243
Defense, U.S. Secretary of, 18, 60, 186, 203, 255; see also McNamara, Robert
    ammunition management, 225, 247, 250, 251, 253
Delanoy, Lieutenant Billie L., 207
*Deliver* (ARS–23), 207, 213, 214
DeLong piers, 88

*Desal II* (civilian barge), 209
Destroyer escorts, 13, 129, 130, 133, 153, 237
Destroyers, 46, 56, 91, 129, 198
Diem, Ngo Dinh, 2, 12, 13
Dien Bien Phu, 11, 126
"Dinassaut," 147, 148
*Diodon* (SS–349), 217
Dixie Station, 42, 46, 47, 49, 50, 57; see also Yankee Station
Dong Ha; see Naval Support Activity, Danang, Detachments
Dong Hoi, 15
Dong Tam, 172–3, 213; see also Naval Support Activity, Saigon, Detachments
Dozier, Captain W. C., Jr., 38
Drain, Captain Dan T., ix, 224
Dredges, 86, 104–5, 121, 123, 182, 209
Dredging, 94, 104, 115, 142, 162, 166, 184, 185
    Cua Viet River, 119, 121, 122, 123
    Dong Tam, 172, 211
    Tourane River, 86, 88
Drydocks, floating, 23–4, 45, 73, 75, 132, 159, 237
Duc Pho, 98, 109, 126, 217

E

Eccles, Rear Admiral (Ret.), viii, 31, 82
*Edson* (DD–946), 234
*Edwards* (DD–619), 15
SS *Ekaterini G.*, 202
*Elkhorn* (AOG–7), 123
*Energie* (German heavy lift craft), 206
*Enterprise* (CVAN–65), 46
Enthoven, Assistant Secretary of Defense (Systems Analysis) Alain C., 250
Esso International, 113, 172, 206
SS *Esso Marikado*, 169
SS *Esso Victory*, 213
SS *Evanthie*, 214
SS *Excellency*, 207
Explosive Ordnance Disposal Teams, U.S. Navy (EOD), 65, 71, 123

F

Facilities Engineering Command, Naval, 154, 163, 180, 190
Fast combat support ships (AOE), 44, 54, 56, 57
Felt, Admiral Harry D., 18
Fifth Fleet, U.S., 17
First Corps Tactical Zone (ICTZ), x, 37, 67–127, 137, 139, 148, 152, 153–5, 194, 217, 229
    construction, 182, 187–8, 191
    logistic responsibilities, 61, 181

First Field Forces, U.S., 156
First Fleet, U.S., 247
First Logistical Command, U.S. Army, 60, 61, 139, 142
Fleet Activities, 29, 45
    Ryukus, 28, 232
    Sasebo, 28, 45, 46, 71, 140, 204, 206, 232, 233
    Yokosuka, 28, 232
Fleet and Force Supply Office, 29, 63, 142, 238
Fleet Air Bases, U.S., 23
Fleet Air, Western Pacific, 146
Fleet Base Force, U.S. Fleet, 22; see also Base Force, U.S. Pacific Fleet
Fleet freight, 43, 44, 47, 52, 54, 56
Fleet Maintenance Office, 29, 136, 235
Fleet Marine Force, 17–18, 31, 70, 72, 231, 244
Fleet Post Office, San Francisco, 25, 230
Fleet train, 21, 33, 231
*Florikan* (ASR–9), 213
*Forrestal* (CVA–59), 234
Fourth Corps Tactical Zone (IVCTZ), 61, 133, 136–8, 142, 151, 154
Frankenberger, Captain N., 235
*Frank Knox* (DDR–742), 39, 197–201, 211
Free World Military Assistance Forces, x, 60, 63, 79, 137
FS–344 (later *Pueblo*), 221
FS–217 (later *Palm Beach*), 221

G

*Gallup* (PG–85), 159
Game Warden (TF–116), 133–6, 139, 141, 144, 154; see also River Patrol Force
    base support, 137, 167, 172, 183
    repair support, 148, 161, 164
USNS *Geiger*, 217
General Agency Agreement, 258
*Genesee* (AOG–8), 71, 72
*George Eastman* (YAG–39), 229
SS *Gertrude Therese*, 208
Giap, General Vo Nguyen, 2, 4
Gio Linh, 192
Global Chartering and Brokerage Company, New York, 202
Gordon, AO1 C. G., 211
Grabowski, Captain T., 218
Grantham, Rear Admiral E. A., 235
*Granville S. Hall* (YAG–40), 229
*Grapple* (ARS–7), 198, 211, 216, 218
*Grasp* (ARS–24), 213, 217
Great Sitkun Island, 202
*Greenlet* (ASR–10), 114, 200, 213
Guam, 219; see also Naval Stations
SS *Guam Bear*, 213
*Guardfish* (SSN–612), 217–18

Guard Force, 100
Gulf of Thailand Support Group, 130
Gunfire support, 42, 46, 56, 111, 161, 243
Gurke, Commander Donald, 72

## H

Hainan Island, 133
Haiphong, 5, 242
Hai Van Mountains, 67, 110, 112, 114
Hai Van Pass, 67, 113, 115, 191
Halsey, Admiral William F., 40
*Hancock* (CVA–19), 15, 42·
Hanoi, 5, 10, 242
*Hanson* (DD–832), 42
Harbor Clearance Team One (HCT–1), 209
Harbor Clearance Team Two (HCT–2), 209, 216
Harbor Clearance Team Three (HCT–3), 214
Harbor Clearance Team Five (HCT–5), 209, 215
Harbor clearance teams, 160, 177
Harbor Clearance Unit One (HCU–1), 45, 149, 203–13, 215
Harbor Defense Forces (Stable Door), 140, 141, 159
Harbor utility craft, 24, 74, 118, 122, 123
Harkins, General Paul D., 14
*Harnett County* (LST–821), 146
Harris, Lieutenant Commander William R., 164
Headquarters Support Activity (HEDSUPP-ACT), Saigon, 14, 25, 59–65, 69, 136, 138, 146
   supply responsibilities, 73, 94, 95, 142
Headquarters Support Activity (HEDSUPP-ACT), Taipei, 25, 44, 54, 232
Heaman, Rear Admiral William M. (CEC), 181, 190
Helicopter Attack (Light) Squadron Three (HAL–3), 143
*Henry W. Tucker* (DD–875), 42
*Hitchiti* (ATF–103), 202, 206, 207, 213, 215, 217
HLC–2, 209, 212
Ho Chi Minh, 8, 11, 12
"Ho Chi Minh Trail," 5, 14, 110
Ho Gio Island, 133
Hoi An, 92, 98, 117
Hospital; see medical facilities
Hospital ships (AH), 21, 77
Howell, Lieutenant Commander Frederick J., 224
Hue, 68, 91, 93, 110, 112–17, 118; see also Naval Support Activity, Danang, Detachments
Huff, Captain K. P., USNR, 73, 81
*Hunterdon County* (LST–838), 176

*Hyde* (Army dredge), 123
Hydrographic surveys, 45, 220, 227–9
Hyland, Admiral John J., 18N, 219

## I

Ignatius, Assistant Secretary of Defense (Installations and Logistics), Paul R., 250
Inshore and inland waterways, 128–52, 164, 194, 202–3, 253, 257
*Intrepid* (CVS–11), 50
Irvin, Rear Admiral William D., 24–5, 34, 36–7, 71, 200, 246
*Iwo Jima* (LPH–2), 200

## J

Jackson, Captain Henry S., 42
*Jamaica Bay* (Army dredge), 211–13
*Jamestown* (AGTR–3), 219, 224
Janney, Rear Admiral Frederick E., 44, 201, 206
Japan, 28, 64, 232, 233, 253
Johnson, Rear Admiral Frank L., 224
Johnson, President Lyndon B., 15
Johnson, Admiral Roy L., 18N, 61, 75, 103, 130–1, 136
Joint Chiefs of Staff, 61, 250
Junk Force, Vietnamese, 129

## K

Kaohsiung, Taiwan, 161, 234
Kelley, Rear Admiral James W., (CC), 151
Kennedy, President John F., 13
Khe Sanh, x, 98, 110, 126–7
King, Captain Herbert, 137, 138, 139, 156
*Krishna* (ARL–38), 131–2, 138, 161, 163–4, 201, 206
Krulak, Lieutenant General Victor H., 4, 72
Kuntze, Captain Archie C., 60, 136, 139
Ky, Premier Nguyen Van, 91, 92, 93

## L

Lacy, Rear Admiral Paul L., 81, 123
Lam, Lieutenant General Hoang Xuan, 93, 106, 112, 113
Landing craft, 73, 81, 83, 111, 114, 147, 166
   mechanized (LCM), 73, 114, 115, 119, 122, 125, 144, 147, 164, 169, 173
   utility (LCU), 73, 74, 81, 86, 104, 107, 113, 114, 118, 119, 122, 123–5, 147, 204
Landing Ship Squadron Two, 145
Laos, 5, 14, 42, 110, 126, 133
LCC–2, 213
LCM–8, 214

LCU–1494, 202, 217
LCU–1500, 214
Lefevre, Bishop (Apostolic Vicar of Cochin China), 68
*Liberty* (AGTR–5), 219
Liberty, Captain Harold F. (CEC), USNR, 189
LLC–1, 207
LLC–2, 209–10, 215
LLC–3, 209
Lieu Chien Esso Terminal, 100
Lift craft, 160, 166, 177, 203–9, 212–13
Lighterage, 74, 81, 82, 83
    covered lighters, 74, 75, 96, 115, 149, 175, 204, 208
*Lipan* (ATF–85), 215
Local Area Coordinators, 26, 28, 61
Lodge, Ambassador Henry Cabot, 60
Logistic Command, U.S. Army, Okinawa, 95
Logistics over-the-shore (LOTS), 6, 71, 88, 103, 109, 119, 258
Logistic Support Plans, 138, 140, 149
Long Binh, 191
Long Tau River, 144, 145, 161, 164–5, 210
    mine operations, 134, 162, 208
Long Xuyen; see Naval Support Activity, Saigon, Detachments
LSIL–331 (Vietnamese), 145
LST (Landing ship, tank), 106, 124, 130, 132, 154, 185, 214, 237, 258
    logistic support, 84, 104, 122, 144–5, 148–9
    off-load facilities, 81, 86, 88, 104, 107, 114–15, 125, 211
    river mouth operations, 134, 143, 146, 161
LT–431, 202
Luoto, Lieutenant Commander H., 79

**M**

McKinney, Captain W. R., 71
McNamara, Secretary of Defense Robert, 131, 185
*Maddox* (DD–731), 15
*Mahnomen County* (LST–912), 211
*Mahopac* (ATA–196), 198, 201, 214
Mail, 43, 45, 47, 52, 54, 56, 230
Maintenance, 26, 30, 45, 58, 59, 61, 75, 142–143, 148, 151, 155, 158, 180, 233, 238; see also Repair
    airfield and airstrip, 97, 126, 143
    of craft, 136, 140, 142, 159, 205, 235
    vehicle and equipment, 64, 98, 148, 166, 189
USCG *Mallow*, 215
*Mansfield* (DD–728), 42
Marble Mountain, 75, 95, 98, 101

Marine Corps, U.S., Air Station, Futema, Okinawa, 189
Marine Force Logistic Command, 101
Marine, U.S., 49, 61, 70, 71, 92, 93, 109, 115, 121
    ammunition support, 36, 244, 249, 250, 251, 253
    construction support, 97, 185, 187, 188, 191
    logistic support, x, 17, 18, 59, 69, 73, 94, 230–3, 255
Marine, U.S., Air Group, 20, 103
Marine, U.S., Air Wing, 35, 104
Marine, U.S., Division Shore Party, 85, 107, 124
Maritime Administration, 258
*Mark* (AKL–12), 131, 138, 144, 145, 173, 220
*Markab* (AR–23), 161, 162
Market Time (TF–115), 38, 129–32, 136, 139, 156, 158, 159, 169; see also Coastal Surveillance Force
    bases in support, 107, 115, 132, 137, 141, 155, 156, 162, 163, 183
    craft repair and maintenance, 75, 132, 136, 148, 155, 157, 161, 234
    logistic support, 38, 46, 47, 104, 130, 131, 140, 251
    underway replenishment, 48, 49, 51, 53
*Mars* (AFS–1), 54, 57
Marschall, Captain Albert R. (CEC), 189, 191
*Mataco* (ATF–86), 202, 213, 214, 216
*Maury* (AGS–16), 105, 228, 229
Maury, Commander Matthew F., 227
Medical and dental services, x, 43, 61, 65, 75–7, 101, 111
    facilities, x, xi, 65, 75, 77, 79, 101, 111, 232
*Meeker County* (LST–980), 115
Mekong Delta, 10, 133–4, 144, 151, 152, 166, 169
    hydrographic surveys, 228–9
    logistic support, 141, 145, 260
Mekong Delta Mobile Assault Force (later Mobile Riverine Force), 147, 148, 150, 172
Mekong River, 133–4, 140, 144, 145, 147, 228
*Midway* (CVA–41), 42, 200
Military Advisory Group Eleven (MAG–11), 101
Military Advisory Group Sixteen (MAG–16), 95
Military Assistance and Advisory Group (MAAG), Vietnam, 14, 59

Military Assistance Command, U.S., Vietnam (MACV), 14, 59, 86, 96, 98, 118, 136, 152, 182, 192
    command relationships, 18, 20, 38, 115, 127, 130, 137, 170, 186, 190, 258
Military Assistance Command, U.S., Vietnam, Advisory Groups, 97
Military Construction Program (MILCON), 185, 235
Military Sea Transportation Service (MSTS), 11, 63, 69, 210, 230, 255–8
    ship availability, 83, 185, 248
    ships, 53, 61, 75, 95, 96, 126, 145, 206, 208, 214, 244
Military Transportation Management Terminal Service (MTMTS), 84; see also Military Sea Transportation Service
Mine Force, U.S. Pacific Fleet, 32, 71
Minesweepers, 13, 47, 122, 130, 153, 164
    minesweeping boats (MSB), 166, 167, 168, 169
SS *Minot Victory*, 214–15
*Mispillion* (AO–105), 52
Mitchell, Commander E. B., 198, 203, 204, 212, 216
Mobile Assault Force; see Mekong Delta Mobile Assault Force
Mobile Inshore Undersea Warfare Surveillance Units (MIUWS), 71, 140
Mobile Logistics Support Group (CTG–73.5), 48
Mobile Navy Post Offices, 230
Mobile Riverine Assault Force, 148, 161
Mobile Riverine Force, 144, 146–51, 160, 174, 191, 205; see also Mekong Delta Mobile Assault Force
Mobile support, 7, 96, 154, 166, 170, 174; see also Underway replenishment
    concept, v, 45
    forces, viii, 24, 46, 153, 160, 170, 234
Mobile Support Base I, 154
Mobile Support Force, 46, 131, 231
Mobile Support Unit Three, 71, 233
Mobile Technical Units, 44
Moinester, Lieutenant (jg) Robert W., USNR, 118
*Molala* (ATF–106), 201, 215
Mole, Commander R. L. (CC), 152
*Mondego* (civilian fishing boat), 213
Monkey Mountain, 81, 83, 91, 187
Monroe, Rear Admiral Henry S., 61
Moreell, Rear Admiral Ben (CEC), 187
Morison, Samuel Eliot, v, 256
*Morton* (DD–948), 15
*Mount Katmai* (AE–16), 53
MSB–54, 210
MSB–14, 213
*Mui Finn* (French ship), 213

*Munsee* (ATF–107), 198
Museum Ramp, Danang, 81, 86
My Tho; see Naval Support Activity, Saigon, Detachments

N

Naha, Okinawa, 206, 232
National Defense Reserve Fleet, 194, 258
National Security Agency, 221
Naval Advisory Group, Vietnam, 38, 130, 136
Naval Air Facility, U.S., Cam Ranh Bay, 158, 159
Naval Air Force, U.S. Pacific Fleet, 18, 32, 231, 252
Naval Base, Subic Bay, 28, 35, 203, 206, 233
Naval Beach Group Detachment, 107
Naval Communications Station, Cam Ranh Bay, 159
Naval Construction Battalion Center, Point Hueneme, California, 29, 71, 78, 190
Naval Facility, Chi Chi Jima, 28
Naval Forces, Japan, 26, 221, 224
Naval Forces, Marianas, 26, 131, 220
Naval Forces, Philippines, 26, 78, 131
Naval Forces, Vietnam (NAVFORV), 137–140, 149, 155, 159, 167, 183
Naval magazines (NAVMAG), 28–9
    Guam, 25, 44, 79, 232
    Subic, 25, 35, 36, 44, 140, 244, 245, 248, 251–3
Naval Material Command, 247, 248
Naval Material Support Establishment, 248, 249
Naval Mobile Construction Battalion Maintenance Unit 301, 98
Naval Mobile Construction Battalions, (NMCB), U.S. Pacific Fleet, 67, 86, 180, 187, 189, 191; see also Seabees
    NMCB–3, 71, 107, 189
    NMCB–4, 189, 192
    NMCB–5, 192
    NMCB–8, 189
    NMCB–9, 71, 75, 192
    NMCB–10, 71, 103, 125
    NMCB–40, 189
    NMCB–58, 189
    NMCB–62, 189
    NMCB–133, 189
Naval Ordnance Facilities, 25, 28–9, 44, 232
Naval Overseas Transportation Service (NOTS), 256
Naval Security Group, Washington, D.C., 221
Naval Ship Repair Facilities (SRF), 28, 233
    Guam, 25, 44, 123, 140, 213, 232, 237
    Subic, 25, 35, 44, 53, 130, 131, 132, 140, 151, 204, 233, 234, 235
    Yokosuka, 25, 44, 140, 149, 173, 175, 200, 232

Naval Shipyard, Pearl Harbor, 223
Naval Shore Electronics Engineering Activity, Pacific, 140
Naval Stations, 28–9, 45, 232, 233
Naval Supply Center, Oakland, California, 78, 94, 95
Naval Supply Depots (NSD), 28–9, 44, 45
    Guam, 25, 26, 44, 232, 238, 245
    Subic, 25, 35, 44, 45, 53, 96, 140, 141, 237, 238
    Yokosuka, 25, 44, 45, 232, 237, 238
Naval Support Activity (NAVSUPPACT), Danang, 61, 69, 72, 73–102, 107, 109, 112, 113, 115, 117, 119, 122, 123, 124, 126, 130, 132, 137, 140, 146, 183, 185, 188, 189, 191, 207, 217, 257
    construction, 71, 75, 83, 183, 187–8
    establishment, 37, 71, 73, 78–81, 153
    logistic support, x, 47, 67, 72, 94, 95, 97, 103, 111, 114, 132, 137, 138, 147
    repair support, 44, 94, 107, 123, 132, 234
Naval Support Activity, Danang, Detachments
    Chu Lai, x, 71, 73, 82, 83, 84, 95, 97, 103–5, 106, 107, 109, 153, 183, 188
    Cua Viet, 119–22, 123, 125–6, 155, 210
    Dong Ha, x, 77, 98, 117, 118, 119–22, 123, 124, 125, 126, 188
    Hue, 14, 64, 98, 111, 112–17, 118
    Tan My, 98, 111, 112–17, 118, 125, 155, 184
Naval Support Activity (NAVSUPPACT), Saigon, 44, 136–52, 155, 167–8, 170, 220
Naval Support Activity, Saigon, Detachments
    An Thoi, 45, 49, 130, 131, 132, 139, 143, 146, 153, 161, 163–4, 177, 215
    Binh Thuy, 143, 146, 176–9
    Cam Ranh Bay, 62, 63, 90, 130, 139, 141, 143, 144, 146, 153, 157–9, 182, 257
    Can Tho, 134, 139, 143, 177
    Cat Lo, 130, 134, 139, 143, 153, 155, 162–3, 165, 209
    Dong Tam, 148, 149, 151, 155, 160, 172–4, 191, 211, 213
    Long Xuyen, 134, 140, 173, 177
    My Tho, 134, 139, 140, 170–2, 207, 215
    Nha Be, 139, 143, 165–9, 210
    Qui Nhon, 63, 130, 139, 146, 153, 155–157, 182, 202
    Sa Dec, 134, 140, 175
    Vinh Long, 134, 140, 143, 174, 209
    Vung Tau, 141, 143, 146, 148, 149, 159–62, 205, 207
Naval Support Activity, Saigon, Liaison Detachment, 149

Naval Support Facility, Cam Ranh Bay, 44, 159
Naval Weapons Station, Concord, California, 248
Navy Post Offices, 143, 230
Navy, U.S. Department of, xi, 17, 26, 256
Navy, U.S. Secretary of (SECNAV), 14, 67, 137, 196, 225
Neman, Captain Sol, 134
*Neptune* (ARC–2), 229
*New Jersey* (Army dredge), 211
*New Jersey* (BB–62), 42
Newport, 167
Nha Be; see Naval Support Activity, Saigon, Detachments
Nha Trang, 140, 141, 192, 214, 228
Ninth Infantry Division, U.S. Army, 148, 151, 172, 213
Ninth Marine Expeditionary Brigade, 68
Nimitz, Fleet Admiral Chester W., 23
Nitze, Secretary of the Navy, Paul, 37
NMCB; see Naval Mobile Construction Battalions
SS *Norbega*, 214
North Korea (Democratic People's Republic of Korea), 1, 4, 219, 225
North Reef, Paracel Islands, 214
Northwest Cape Facility, Australia, 208
*Noxubee* (AOG–56), 216
Nucleus Port Crews, 71, 79

O

*Oak Hill* (LSD–7), 215
Oakland, California, 86
*O'Brien* (DD–725), 234
Observation Point, Danang, 89, 90
SS *Oceanic Tide*, 214
Oceanographic Office, U.S. Navy, 143, 146
SS *Ohio*, 207
Oilers, 44, 48–9, 51–2, 57
SS *Old Westbury*, 210
Ordnance Facilities; see Naval Ordnance Facilities
Ordnance Systems Command, Naval, 28, 249
Orem, Commander John, Jr., 211, 214, 216
*Oriskany* (CVA–34), 53, 234
Osborn, Rear Admiral James B., 81
*Oxford* (AGTR–1), 219, 224
*Ozbourn* (DD–846), 234

P

Pacific Architects and Engineers (PA&E), 144
Pacific Area Movements Priority Agency (PAMPA), 86

Pacific Fleet, U.S. (PACFLT), 22, 34, 225
   command relationships, 28, 31–2, 38, 161
   logistic support, 7, 18, 25, 26, 36, 43, 162
*Palm Beach* (AKL–45) later (AGER–3), 221, 222
Paracel Islands, 13, 15, 207, 214
"Passage to Freedom" Operation, 11
*Patapsco* (AOG–1), 115
PCF–4, 206
PCF–76, 217
PCF–97, 215
Pearl Harbor, Hawaii, 39, 44, 141, 182, 223–4
Percival, Captain (Mad Jack), 68
Perfume River, 111, 113, 118–19, 122, 125, 154–5, 228
*Peregrine* (AG–176), 229
"Personal Response Project," 151–2
Petroleum, Oil, and Lubricants (POL), 23, 44, 48–53, 79, 95, 101, 165, 169
   delivery, 56, 57, 72, 95, 103, 104, 115, 119, 125, 255, 257
   requirements, 43, 46, 52, 79, 255
   ship-to-shore (offshore) fuel lines, 72, 103, 104, 107, 109, 114, 115, 119, 122, 217
   stowage, x, 95, 107, 123, 169, 172
Phan Rang, 228
Phu Bai, x, 77, 97, 100, 112–17, 188, 191
Phu Qui, 42
Phu Quoc Island, 13, 163
Phu Thien, 133
Phu Thu, 202
Pile Drivers, 86, 155, 172, 173, 182
Plain of Reeds, 140
Planning, 24, 40, 70, 85, 128, 141, 148, 159, 227
   base development, viii, 11, 80, 140, 170, 183
   construction, 86, 182–4
   logistic support, 31, 38, 83, 85, 131, 136, 148, 245, 257
Pleiku, 191
Pleiku Air Base, 15
Poage, Captain Robert B., 136
*USCG Point Young*, 201
*Ponchatoula* (AO–148), 52
Poro Point, Philippines, 84, 185
Port Hueneme, California; see Naval Construction Battalion Center
Port operations, 59, 61, 69–70, 79, 81–6, 107, 121
   cargo handling, 35, 61, 78–9, 83–4, 89, 91, 93, 96, 104, 107, 115, 122, 124, 126, 149, 165–6, 185, 245
   cargo throughput, 36, 88–9, 109, 115, 117, 122, 125

Poulo Obi Island, 143
*SS Prairie Grove*, 210
Pratas Island, 198
Pratas Reef, 39, 197, 200
Prepositioned War Reserve Stocks, 36; see also Ammunition
President of the United States, 18, 225, 256
Principal Logistic Agent, 25, 31–2, 38
Provisions, 43, 44, 54, 59, 60, 62, 63, 73, 81, 94, 95–6, 107
   chill and freeze (perishable), 43, 45, 54, 62, 63, 115
Public works, 29, 59, 64, 97–8, 107, 143, 144
*Pueblo* (AKL–44) later (AGER–2), 4, 19, 191, 219–20, 221–5, 241, 253
Puget Sound Naval Shipyard, Bremerton Washington, 220, 221, 222
*Pyro* (AE–24), 53

**Q**

Quang Ngai, 37, 67, 93, 98, 117, 191–2
Quang Tin, 93
Quang Tri, 14, 98, 110, 111, 117, 119, 123–5
Qui Nhon, 15, 40, 62, 109, 214; see also Naval Support Activity, Saigon, Detachments

**R**

Rach Gia, 65
*Radford* (DD–446), 207
Ramage, Vice Admiral Lawson P., 18N
*Ranger* (CVA–61), 15, 42
Raymond, Morrison, Knudsen (RMK), 86, 106, 107, 184
Raymond, Morrison, Knudsen, Brown and Root, J. A. (RMK–BRJ), 184
*SS R.C. Stoner*, 215–17
Real estate, 64, 96–7, 142, 165–6, 175, 232
*Reclaimer* (ARS–42), 206, 207, 208, 213, 214
Red Beach, Danang Bay, 68, 95
Refrigerator ships, 21, 75, 96
*Rehoboth* (AGS–50), 228, 229
Renken, Rear Admiral H. A., 189
Repair, x, 23, 31, 38, 44, 94, 100, 138, 142–143, 151, 154, 166, 173, 217, 229, 233–7, 251–3; see also Maintenance
   air facilities, 124, 126, 188
   capabilities, 45, 130, 159, 174, 178, 256
   engine, 151, 168, 223
   requirements, 43, 158, 194, 233
   of vessels, 30, 44, 58, 75, 107, 123, 132, 140, 155, 157, 161, 168–9, 177, 196, 206, 209, 210, 214–15
   vessels, 44, 75, 130, 132, 148–9, 158, 160, 161, 233–4

Repair parts, 31, 141, 142
    logistic support, 45, 57, 146, 161
    requirements, 43, 141, 189, 237
Repair ships, 21, 44, 45, 130, 160–1, 233–4
*Repose* (AH–16), xi, 77, 111
Rest and recreation (R&R), 58, 63–4, 97, 231
River Assault Group, Vietnamese (RAG), 142, 166, 170, 172, 174, 177
River Escort Group, Vietnamese, 148
River Force, Vietnamese, 134, 147, 148
Riverine Assault Force (TF–117), 151, 170, 173, 215
Rivero, Admiral Horacio, 100
River Patrol Force (TF–116), 134, 140, 143, 169, 170, 174; see also Game Warden
River Support Squadron Seven, 150
Roc Gia, 146
*Rochester* (CA–124), 215
Roeder, Vice Admiral Bernard F., 131, 132
Rosemary Point, Chu Lai, 104, 106, 153, 211
Route Nine, 126
Route One, 67, 104, 114, 115, 119
Rukon Shoal, 206
Rung Sat Special Zone (RSSZ), 134, 151, 161, 162, 167, 228
Rydeen, Captain Francis C., ix

S

*Sacramento* (AOE–1), 54, 56, 57, 253
Sa Dec; see Naval Support Activity, Saigon, Detachments
*Safeguard* (ARS–25), 202, 206, 208, 209
Sa Huynh, 67
Saigon, 6, 59–65, 68, 89–91, 134, 139, 167
Saigon Naval Hospital, 63, 65
Saigon River, 203, 207
*St. Can* (French Patrol Boat), 148
Salvage, 23, 38–9, 43, 149, 177, 194–218
Salvage ships, 45, 195, 197, 200–201, 210, 217, 225–6
*Sanctuary* (AH–17), xi, 77, 111
San Diego, California, 24, 222
San Francisco, California, 25, 48, 54, 84
Sangley Point, Philippines, 131, 158
Sea Force, Vietnamese Navy, 129
Seabee Maintenance Unit 301, 126
Seabee Maintenance Unit 302, 144
Seabees, x, 14, 64, 75, 86, 95, 107, 122–4, 144, 158, 173, 180, 186–93; see also Naval Mobile Construction Battalions, Construction
    air facilities construction, 71, 106–7, 109, 111, 119, 123
    other shore facilities construction, 75, 94, 106–7, 111, 156, 159, 172, 183
    ramp construction, 104, 107, 115, 125

Seabees—Continued
    road construction and maintenance, 83, 94, 115, 119, 158
Seabee Technical Assistance Teams (STATS), 14
"Sea Dragon" Operation, 42, 46, 50, 53, 243
Sea Hawk helicopters, 179
Sea lines of logistics, 40, 71, 113, 119–27
    operation of, 104, 109, 115, 131, 144–6
*SS Sea Raven*, 206
Searle, Captain W. F., Jr., 198, 203
*SS Sea Train Texas*, 210
Sea Wolf helicopters, 143, 160, 167, 168
Second Corps Tactical Zone (IICTZ), 61, 136–8, 142, 149, 155, 157
Security, 59, 64–5, 89, 96, 98–101, 103, 106, 147, 156, 166, 175, 222
    harbor defense, 79, 90–1, 104, 106, 122, 136, 140–1, 160
*Serrano* (AGS–24), 228, 229
Service Force, U.S. Atlantic Fleet, 189
Service Group One (SERVGRUONE), 24, 222
Service Group Three (SERVGRUTHREE), 201, 208
    logistic support, 38, 44, 51, 140, 221, 233, 243, 244, 247
    salvage, 196, 198, 200, 210, 211, 214
Service Squadron One (SERVRONONE), 24
Service Squadron Three (SERVRONTHREE), 17, 221, 224
Service Squadron Five (SERVRONFIVE), 17, 48, 218
Service Squadron Seven (SERVRONSEVEN), 25, 48
Service Squadron Nine (SERVRONNINE), 48
Seufer, Rear Admiral P. E. (CEC), 190
Seventh Fleet, U.S., 11, 13, 15, 17, 40–58, 67–8, 74, 91, 132, 153, 200, 227, 232–3
    logistic support, 18, 35, 45, 56, 96, 143, 158, 232, 234, 237, 247, 251, 260
    logistic support ships and craft, 96, 114, 145, 215, 224, 232
    subordinate commands, 44, 71, 130, 205
Sharp, Admiral U. S. G., 18, 85, 86, 90, 103, 186
    logistic support responsibilities, 37, 61, 70, 95
*Sheldrake* (AGS–19), 228
Ship Repair Facilities; see Naval Ship Repair Facilities
Ships systems command, naval, 28, 195, 223
Shultz, Rear Admiral Floyd B., 220
Siam, Gulf of, 13, 130, 133, 163, 201, 206
Sihanouk, Prince Norodom, 6
Sihanoukville, Camodia, 6
*Sioux* (ATF–75), 200, 211, 214

Smith, Camp, Pearl Harbor, Hawaii, 85, 103, 250

Soirap River, 165, 169, 228

Southeast Asia Treaty Organization (SEATO), 11, 40, 233

Spore, Captain Burns W., 139, 142

Stable Door; see Harbor Defense Forces

*SS Steel Flyer*, 217

Stores, 47, 54, 56, 57, 63

Store ship, combat (AFS), 44, 45, 54, 57, 96

Stowage (storage), x, 79, 95, 100, 115, 169, 257

    facilities, 59, 63, 94, 139, 187

"Street without joy," 14

Subic Bay, Philippines, 215, 228, 234

Submarine Force, U.S. Pacific Fleet, 32

*SS Sudbury Two*, 202

*USNS Sultan*, 206

*Summit County* (LST-1146), 206

*Sunnadin* (ATA-197), 210, 228

Supervisor of Salvage, Bureau of Ships, 195, 196, 198, 200, 201, 203

Supply, 107, 138, 140, 141-2, 154, 174, 237-8

    common support, x, 8, 20, 32, 59, 61, 63, 70, 79, 94, 95, 132, 142, 149

    service peculiar support, 18, 59, 142, 149

Supply Depots; see Naval Supply Depots

Supply Systems Command, Naval, 28, 142

Support Command, U.S. Army, Vietnam, 59, 149

*Surfbird* (ADG-383), 207

Surveillance, 46, 50, 90, 129, 153, 159, 219-225

Sutherling, Rear Admiral Elton W., 238


T

*SS Tai-nam*, 202

Taiwan, 54, 64, 84, 233

*Takelma* (ATF-113), 213

Tam Ky, 117, 192

Tan An, 215

Tan Chau, 134, 140, 175, 178

Tankers, 53, 114, 119, 122, 125, 255, 257

Tan My; see Naval Support Activity, Danang, Detachments

*Tanner* (AGS-15), 228

Tan Son Nhut Airport, Saigon, 63, 130, 167

Task Force Clearwater, 126

Task Force 72 (Patrol Force, Seventh Fleet), 131

Task Force 73 (Mobile Logistic Support Force), 130, 140, 162, 205

Task Force 77 (Attack Carrier Striking Force), 15, 50, 225-6

Task Force 96; see also Naval Forces, Japan, 224

Task Force 115, 158; see also Coastal Surveillance Force

Task Force 116, 167, 178; see also River Patrol Force

Task Force 117, 174; see also Riverine Assault Force

Task Group 76.4 (Amphibious Ready Group Alpha), 73

*Tawakoni* (ATF-114), 202, 214

*SS Teh Hu*, 213

*Terrell County* (LST-1157), 201

Thailand, 11, 133, 181, 182

Thanh Hoa, 15

Thi, General Nguyen Chanh, 91-2, 106

Third Corps Tactical Zone (IIICTZ), 61, 136-7, 138, 142, 149, 154

Third Field Hospital, U.S. Army, 63

Third Fleet, U.S., 17, 40

Third Marine Amphibious Force, 71, 85, 154; see also Third Marine Expeditionary Force

Third Marine Expeditionary Force, 71, 78, 136; see also Third Marine Amphibious Force

Third Marine Division, 110

Third Naval Construction Brigade, 191

Third Naval District, Commandant, 79

Thirtieth Naval Construction Regiment (NCR), 71, 189, 191

Thirteenth Naval District, Commandant, 221

Thirty-First Naval Construction Regiment (NCR), 190

Thua Thien, 110, 111

Thuong Duc, 192

*Tiburon* (civilian motor vessel), 210

*Ticonderoga* (CVA-14), 15

Tien Sha, 77, 80, 81, 96, 98

*Tiru* (SS-416), 210

Tonkin, 10

Tonkin Gulf, 11, 15, 45, 226

    underway replenishment cycles, 47-8, 50, 51, 54

Tourane; see Danang

Tourane River, 69, 74, 81, 86, 88, 93, 101

Towing, 43, 45, 195, 202, 203, 206; see also Salvage

*Towhee* (AGS-28), 228

Training, 8, 11, 17, 206, 222, 224, 232, 240, 245

    salvage, 196, 200, 201, 205

Transport aircraft, 59, 60, 62, 127, 146, 254

Transportation Management Agency (TMA), Military Assistance Command, Vietnam, 84, 147

Transport Group, Vietnamese, 148

Thuan an Island, 114, 115

Truman, President Harry S., 10

Truong River, 104

Tsoying Harbor, Taiwan, 217
Tubbs, Captain Joseph J. (CC), 152
Tu Doc, Emperor, 113
Tugs, 74, 197, 206, 209
    auxiliary ocean tug (ATA), 45, 201, 214
    fleet ocean tug (ATF), 45, 195, 196, 214, 225
    large harbor tug (YTB), 74, 148
*Turner Joy* (DD–951), 15, 234
*Tutuila* (ARG–4), 148, 151, 160, 162, 164
Tuy Hoa, 201

## U

Underway replenishment, 23, 35, 36, 44–58, 130, 140; see also Mobile Support
*Ute* (ATF–76), 207

## V

*Valley Forge* (LPH–8), 42
Van Truong Peninsula, 106
*HMAS Vendetta*, 210
Veth, Rear Admiral Kenneth L., 137
Villasenor, Chief Boatswain's Mate Richard, 206
Vinh Long; see Naval Support Activity, Saigon, Detachments
*Virgo* (AE–30), 53
VQ–1 (Navy) squadron, 213
Vung Ro Bay, 129, 210
Vung Tau, 151, 159, 160, 210, 215, 228; see also Naval Support Activity, Saigon, Detachments

## W

*Waddell* (DDG–24), 213
Wake Island, 209, 215, 216
Walt, General Lewis K., USMC, x, 71, 85, 91–3, 106, 183, 188
*Wandank* (ATA–204), 210, 216
Ward, Rear Admiral N. G., 38, 44, 130, 134, 136–8, 183, 224
*SS Washington Maid*, 207

Weapons Division, Service Force, Pacific, 29, 37, 249
Wells, Captain Wade, 149
Weschler, Rear Admiral Thomas A., 81
Western Sea Frontier, 84
Western Pacific Area (WESTPAC), x, 141
Westmoreland, General William C. (USA), 60, 109, 117, 124, 126–7, 153, 167
    construction management, 86, 183, 186
Williams, Rear Admiral Joseph W., Jr., 38, 44, 200
Wooding, Rear Admiral R. R. (CEC), 190
*Wrangell*, (AE–12), 53
Wulzen, Rear Admiral Don W., 71

## Y

Yankee Station, 42, 46–8, 50–1, 57, 219, 227, 253; see also Dixie Station
YC–51, 217
YD–220, 151, 173
YFNB–9, 174, 178
YFNB–16, 166
YFNB–24, 173
YFR–866, 144
YFR–889, 144, 146, 173
YFR–890, 144, 146
YFRN–412, 210
YFU–59, 123
YR–70, 94
YRBM–9, 178
YRBM–16, 175–7, 178
YRBM–17, 149
YTB–657, 218
YTB–761, 218
YTB–784, 151
YTB–785, 151
YTM–195, 218
YTM–757, 218

## Z

Zumwalt, Vice Admiral Elmo, 137
*SS Zuna*, 208

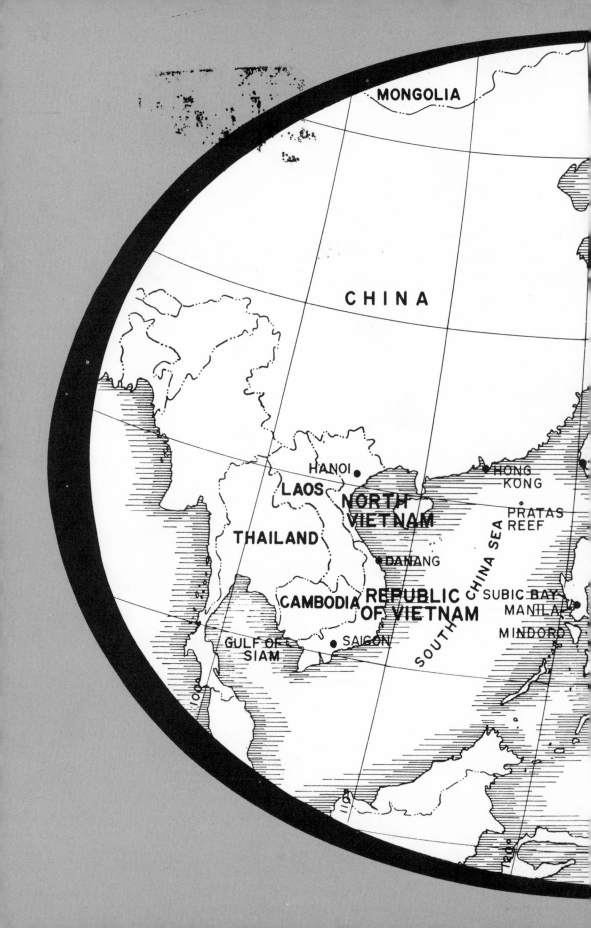